Healing the Soul

Healing the Soul

Pluto, Uranus
and the Lunar Nodes

Mark Jones

RAVEN
DREAMS
PRESS

Portland, OR

Published in 2011 by Raven Dreams Press
An imprint of Raven Dreams Productions, LLC
9524 N Kalmar St.
Portland, OR 97203
www.ravendreamspdx.com

ISBN 978-0-9840474-0-6

Library of Congress Control Number: 2011939932

Cover design: Clare Phillips - clarephillips.com

Edited by: Tony Howard

Book design and production by:
Raven Dreams Productions, LLC
www.ravendreamspdx.com

Printed in the United States of America

Table of Contents

Acknowledgments

Thank you to all my clients and students with whom I have shared many journeys and learned so much. I feel a tremendous gratitude to all of the people that I have worked with, or am still working with, and a specific acknowledgement is needed to all of those who have given me permission to use their charts as examples in my classes and in this book, thank you.

Thanks to my good friend Jonathan for the initial edit and tidying up of my first draft and to Keith for proof-reading and sharing ideas.

For the tireless work of my friend and collaborator Tony Howard who edited and arranged this work, I extend gratitude.

And I wish to acknowledge the dedication of my partner Clare who was so dedicated in the pursuit of excellence in her Art during the period of writing this book that I was finally inspired to convert long held ideas of my own into actual form.

Introduction

Consciousness and the Zodiac

This book explores astrology from the starting point that all 12 signs of the Zodiac represent archetypes that are symbolic of the complete range of experience of human consciousness. The totality of consciousness can be likened to a field that contains every possible state of being, action or experience. This is the ultimate context from which all content emerges, and in which humans find their place as co-creative aspects of the Cosmos.

In their highest expression, the 12 archetypes of the Zodiac represent a symbolic correspondence between the infinite potential of the total field and all possible ranges of human experience within that field. The critical fashion in which the 12 archetypes manifest within the individual natal chart corresponds to the nature of the particular "charge" that an individual emanates: the expression of the creative and spiritual will of the individual. Emanating the energetic of this charge, the individual then aligns with the multiplicity of potential realities.

When explored in depth, the birth chart is a powerful asset for understanding the nature of the charge and therefore the reality of the individual as experienced on both a conscious and unconscious level. We enter the doorway for this exploration through Pluto, Uranus and the nodal axis of the Moon. The central purpose of this book is to illustrate how this analysis can be achieved and how the innermost concerns of the individual life can be contextualized through this understanding.

Connecting With the Deep Self

Conventional medicine and therapy all too often fail the client by not acknowledging the meaning of their suffering, the potential insight behind the apparent struggle in the ordinary world. It is far too common for over-extended medical professionals these days to hand out unnecessary medication or simplistic diagnoses. In an effort to ameliorate our symptoms in the easiest way possible, we have turned away from the language of soul, the true meaning of psychotherapy, towards a confused marketplace filled with promised cures for our ills.

The deep self is the true nature of psyche or soul. By focusing on the deep self within the individual the astrological approach I outline here serves as a corrective to this collective imbalance. From the reality of the deep self we can see that our depression, anxiety, existential confusion and despair can be linked to a loss of soul perspective – a loss of the capacity to see through to the *nature of the field*, the underlying reality from which we can never be truly separate (though we may experience the suffering of seeming to be so). The reality of the deep self is multi-dimensional. It includes all of our past experience as well as our potential for the future. From this perspective the soul is viewed through the lens of Pluto, in all its incarnational history, with its stored potential and wounding, without taboo, without judgment, but with absolute honesty, necessity and intensity. The idea of intensity is of central importance: the innermost psyche measures prior experience by impact not by duration.

Time itself is not just a quantitative phenomenon. It also has a qualitative dimension, measurable in terms of intensity. An experience that only last a few seconds might be of sufficient intensity to vibrate through space and time for millennia whereas an event that took centuries to unfold can be easily forgotten. This paradoxical language of intensity is the domain of Pluto, Uranus and the nodes of the Moon. They speak to us of what has mattered most to the deep self of the individual into whose natal chart we are gazing.

The focal point of the psyche may include events, memories or feelings from early childhood, from life in the womb and from events in prior lives or in-between lifetimes. For the deep self does not seem to hold to the boundaries of the body, mind or specific arc of just one lifetime. Events may be of such importance or high impact that they echo throughout the psyche without limit.

Why Pluto, Uranus and the Nodes of the Moon?

Pluto holds the key to unlocking the mystery of primary events – moments of intensity that have reverberated throughout millennia. We may be born time and time again but, like the circle of the Zodiac, perhaps we just spiral around the same key events and issues. Prior-life analysis in the horoscope is not an attempt to delineate the quantity of prior experiences, their locations or characters (though it may touch upon these) but is instead a vehicle to assess the quality of the life in the present from the point of view of the deepest reverberating impacts. Such impacts may have happened in a yesterday of 24 hours duration or of 2,400 years duration. Time is not the central to our understanding of the experience Pluto represents. Understanding the nature of the impact is the key to entering Pluto's domain, which we will explore in great detail.

Uranus represents the corresponding aspect of the mental body: the part that can, in certain heightened states, recognize consciously the "stored residues of our own prior lives as information in the here and now."[1] Therefore Uranus holds the blueprints in the subtle mind of potentials as well as past traumatic memories that may still shape the current life.

Prior-life material, traumatic or otherwise, can be included within the therapeutic encounter, whether an astrology reading or on-going counseling. It is my experience that it adds a profound extra dimension to the work of healing. You cannot begin to heal any problem until you understand its origin, for it is much easier to surrender or come to terms with issues that you have begun to make conscious. The approach I present here allows for an expanded conception of what one can become conscious of, and therefore carries a profound healing potential.

The nodes of the Moon refer to the prior life dynamics of the individual on the conscious level – the kinds of egos (Moon) that were manifest in the past in order to express the psychological (Pluto) and mental (Uranus) needs of the deep self. The Moon corresponds to the responses we make as a result of our family conditioning and the development of our conscious and unconscious identity in this life. Through the South Node of the Moon, we can understand the background layer of the deep unconscious which includes the main residues of the intense events of the past that have shaped the psyche (Pluto) and subtle mind (Uranus).

The Infinite Field and the Karmic Dimension

In *Along the Path to Enlightenment*, Dr. David Hawkins describes "the field"– a foundational concept in this work.

> The infinite field of consciousness is All present, All powerful, and includes All of Existence. Thus nothing can possibly happen outside its infinite domain because it is the Source of Existence. Within this infinite field of power, there are decreasing levels of energy fields. As they are expressed progressively in form (linearity), their relative power decreases all the way down to the individual.
>
> The giant field could be compared to an immense electrostatic field in which the individual is like a charged particle that, because of the infinite power of the field, is automatically aligned within the field according to its individual "charge." The charge of the karmic spiritual body is set by intention, decision, and alignment by intention.
>
> It appears to naïve perception that what is not intellectually explicable seems to be "accidental", especially when the event is unpredictable. Inasmuch as the infinite field of consciousness is unlimited in dimension, nothing can happen outside of it. All that occurs within it is under its influence, and therefore, nothing "accidental" is possible in reality.[2]

The ultimate origin of this field is that of spirit, the inherent presence, the silent awareness burning within the heart of life. This is divinity and from that ultimate presence manifests the field of reality. The idea that within this infinite field there is no such thing as an accident is an expression of the law of karma as it operates as a universal law: what happens to us, what we experience, think, feel and act upon is an expression of who we really are and have ever been. From our true nature reality aligns to our intention and provides a perfect opportunity for us to evolve through observing the experience of who we really are being mirrored back to us by reality.

This is the perspective that informed Sri Yukteswar, astrologer and guru to Paramahansa Yogananda, when he explained that an individual is born at the moment of the perfect correlation of their individual karma with the movements of the heavens.[3] From this perspective the birth chart is a symbolic representation of our karma. Karma, from the perspective of the infinite field is simply the nature of who we are returned to us through our experience of our circumstances and our consciousness.

There is no outside agency manipulating our fate. The stars, as Plotinus ruminated upon so splendidly, are not causes of our experience, merely they correspond to our nature as the potential that we contain as we are born into this field, or into life.[4] There is no personal God that is somehow, like a powerful Santa, sitting apart from creation pulling the strings. This conception of God is merely an anthropomorphic projection onto the multidimensional field of potential that contains and enfolds us. God *is* the infinite field. This is the profound insight found in non-dualist teachings from Buddhism, the Hindu Vedas and even Christian mystics such as Meister Eckhart. This revelation does not deny one a personal relationship with God, for the infinite field is all-knowing and one can relate to that knowingness in a very personal way.

In *The Meaning of the Creative Act*, Nicholas Berdyaev, the Russian mystic and philosopher said "freedom is love."[5] By this he means that the creative act in its true potential transcends the world of necessity, the linear notions of cause and effect. The idea of non-linear, non-literal meaning and significance is central to the understanding of the context in which astrology works. The natal chart is not a cage from which we must be released. It is not a reality imposed upon us from without. The natal chart is the symbolic expression of the infinite field as it has been translated into human form and it is the expression of our karmic potentiality as held within that field. That potentiality emerges from the nature of who we really are. Karma in this sense is the creation of reality from our nature, not a punishing or rewarding system of pulleys and levers.

So the planetary aspects in our birth chart that we might see our struggle in do not *cause* our struggle. The planetary bodies are symbolic correspondences to the inner struggle we already experience as played out into the Cosmos, of which we are a living part. To understand the karmic potential within the birth chart is to approach an astrology in which the individual reality of the person whose chart is being examined is validated and given a deeper context from which the process of understanding, healing and surrender can proceed. From this perspective astrology becomes a powerful tool for generating awareness about the most difficult questions in life: Who am I? Why am I here? What am I meant to be doing?

It is with great pleasure that I share with you these profound techniques that I have so often seen aid others in healing the soul.

My Personal Evolution

The body of work introduced in the present volume comes from many years exploring the interface between spirituality, psychotherapy, hypnotherapy and astrology, each of which is in some way integral to my experience of life. In my early twenties, at the end of completing a master's degree in creative writing, I had a temporary experience of awakening that has never left my awareness. The origins of a spiritual consciousness, while already present within me latently, suddenly came upon my conscious awareness in an arresting and undeniable light. This experience of awakening to the nature of the field led me to begin my real education just as I left the higher education system. A series of teachers in London (William Bloom from the Open Mystery School and Yiannis Pittis, a Kabbalist) supported me as I read and meditated upon a variety of teachings of which I had remained completely unaware throughout my conventional education.

In 1995, at the age of twenty-four I studied Kabbalah and astrology with Warren Kenton (Z'ev Ben Shimon Halevi) and this led me to study my own charts and the charts of my friends. I became an astrologer almost overnight as I was the only one within my community with any interest in the subject. And initially interest took the place of any competence. I voraciously devoured works by Howard Sasportas, Liz Greene, Stephen Arroyo and then Heindel, Foster Case and Alice Bailey. I began to facilitate an informal series of classes on Kabbalah, Tarot and astrology within my community. At twenty-seven I began Noel Tyl's correspondence master's program and his support and encouragement through a difficult time was instrumental in developing an awareness that my gifts might reach beyond merely my personal community.

While the master's program gave me a whole new series of technical skills, Tyl's encouragement also led me to America for the first time and to two Astro 2000 astrology conferences in Denver. At the first one I was introduced to the work of Jeffrey Green whose talk on Saturn in Taurus gave me the most penetrating insight on my approaching Saturn return that I had ever received. Through the help of a German student of Jeffrey's, Ulrich Bold, I learned of a program in London that was to be taught mere months later which I was fortunate to attend as it became the only school of its kind in the U.K. In this school Jeffrey Green presented a form of astrology in which the spiritual nature of reality was the central premise making sense of the natal chart in a whole new way for me. At the same time I also began my training as a psychosynthesis therapist, learning a form of psychotherapy with an explicitly spiritual orientation.

During the week of my Saturn return I began my first public astrology class on the nature of the 12 archetypes and by 2002 I graduated from Tyl's mastership program, Green's Evolutionary Astrology school, and became an official psychosynthesis therapist. I also then began to teach the school of Evolutionary Astrology in the U.K. In 2005 I trained as an Alchemical hypnotherapist with David Quigley to further support my client work.

I have been teaching Astrology classes since 1999 and seeing clients as a therapist since 2001. I have accumulated over a decade of clinical work and many thousands of hours one-to-one in client work, readings and classes.

While any body of work must necessarily have a philosophical overview, much of mine has been shaped directly by my work with specific individuals both in one-off readings and in therapeutic dialogue. My current approach is formed by the intersection of Robert Assagioli's Psychosynthesis, Green's Evolutionary Astrology, the spiritual teachings of Mahayana Buddhism, Esoteric Christianity and the integrative work of Dr. David Hawkins.

The Structure of the Present Volume

This book is an introduction, though many might find it rather in-depth. Although this work has many influences it is self-explanatory; the reader is not charged with the task of having to read an outside source in order to fully comprehend it. The dedicated beginner can follow this book just as easily as a more experienced astrologer and I hope within it to clearly speak to both.

This book is arranged into 4 main sections:

- The "Pluto Complex"
- The Nature of the nodal axis of the Moon
- Uranus as both a signature of trauma and of liberation
- A final case study to illustrate the methodology in a step-by-step fashion

The first chapter is a re-examination of the seminal work of Jeffrey Green presented in *Pluto: the Evolutionary Journey of the Soul* in which he clearly articulates the power of Pluto as the planetary symbol that correlates to the evolutionary process from a collective and individual point of view.[6] For the sake of both the structural balance of the present volume and its therapeutic emphasis it is the individual's evolutionary processes that will be emphasized within the current text.

The radical insight, in a way the genius of Green, is to identify the source of deepest unconscious security as lying within that part of the consciousness that experiences itself within the Bardo, or that continues to experience itself in some subtle stream before birth and after death and therefore, symbolically at least, in prior lives or in states of identification with other more subtle forms of consciousness. Detractors of Green, or indeed the entire growing movement of Evolutionary Astrology criticize the work from this very same premise: the idea being that to say that you can see prior lives in the natal chart is hubris or plain fabrication. It is not my intention in the present work to engage with such criticism, which seems more to do with a question about the reality of reincarnation. But as we will explore explicitly within the second chapter, solely because clients experience recall of 'prior lives' it is therefore therapeutically valid, if not essential, to explore the memories, traumas and insights as they are presented by the individual *as if* they are real. For the client, the experience *is* real and therefore worthy of our respectful attention.

It is possible to explore the contents of this book without a belief in reincarnation. I present this material as a working hypothesis, alongside my understanding of verified spiritual and therapeutic traditions, which I have explored deeply in the service of my clients.

In Chapter 2 on the nature of the nodal axis of the Moon the idea developed in Green's work about Pluto as a depth unconscious signature will be expanded alongside his teachings on the nature of the ego, the Moon. In my client experience I have found that Pluto refers to a strata of the consciousness that is both fundamental and primarily unconscious, whereas the nodal axis of the Moon refers to experiences from the past that manifest on a more conscious personal level. If Pluto represents the soul, as Green suggests, the immutable aspect of the consciousness, or what I term the core of the deep self, then the South Node of the Moon represents the prior life, inter-uterine, early childhood 'ego' experiences that have arisen to express those deep unconscious drives.

The approach presented in this book, originated by Jeffrey Green, of fusing Pluto and the nodal axis of the Moon will henceforth be referred to as the "Evolutionary Axis" to delineate its critical role in determining the intended direction within the life path of the individual. The detailed case study in this section adds experiential validity to the nature of the concepts being discussed and reveals the therapeutic benefits that can be enjoyed as the result of exploring the Evolutionary Axis.

Chapter 3 on the nature and function of Uranus considers the critical importance of the Uranian archetype regarding the issues of trauma and liberation. This work has seeds in Green's first and lesser known work *Uranus: Freedom from the Known* that I have further developed through extensive client work.

Uranus is explored here as a signature of events within the mental body of the individual. As a higher octave of Mercury, Uranus refers to a long-term memory that can contain detailed memories of childhood, inter-uterine and prior-life experiences. The work of Stanislav Grof and his systems of condensed experiences (COEX's) will be evoked to explain the multi-leveled symbolism contained within the archetype. I argue here for the importance of Uranus in understanding trauma and healing by presenting a brief overview of the subject clinically with examples from client work. I argue for the importance of including Uranus alongside Pluto and the nodal axis of the Moon in the Evolutionary Axis.

In Chapter 4 I present a long case study with special emphasis on the methodology used to read birth charts presented in this volume in order to give step-by-step guidance to the reader who may wish to further explore this technique.

Chapter 1

Pluto: The Poet's Cookbook

The mast of a ship, a gallows, a cross at the cross-roads...
may be made of the same kind of wood, but in reality they
are *different* objects made of different material... They are
nothing but the *shadows* of real things... The shadows of a
sailor, a hangman and a saint may be completely identical...
Nevertheless they are different men and different objects...
A poet understands... the difference between a stone from
a wall of a church and a stone from the wall of a prison... He
hears the voice of the silence, understands the psychological difference of silence, realizes that *silence may be different*.
- Peter D. Ouspensky[1]

In this rather mysterious and yet beautiful passage, P. D. Ouspensky (the Russian mathematician, explorer of the fourth dimension and renowned disseminator of the trickster Gurdjieff's ideas)
sets out to show us that no two objects are the same and that context always supplies additional meaning. The stone in a church is
different in quality than the stone of a prison wall though they both
might be made of limestone, and have the same shape and weight.
The context of any given object, symbol or event is just as important
as the content.

As I face the prospect of sharing with you an astrological cookbook – one of the favorite tools of the modern astrology student – I
encourage you to hold this understanding in mind, realizing that
the context of the birth chart will dictate the ultimate meaning of
its parts in the end. Two people may have the same configuration

– say, Mars in Leo. But each person will have a completely unique experience of that Mars relative to their chart, and their personal history. That there are advantages for the student of astrology in using a cookbook is clear. At least initially, when trying to grasp a complex symbol system it can help to have the different components broken down into constituent parts in order to better understand them. This book aims to provide such a framework. However just as the inquisitive child might have tremendous fun taking apart an old transistor radio, it can be a lot more difficult putting it all back together again.

For example, let's consider the Pluto in Leo archetype. Pluto in Leo will have a strong inner sense of its own creative path, a self-conscious narcissism and need to engage with the expression of the self in a fashion that benefits from positive feedback from others. However the Pluto in Leo person will express these qualities and needs completely differently through a South Node in Pisces with the ruler (Neptune) in the 12th house in Libra, as opposed to a South Node in Aries with the ruler (Mars) in the 1st house. In the first example the person experiences creativity on a sacrificial basis and will likely express their need for power and approval through passive-aggressive or self-sabotaging strategies. In some cases such a person might manifest illness in order to attract the necessary feedback and concern from others that they cannot bear to relate with directly. In contract, the Aries South Node person is capable of direct action in order to feed the self, and may indeed tend towards another extreme – that of aggression and overt selfishness in order to fulfill the inner directive and need to express the self as it actualizes via creative pursuits.

So you see, the further we try to explain the chart through the content of specific placements to which we've attributed a universal meaning, the further we stray from the complex truth of the individual's experience. We must read each part in its greater context of the whole.

And how might we do that? This is a good question, but one without a simple answer. Though I do teach a method, for that is always a good starting point, the method is not fixed, and is not to be taken as such. I continually refine and adapt my method according to the input I receive from the real-life context of working directly with clients. When we read a chart, we have before us a unique being, with specific karma, and a specific set of issues and concerns. Only by relating to this individual *in their context* to the best of our ability may we begin to access the full potential of Evolutionary Astrology.

So use the following chapter not as an astrological cookbook, but as a poet's cookbook. It consists of twelve archetypal ingredients, from Aries to Pisces, which are interwoven in a unique way for each individual. The paradox of the poet's cookbook is that every ingredient, no matter how familiar, has the potential to add a completely new dimension to the meal in preparation. As astrologers we must always remind ourselves that while we may feel comfortable with our conceptual understanding of chart dynamics we can only ultimately aspire to an incomplete understanding of an individual's life and selfhood. If we approach each chart with the natural humility that arises with this revelation, we will provide the best service to our clients that we are able.

Technicalities

Before we get into the details, let's take a look at some of the technical ground rules I use in my practice. For all chart analysis, I use porphyry houses and modern planetary rulerships (Pluto as the ruler of Scorpio, Neptune as the ruler of Pisces, and Uranus as the ruler of Aquarius).

I will describe the potential of each placement while equating each sign with the house that it naturally rules, for instance, Pluto in the 1st house or in Aries. I am treating these two placements (1st house and Aries) as archetypally one and the same. Pluto in Aries is a generational signature (last evidenced in the 1850s) and so the house position of Pluto is the priority for understanding the archetype in the birth chart, even though the meaning of Pluto in the 1st house is essentially the same as Pluto in Aries.

Following the same line of thought, Pluto in the 1st house is archetypally similar to having Pluto conjunct or in very close aspect to Mars. The effect Pluto has on Mars in proximity via the fourth harmonic aspect (conjunction, square or opposition) is essentially similar to the effect of the 1st house Pluto. The 2nd house Pluto is similar to Pluto in aspect to Venus, and so on. I apply this same logic to the Nodes of the Moon in the next chapter. As we begin to blend the archetypes in the unique combination presented by each birth chart, we add detail and complexity to our overall understanding.

As we approach each archetype, we will consider its relationship by aspect to the others. The graphic that follows shows an empty chart with Aries on the Ascendant (see fig. 1). So for example, the two signs that naturally square Aries are Cancer and Capricorn. We'll consider the impact of this extra information when we explore each archetype. In some cases we will also consider the sequential relationship of each archetype with the idea that the progression of one archetype to the next can add insightful information to our understanding.

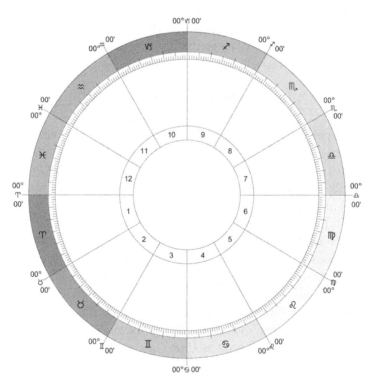

Figure 1. *Natal chart with Aries on the Ascendant*

The Pluto Complex

In the practice of Evolutionary Astrology an analysis of the Pluto placement of any given chart provides the baseline understanding – the context – for the entire birth chart. From its Greek association to Hades and the underworld, Pluto represents the idea of hidden riches and treasure (Hades being the brother of Zeus and ruler of the depths as his brother ruled the sky). With Evolutionary Astrology, we can identify the source of these riches in each chart, as Pluto relates to each soul's unconscious security needs and the issues held within.

By deepening our understanding of this complex in each person's chart, we can not only see the chart as a whole from a rich foundation, we can become aware of the specific content of the subterranean wealth guarded by the Lord of the underworld. Pluto adds the capacity for depth and compulsion to the range of expression signified by its sign and house placement. To identify the Pluto complex is to establish a foundation from which we can understand the entire birth chart. Through Pluto, we become aware of the central evolutionary concerns stemming from deep within the soul. When we register these potentials and underlying motivations, we can experience the rest of the chart in its naturally profound complexity.

Pluto relates to our deepest unconscious security needs and as a result, those behaviors that we (primarily unconsciously) default to under stress. We build a feeling of security on the foundation of what is most familiar, those experiences which have occurred before. Our deepest unconscious security needs are linked with repeating clusters of prior life and early childhood feelings and experiences. For instance, if a person is raised by cold and distant parents, their adult relationships might take on that same (familiar) form. If this pattern repeats, the unconscious gets used to the pattern and will require great energy to change. Pluto symbolizes the gravitational pull of the past. Green writes:

> From a purely psychological point of view, Pluto correlates to the deepest emotional security patterns in all of us. These security patterns are unconscious. Most of us automatically gravitate to the path of least resistance. The

patterns in identity association that are carried over from the evolutionary past are directly linked to the path of least resistance and, therefore to our security needs at an unconscious level.[2]

It is this deep source of unconscious security that forms the essence of what I call the "Pluto complex." To the extent that we form our deepest security on what we already know or have been, we rest on the past. To the extent that we feel comfortable evolving into new forms, we leave the past behind and grow towards the future. From this paradox arises the Plutonian problem of attraction and repulsion. We are attracted to people, places, and ideas that symbolize our evolutionary intentions just as we are repulsed by them if they threaten our pre-existing security, which is formed through identification with the past and what we already are. This conflict, or process, is symbolically portrayed in the birth chart by the natal position of Pluto and the point opposite to that (whether a planet is there or not). The polarity point of Pluto (the point opposite) represents the promise of the Pluto level of identification to evolve towards the future.

Pluto represents the core psychological realizations of what occurred in the past: the events of highest intensity that have marked the development of the self. Pluto represents the behaviors and orientations in consciousness that allowed the self to manage or cope with what occurred before. If a person is too attached to a prior orientation because it provided a feeling of security, then compulsion or obsession can arise as one possible expression of the Pluto complex. In this way, the compulsion to repeat old patterns is born out of resistance to the evolutionary impetus to grow or transform. Such resistance can become a source of major stress, illness or dysfunction. The way this might manifest can be explored through the birth chart.

The Pluto complex also relates to the deepest level of attraction within the soul. To the extent that the needs symbolized by the Pluto complex are understood and approached by the individual, there are consequent attractions to people, places and ideas that symbolize the soul's desires. However a conflict can arise between ego and soul as the awareness of the Pluto complex comes into consciousness, because the ego can become afraid of its own non-existence in the face of the awareness of the greater depth of the deeper self. If this conflict arises, there is subsequent resistance, and a person may experience a corresponding repulsion towards the very thing that they had been drawn or attracted to. This attraction/repulsion dynamic is a core part of how the Pluto complex expresses itself in an individual's life.

The Pluto complex revolves around the tension between ego and soul. The nature of the soul is freedom, infinite love and gratitude to the divine. The nature of the ego (an aspect of soul unaware of its origins) is that it is in love with its own bondage. In *The Republic*, Plato's "Allegory of the Cave" provides an excellent image of the ego's self-imposed imprisonment, symbolized by shadows on a cave wall. In the allegory, which is an imagined conversation between Plato's brother and his teacher Socrates, Socrates tells the story of a group of people who have lived all of their lives chained to the wall of a cave, in which their only view is the blank wall before them. The people watch the shadows that are projected on the wall by the changing light and begin to ascribe forms to the shadows. The shadows account for the entirety of the prisoners' limited experience of reality. Socrates then likens the philosopher's experience to that of one of these prisoners suddenly freed from the cave and coming to understand that the shadows on the wall do not comprise the complete picture of reality at all.

Our entranced ego ascribes meaning to the shadows of life, engaging in the drama as if it were the most gripping soap opera, and yet ignorant of the source that creates the shadows before it – the light of the spiritual Sun. Whereas the soul sees change as an adventure, the ego sees the same change only in terms of what might go wrong, what might be lost. This fear of the loss of the known compels the ego, even paradoxically, if the known experience is actually a burden. The burden is at least familiar, and less frightening than the unknown represented by freedom. But in that freedom lies the essence of the true identity – the more complete picture of who we are, including the source of the light within us.

The Course in Miracles teaches that all decisions can be essentially boiled down to the choice between Love and Fear. Similarly we can think of each life choice as one between ego and soul.

The Pluto complex is a paradox of dualism between the ego and the self which can only be ultimately transcended through the realization of the non-dual nature of reality.[3] From the vantage point of the ego which sees before it a linear world of cause and effect, the polarities of astrology (Aries-Libra for example) appear to be real. The apparent dualism of ego and self (or Samsara and Nirvana) also appears to be real. But as the Buddhist Heart Sutra beautifully teaches, Samsara is Nirvana and Nirvana is Samsara: they are both the same. This is the radicalism of non-duality, which we will explore throughout this text. In non-duality, the kingdom of heaven is already here. There is no need to strive after it, and like the prodigal child we can return whenever we chose.

While it is important to contextualize this work within the field of non-dual truth as the highest expression of enlightened insight, it is equally important to remain grounded in material reality. Within the relative world, the astrological polarities are relevant to our divided experience and they are explored in this section as the critical indicator of the fundamental starting position of the individual coming into this life. The aim of astrological counseling is to help generate the energy required by the individual to resist the gravitational pull of the compelling but destructive material Pluto points to in the birth chart.

With that, let's take our first steps toward understanding the Pluto complex by taking a closer look at Pluto's expression through each archetype.

Pluto in the 1st House/Aries

Pluto in the 1st house or Aries symbolizes the beginning of a whole new cycle. Fresh from the ocean of Pisces, the potential for new being emerges through Aries, and as such there is a natural sense of possibility, an instinctual sense of purpose or destiny. With Pluto symbolizing the evolutionary desire of the soul we can see that in the 1st house or Aries the deepest impulse is towards independent experience, the freedom to perpetually grow and express one's will. This desire will be felt primarily on an instinctual level, as an inner pulse driving the person forward. Consequently there may be little or no conscious understanding of these dynamics.

As the ruler of this first archetype (Aries and the 1st house), Mars represents the instinctual will, the expression of desire, the gut response to others and to life.

With Pluto ruling Scorpio, the eighth archetype, there is a natural quincunx (150° aspect) between Scorpio and Aries. This is indicative of the potential conflict or inner crisis between the soul desire or attachment in Scorpio and the instinctual desire for perpetual expansion in Aries. The quincunx between these archetypes is indicative of the potential for increased crisis between the soul and ego based on their differing attractions. The evolutionary purpose for Pluto in Aries/1st house is the search for self, for the fulfillment of one's individual potential. This purpose is actualized through the attractions of the instinctual body toward immediate experience.

The Aries impulse demands freedom, novelty, and the unchecked expression of desire, whereas Pluto relates to the deepest unconscious security. The need for security, which is often experienced through familiarity and repetition, stands in marked contrast to the martial will that wishes to push into ever new territory. Pluto represents the core of our impulse to seek meaning, the part of us that asks "why?" This differs innately from the purely instinctual expression of the will in Aries. The conflict arises in the Pluto in Aries person because Aries is not self-referential, while Pluto/Scorpio is.

In his book *The Act of Will*, Roberto Assagioli, the Italian founder of Psychosynthesis, underscores the primacy of the will in life as critical to our evolution.[4] In addition he makes the point that there are many different components to the will – that the will is not a singular expression. It is important then to ask, "Who is will-ing at this precise moment?"

Assagioli concludes that there are many different parts that make up our experience of self and calls these sub-personalities. These diverse parts of the overall personality may take on a life of their own if they are not ordered by a central principle, which he labels the individuality or "I." This "I" is in a constant dialogue with the soul or Higher Self, an on-going relationship that he named the I/Self Axis.

That the will has many different expressions or sub-personalities is an idea that is also embedded within the framework of the twelve archetypes of the Zodiac. The will evolves by a progression through all twelve archetypes. In the first stage of the evolution, in Aries, there is a purely instinctual, self-orientation. In Taurus there is the foundation of inner values; in Gemini, the establishment of language and conceptualization of the world, and so on. By the time we get to Scorpio we experience the will in a highly intensified form; compressed and internalized in order to focus on the inner meaning of experience. The conflict between the Aries and Scorpio styles of expressions of the will suggest the possibility of a core identity crisis within the Aries/1st house Pluto individual as they struggle with the perpetual impulse toward the new alongside a growing need to understand what is happening to them. One is a constant reaching out, the other the need to reflect on what has already been in order to understand it.

At its best the Pluto/Scorpio process is like a well of deep clear water refreshing the individual with meaning. But the need for the familiar can become like stagnant water and the individual can feel trapped, stifled and purposeless. Such a state will lead the Pluto in Aries/1st house person to one of two possible expressions of martial anger – explosion or implosion. The Pluto in Aries/1st house person will rage against another (or against the self) in defense of the on-going need to break beyond pre-existing limitations. This expressed rage can be very destructive. If the anger is instead repressed (as signified by other factors in the chart, for example a strong Saturn influence) then it can become the source of cyclical and deep depression.

These feelings of anger, internalized frustration and/or depression can potentially lead this person to a breakdown of their instinctually narcissistic focus. The loss of identity precludes their capacity to grasp what they want because they simply are not clear enough about what that is. This limitation can lead them the need to initiate relationship, to reach out to others. This need is expressed by the polarity point (the opposite) of the 1st house Pluto which is the 7th house or Libra. The individual turns towards others for that which is new, in the hope that shared experience will take them beyond their current impasse.

Since Pluto in Aries/1st house individuals are highly magnetic and have a strong sense of purpose they tend to attract others who can match that. Often these people will support the individual in rediscovering the sense of adventure that they need so strongly in order to feel alive. Others to whom they are attracted by virtue of their strong physical or psychological charisma will shock and inspire them into a new path or direction.

The Pluto in Aries/1st house individual is often instinctively drawn towards certain people just as they are repelled by others, but all of these relationships originate on an intense physical/sexual level, or a strong animal magnetism. Some of these relationships are sexual, others are not; yet the intensity of the attraction will be apparent. At times these individuals may experience the paradox of attraction and repulsion co-existing towards the same person. This can happen if what they are attracted to calls into question their nature or their path. Often such relationships play out in extremis. For example, the individual may totally fall for someone, completely obsessed with everything about the object of their desire, hanging on every word and feeling as though this person exists just for them.

Conversely if someone turns them off these individuals may completely ignore everything they say or do, as if they simply did not exist. In those cases where attraction and repulsion co-exist (because what the 1st house Pluto person is attracted to in the other represents a threat to their existing security) the person may be in for an emotional roller-coaster ride whereby they cyclically are consumed by their attraction to the other only to later totally reject or ignore them.

Returning again to the quincunx aspect between Aries and Scorpio, we can understand that the conflict between the desire for the new and the desire to maintain security plays out externally in relationships. For example, if the person develops a strong sexual attraction to another person but they are already in a relationship, the dilemma is played out literally. Their desire to maintain security and stay in the current relationship is eclipsed by the desire to pursue the new object of their attraction.

Sometimes a more complex dynamic arises. The Pluto in Aries/1st house individual often initiates relationship when they have reached an impasse within themselves. Such relationships suffer with the paradox of the strong subconscious need for security alongside the ever present impulse toward the new. When the new relationship is just beginning, the other person embodies that new potential and becomes a portal through which the individual re-engages with their life path. But as the relationship progresses, by nature, the new person becomes familiar, thereby meeting the deep unconscious (Pluto-Scorpio) security needs. As such, the basis for the initial attraction – the freedom of the new – becomes completely transformed over time into the very quality that this person had been struggling with before meeting the other: the comfort of the familiar.

The word familiar itself expresses a resonance with the family. We learn what we are familiar with through our early childhood conditioning. Aries/Mars/1st house stands in archetypal conflict with the family conditioning as signified through the natural T-square from Aries to Cancer/Capricorn (and the 1st house to the 4th/10th houses). The instinctual will (Aries-Mars) stands in archetypal conflict with the early childhood ego formation (Cancer-Moon) and the conditioning structures of the family and society (Capricorn-Saturn). Simply put, the instinctual will does not like to be told what to do, either by mom and dad or by society. As Sigmund Freud's concept of the super-ego explicates, at times the suppressive influence of the father-society (Saturn) and the emotional shadow of the mother-home (Moon) becomes the basis for neurosis because they can both suppress the instinctual sexuality and will (Mars).[5]

Bringing this awareness into our analysis, to the extent that the experience of a new partner (who initially represented freedom) begins (through time and proximity) to represent the familiar, then the potential for all the conditioning impulses from childhood and the unresolved anger symbolized by the Mars-Pluto quincunx crisis can come to bear on the relationship. In extreme cases this is a process that culminates in acts of physical violence.

In one common scenario, the Pluto in Aries/1st house person unconsciously attracts a partner that has some fundamental flaw, thereby guaranteeing that the relationship will not last. In this way they leave the back door perpetually open for someone else. Why? So that their inner fear of imprisonment is never realized through excessive proximity to someone else. If the relationship does not last long enough, it will not trigger any family conditioning or feelings of entrapment. In this way the person maintains the ultimate freedom to explore their own will and desire unchecked.

Other scenarios involve a critical distortion of the 7th house/Libra polarity point, in that relationships will develop in which there is some kind of fundamental inequality between the partners. The Pluto in Aries/1st house person may be the dominant force, subconsciously attracting a weaker-willed individual to guarantee eventual separation. The weaker person's neediness and security issues (Aries square to Cancer) are experienced as distracting them from their desire to be free to do what they want. Conversely they may attract a totally dominating partner, again guaranteeing a finite time limit on the relationship. Yet other 1st house Pluto individuals avoid relationships altogether in order to keep the subconscious fears at bay.

For many people with this placement, the lack of relationship, or the repetitive cycle of all-too-brief relationships can become a source of great disappointment and frustration, even though their own deeper subconscious fears are instrumental in maintaining that situation. The polarity point of Pluto in the 7th house or Libra reveals that the loner karma of the past is seeking to shift by way of experiencing the self-knowledge and growth that can occur through the mirror of meeting others face-to-face. In order to evolve past the point of what is already known, the soul needs others through which to experience feedback as to the nature of the self-consciousness that it has developed.

The critical factor in transcending the intimacy paradox lies in the nature of the partner who is chosen. If the couple can understand the early family or prior-life conditioning and make room from the subconscious fears of entrapment to be experienced in a meaningful context, then a place for healing is made within the partnership. If the partner can then be secure enough within themselves to allow the 1st house Pluto person to go off on their own and continue to experience their journey of self-discovery, then the relationship need not necessarily be experienced as restrictive. These are not simple dictates – they require dialogue, listening and compromise, all of which are Libra/7th house issues that the soul is seeking to develop and integrate.

Pluto in the 2nd House/ Taurus

Following the yang archetype of Aries is the yin Archetype of Taurus. In contrast to being driven by the outgoing need for instinctual fulfillment, the person with this placement withdraws somewhat in order to experience the nature of their own values and needs from within. Over lifetimes, people with Pluto in the 2nd house and Taurus have had an on-going need to develop self-reliance and internal security. Taurus correlates with biological survival and these people are often harboring memories of prior-lives in which their survival was threatened or they had to develop simple coping mechanisms in order to survive intense and difficult experiences. They enter this life with a highly internalized energy structure, a strong physical/ sexual energy and a strongly developed sense of self-sufficiency.

This person has had a tendency to withdraw from external circumstances and activities which has led to the development of an internal fixed identity as the basis of inner security. This is an innate strength, developed by coping with experiences that have been threatening to their identity. To the extent that this has included prolonged periods in prior lives (or in this life) spent in survival mode (where each day one is tested to the very limits without the absolute minimum resources needed to get by) then there is a tendency for a narrowing of focus to occur. A limiting of the personal field of vision was necessary in order to cope with harrowing or edgy experiences. While useful at the time, this has created the karmic potential for stuckness and habitual self-imposed limitation. Now this limited vision no longer supports the soul's real potential for growth.

Survival issues often involve money. Relative to the difficulty people with these signatures have had in their current or prior lives with issues of survival there may be excessive or distorted significance applied to money. This might manifest as a relatively complete identification with money as possessing the power that can magically prolong life or give it meaning. This viewpoint ignores the obvious existential truth that the richest Pharaoh and the poorest peasant all die just the same. This is also problematic because an attachment to a solely monetary system of valuation can distort all other forms of value (human relationships, creativity etc.) and lead to problems of avarice, and in extreme cases, manipulation and lies used in order to achieve material prosperity. If this is the working pattern in a person's karma, it will almost inevitably exist within a cyclic framework of gain and loss, and any highs of deception will contrast with lows of internal and external confrontations.

The confrontations described above are symbolized by the polarity point from Scorpio and the 8th house. The Scorpio/8th house polarity point encourages confrontation in order to break free of pre-existing limitation. In some cases the survival-threatening experiences that led to the (necessary) limitation will have been caused by material loss (personal or collective) through natural disaster, the change of a political system, a personal failing, or in rare cases through the consequences of the unfair acquisition of wealth (revenge, guilt and betrayal).

As a person begins to individuate, their identification with external things as expressions of personal power lessens and the identification with the self increases, which then becomes the central resource. In the process of individuating, withdrawal from the external world is necessary at times in order to clear the prevailing consensus influences and to reconnect with personal values.

To the extent that survival concerns become limiting, confrontations are implicit by the polarity point of Scorpio/8th house. These can take both internal and external forms, through facing limitation or through negative feedback from intimate others. Those close to the Pluto in Taurus/2nd house individual, on perceiving their unavailability and withdrawal, may feel compelled to initiate a confrontation. In this way personal frustration becomes the basis for evolution.

In fact, the 8th house polarity point suggests the very direct lesson of learning to work with others in a more open way. It is not enough for the 2nd house Pluto person to just work with others from the confines of their pre-existing limited view of themselves. If their creativity and vision is to be successful or meaningfully manifested they must realize their full potential and experience it through shared effort. Initially this may take a very practical direction. One person is frequently not enough to accomplish a goal no matter how energized or talented. If you want to have a successful band, you need several musicians. Even if you are the greatest solo flautist you still need musical and practical support to form a full sound and to produce your product. Initially the practical realization of how much more could be achieved in collaboration with others will draw the 2nd house Pluto person into shared projects and collective experiences. Eventually that experience can lead to an insight that the shared experience is inherently valuable rather than just a means to an end.

The 2nd house describes how we internally relate to ourselves, how we identify and begin to meet our base needs. In contrast, the 8th house polarity point includes the nature of powerful people we attract to ourselves in order to have an impact on our sense of personal power. In this way the 8th house polarity point speaks of an evolutionary crossroads between the self-reliance of the past and the need to confront the existing limitations that such a self-imposed sense of meaning has generated. We've explored some of the ways significant others will enter the 2nd house Pluto person's life to great impact. Such significant relationships may also include profound (internal or external) struggle as they represent that which is most deeply longed for, and most deeply resisted at the same time. This is how the attraction/repulsion issue at the heart of the Pluto complex expresses for this archetype.

If we return to Plato's image of the shadow on the wall, we see that the Pluto in Taurus person faces a similar challenge in needing to expand their perceptions beyond a limited view. They must face the fear that moving outside of their perceived limitations will threaten their survival and the loss of self-reliance. The soul (signified by both the natal Pluto placement and its polarity point) sees that operating from survival mode inherently narrows experience and that one can learn to live again through the opening of personal boundaries to new encounters, to let in more of the sky. In this way the pre-existing self-reliance of the Pluto in Taurus/2nd house person becomes an inner strength brought to the new adventure rather than a stance that exists only by habit or for its own self-preservation.

Pluto in the 3rd House/Gemini

As we move to the third archetype in the Zodiac, we can explore the context from which it arises in the cycle. If we view the twelve archetypes of the Zodiac as a symbolic story of human life and evolution, then on a psychological level the 1st house/Aries can represent birth and the nascent identity instinctually striving to meet its needs within the early environment. The 2nd house/Taurus represents the phase of object constancy that follows the initial purely instinctual phase of life. In early infant-family relations the parental figure is internalized to a sufficient degree that the child is able to be left alone or play by themselves to a certain extent. The child has an inner knowingness that the parent is still *there* even when not actually physically present. Traumatic events or serious neglect at either of these key stages can be enormously detrimental to the development of a healthy personality. Both the Aries phase and the Taurus phase consist of a critical pre-verbal or partially verbal stage of the development of the self.

The Gemini/3rd house phase relates to the child's verbal development and the experience of intense curiosity about its environment. Recent studies on healthy children show how the development of the language faculty depends upon contact, touch and holding by the parents to stimulate areas of the brain related to the acquisition of speech. Studies on so-called "feral children" (those brought up in captivity or by animals) reveal that the development of the verbal centers of the brain comes about through mimicry and specific human contact. Children raised by dogs often whine, howl and bark and are more comfortable communicating in the canine idiom.

In the alleged "forbidden experiment" of Holy Roman Emperor Frederick, eleven children were raised without any human interaction in order to discern whether Latin or Hebrew was the "innate" language. All died before any could prove anything other than that human contact is required for children to survive and thrive. It follows then that touch and holding are necessary healthy components of the Taurus phase, directly related to the proper development of the Gemini function in the next phase. Before we can begin to develop language (Mercury), we need to have survived (Aries), and we need to be have been held and touched, hence able to establish a link to our real inner needs (Venus). In fact, with this information we can now observe the theme with Pluto in any given archetype that the greatest potential problem we face is the failure to evolve through the pre-existing archetype.

Those with Pluto in Gemini/3rd house are learning how to expand into their environment in order to intellectually engage in life. Ideally the person has internalized the gifts of the prior 2nd house/Taurus phase including inner strength and a feeling of self-sufficiency such that the individual now wishes to engage with the world around them through collecting data, naming things, and passing on that information to others. This is the "Adamic" act of the 3rd house Pluto: the giving of names and classification. This act leads to an intellectual security that can be added to what was (hopefully) the emotional security of the 2nd house experience.

With Pluto in Gemini/3rd house the *idea* of who one is becomes as important as the biological or felt needs. The compelling need is *to know* – to structure the knowledge of their environment and to intellectually organize that environment so that it makes sense to them. Interestingly the Swiss thinker and education reformer Rudolf Steiner argues for a delay in learning language during childhood so that the child does not develop the capacity to label faster than their inner ordering of reality can manage (Taurus-Gemini in harmony). That philosophy underlies Waldorf School education, one of the fastest growing independent educational movements in the world.[6]

The attraction/repulsion aspect of the Pluto complex conflict is played out for this placement through their need to intellectually organize of the environment. The desire to know more is based on curiosity and need for expansion, yet emotionally the nature of security is generated through familiarity. So the temptation for this placement is for the person to create an intellectual structure of a known and familiar kind. This (safe) structure is then consistently threatened by the very curiosity and need for intellectual expansion that underlies the Gemini archetype. Words are used to construct concepts of identity – safe and "known" ideas – and yet the natural tendency towards curiosity leads to new words and new ideas that threaten their pre-existing safe constructs. Such a dilemma leaves the individual with a perpetual choice at the level of the will: to embrace the new or stick to a comfortable intellectual framework.

This issue forms the basis of the cyclic destruction of familiar intellectual worlds for the individual, with all the potential for emotional fallout that can accompany such loss. Pluto in any given archetype indicates the prominence of the issues of that archetype in establishing and maintaining the core security of the individual psyche, and here those issues include communication, information and the intellect.

If someone threatens our existing intellectual framework it can feel like an attack. If the process of internalization symbolized by the Taurus/2nd house archetype has been problematic (e.g. the parents were too forceful or chaotic, or prior-life traumas too destructive) then the threats to the intellectual framework can be capable of threatening breakdown. Threats to how we make sense of our environment can lead to a fear of overwhelm, even insanity. This kind of conscious or unconscious fear can lead people to rigidly adhere to one "safe" intellectual framework in order to resist potential change or breakdown of meaning.

We can also infer from Gemini's relationship to the preceding archetype that a counter-reaction to the self-imposed limitation of Taurus can manifest as constant restlessness when Pluto is in Gemini or the 3rd house. The desire to learn new information is ever-present but is also accompanied by the fear that one will never have enough time to learn everything, or that one can never know enough. The evolutionary intention behind this placement is movement. The individual is meant to expand and grow but this process can be compulsive to the extent that they feel incapable of storing or making use of all the information that they are amassing. This can become its own problem: a disintegration process whereby the individual loses all sense of meaning, plunging blindly into more and more compulsive experiences that they have no real capacity to digest or integrate.

The polarity point of Sagittarius/9th house suggests a need to begin to develop an intuitive conception of meaning, a bigger picture in which this person can situate the diverse strands of their learning in order to weave together an integrative vision. If they achieve this, the constant pressure to learn can begin to relate back to a larger meaning whereby what is being learned gains new relevance. The container of the larger context of meaning is the antidote to the addiction to content that the Gemini/3rd house Pluto person has. For example, this person might align with a larger belief system (Humanism, Buddhism, Theosophy, or Jungian Therapy, etc.) and then relate all that is being learned to the meta-system, which serves as a protective canopy. This will allow the multiple forms of information taken in to be digested into some kind of context.

However, one person's meta-system is another person's poisonous restriction. For some, this approach will seem too restrictive and they will seek to create a larger framework of meaning via the interlocking of a number of different systems. However, a potential problem in doing so is that if the various systems are contradictory they can result in confusion and an inability to articulate and interact with the container of the greater context in a meaningful way. Many people with this problem reduce their interactions with larger systems to the magpie level, taking in only what catches their eye and leaving the rest. The problem then becomes lack of depth. People with this placement will need to seek out balance in their approach between adopting systems that are too restrictive, and trying to integrate too many systems. Once that balance is achieved, through developing a belief system they begin to have a subjective experience of knowing that goes beyond mere categories.

Whatever the path chosen, the soul intention is the development of the intuition to perceive reality in a more direct and inclusive fashion. This person is learning that the capacity of the mind to label reality is not the same as the capacity of the soul to fully experience reality. In his *Critique of Pure Reason*, Kant argued that we cannot *know* reality via the mind; we can only know the various categories of perception we place between us and it. This epistemological dilemma is at the heart of the modern problem of knowing the world. The 9th house polarity to the 3rd house Pluto holds the potential for transcending such Kantian categories of mind and perceiving reality in a more holistic fashion. This can occur via development of the personal intuition, which is akin to the Kabbalist path of probation, or the Middle Way of the Buddhists. The idea is to develop the capacity to perceive reality at the point of fusion of the self and world, instead of always keeping the world at arm's length via the conceptual powers of the mind.

Rudolf Steiner sees this process as following the path of Imagination-Intuition-Revelation whereby the development of the imaginative faculties (for instance by contemplating the nature of the plant within the seed) lead eventually to a direct perception of the life force.[7] In a beautiful illustration of Steiner's point, Brother Lawrence in *The Practice of the Presence of God* writes how while contemplating a tree in winter he saw the coming spring arrive and had an understanding/experience of the resurrection that led him into a contemplative life.[8]

The Pluto in Gemini/3rd house person need not have this kind of profound integration to benefit from the attempt to integrate their ideas into a larger context of meaning. The process of integrating alone will allow them to overcome the confusing merry-go-round of ideas which can lead to a complete loss of direction in life. If, however, the innate security of the individual is predicated primarily on intellectual foundations, then the potential exists for rigid thinking, argument instead of discussion, reaction instead of response, to occur compulsively. The intensity of these difficult exchanges will be directly proportional to the degree of personal security invested in them.

The potential exists with this placement for the development of a powerful mind. However, this presents another problem. Because in this case the mind is fused with the Pluto complex, the person may have a natural intense attraction to fellow thinkers, which can lead to intense conflict if they do not see eye-to-eye. The Pluto in Gemini/3rd house person may react to this kind of challenge by using intellectual manipulation, relying on their powerful mind to attempt to control the other by exposing the inherent weakness of their argument, regardless of whether or not what their opponent is saying is true. This can be likened to the skilful lawyer's dilemma: the successfully developed argument which may or may not be in service to the truth of the person who committed the crime.

With this placement the individual may have experienced profound psychological conflicts with regard to lies and deception of various kinds. This could take multiple forms: those around them not believing them, others experiencing them as profoundly incongruent, or others lying to them. One client of mine with Pluto conjunct Uranus in the 3rd house experienced her siblings as seeing her as incompetent in situations where she was helping out. In life outside of her family she was really successful, but in their eyes she remained the young helpless child to an extent where her siblings' experience of her was distorted enough to consistently support that view. These kinds of situations often have roots in excessive prior-life dependency on others, or in a past struggle to maintain an inner authenticity that is being tested now.

Another possible deception is the inner lie – the story that we tell ourselves to rationalize our difficult experiences and to protect our core identity from the shocking realization of our own motivations and weaknesses. Such inner lies can form the basis for identity crisis and for living out "double lives."

The potential exists for this person to have a powerful mind and be a charismatic speaker or writer. But people with this talent who also believe their own myth/lie can be powerful manipulators of the truth, and some even manage to fool lie detectors. This Gemini/Sagittarius issue shows up publicly within politics and the media, as we often see the gifted communicator who turns their inner fiction into a spectacle on the world stage. But the potential also exists for this individual to actually use their mental gift in service of the reality of their situation.

A frequent issue with this placement and related signatures is the ongoing need to know rationally what is going on at all times. This quality can drive some towards success and others to high anxiety, often both at the same time. There is a powerful need to know in order to satisfy an inner compulsion or concern. Sometimes these issues originate in prior-life traumatic memories of being persecuted for what they have written or said, or of being forced to speak out against themselves or others close to them, sometimes under torture or threat of loss and the terrible consequences of such events. Through coercion they may have been made to feel responsible for implicating someone in a crime and then felt responsible for the fate of that individual.

Whatever the roots of the issue, the constant pressure to rationalize ultimately stems from a kind of fear in the face of the unknown within life and surrendering it can bring greater peace of mind. The mind's desire to know cannot be underestimated. The value of that knowing is too easily over-estimated. Releasing the desire to know can bring profound relief – that one simply does not need to know everything.

Pluto in the 4ᵗʰ House/ Cancer

Returning to our image of the Zodiacal cycle mirroring the phases of childhood development, we arrive at the 4ᵗʰ archetype: Cancer/4ᵗʰ house. In the 3ʳᵈ house/Gemini phase of development we see the desire to learn about the environment and with it the capacity for intellectual classification and language. We may conceptualize this process as the initializing of the physical-etheric body (Aries), the instinctive and emotional body (Taurus) and the mental body (Gemini), all of which coalesce in the formation of the ego, understood here to mean the conscious emotional body, symbolized by Cancer and the 4ᵗʰ house. It is with the development of the ego in Cancer that the personality becomes conscious of its surroundings in a more integrative fashion: my family, my society and my formative experiences. This is the central lens from which the individual then focuses on the world.

The Cancer archetype is cardinal. Pluto in any cardinal house or sign indicates the start of a new cycle. The cardinal sign Aries represents birth, a completely new experience in being. In Cancer and the 4ᵗʰ house the new cycle relates to the experience of emotional security. The soul intention here is to generate security in response to excessive attachment to *external* sources of security such as lovers, parents and family, work or ideological concerns. True happiness and contentment are impossible to achieve when there is excessive attachment to centers of meaning outside of the self. So the intention here is to come into right relationship with nurturing relationships of a familial nature.

With this being the beginning of a new cycle, likely as not, the individual has not yet grasped the evolutionary intention and many will be born into a family situation wherein one or both parents fundamentally misunderstand the true nature of the Pluto in Cancer/4ᵗʰ house individual. There may be some kind of traumatic shock or abuse, or the family may simply fail to meet the basic needs of the child. All of these experiences effectively cause this individual to rely on their own emotional resources from a very young age. As an infant one is naturally dependent on parental figures. The length of time the human infant is dependent on the parents is long relative to other mammals. As such the impact of emotional shocks or failures of care during early development is profound, forcing the person into a long-term sensitivity about the nature of their emotional body and the way in which they constitute their sense of security.

This placement may indicate a situation wherein one or both parents have complicated karmic back-stories with the 4th house Pluto individual, perhaps in cycles of letting each other down or through some kind of collective (familial, tribal) event in which the family were lost to each other, thereby fostering an ongoing unconscious insecurity. Such memories and the resultant stress can lead to a childhood situation in which compulsive emotional patterns of behavior are the norm, because difficult prior-life associations and present-life emotional transferences are recycled. The specifics of such karmic dynamics can be found by studying the chart of the 4th house Pluto individual alongside the chart of one or both of the parents. In addition, much can be learned by exploring the subjective dimensions of the early childhood experience and the existing karma can be intuited via the parent-child relations in early life.

I have found that the early childhood experiences which show up as transference dynamics in later intimate relationships (with best friends, lovers, therapists) contain the keys to prior-life dynamics. The strong feelings that are elicited from close adult relationships hold the key to intense childhood feelings, which if understood with a certain openness and depth lead directly back to the experiential level of prior-life dynamics.

This level of insight is of critical importance with the Pluto in Cancer/4th house person as they will likely develop emotional problems to the extent that their fundamental emotional needs were not met during childhood. Intense emotional memories from prior lives are evoked upon incarnating into this life which then permeate this person's childhood like a mist. These feelings can follow the individual into adulthood until the evolutionary intention of learning to meet those needs in oneself is addressed.

The nature of the prior-life wounding can be so intense as to leave an emotional void in this person that is near-impossible to fill even if the parent is relatively loving or adjusted. In such cases the simple fact that the parent might have other concerns (e.g. working long hours, an ill relative to care for) might trigger unresolved feelings related to prior-life memories of abandonment and familial destruction.

The Pluto complex always contains the potential to manifest compulsively or as a cyclic power struggle. At times the Pluto in Cancer/4th house person has a parent who secretly or overtly manipulates them or seeks to dominate them in order to satisfy their own unmet childhood needs. This narcissistic wounding can form the basis for cycles of abuse that grow within the family as the abused person adopts the language of abuse as synonymous with love and family. They have repetitively experienced that familiar figures hurt them and as such when they have their own family they might express their love through the same abusive patterns that were modeled for them, perpetuating the cycle. Inevitably such cycles can cause tremendous pain and personal disillusionment and the individual can come to a place where they feel powerless to do anything to change. The inner guilt for doing to others what felt so terrible to themselves can contribute to despair.

For the Pluto in Cancer/4th house individual who has not had their childhood needs met, the potential exists for them to enter adult relationships with those same displaced needs, attracting partners onto whom they unconsciously project their unmet childhood needs. They can also attract partners who mirror back to them the same unsuccessful parental responses, re-traumatizing themselves over and over. Thus they are forced via the evolutionary impulse to look within for the source of security, to find the inner emotional centre of their identity. In fact such cycles of behavior will repeat over and over until the removal of external dependencies reaches a critical mass and they experience themselves in a new light.

This process of uncovering the roots behind problematic relationship dynamics is a staple of therapeutic work and it almost always involves having to understand the way the child learned to love and seeing how that same child is involved in seemingly adult relationships. This is true of a number of signatures, not just Pluto in the 4th house or Cancer. We might see this kind of dynamic involving planets in the 4th house square planets in the 7th house or their rulers, or aspects to the Moon, etc.

The archetypal square between the 4th house and the 7th represents the conflict between family of origin and one's partners. This can be enacted on a literal level (mother does not think girlfriend good enough) or through psychological identification with the dysfunctional parental dynamics. The critical issue with the 4th house

Pluto is that the underlying theme of the internal sourcing of one's emotional security applies across the board and at a high level of intensity.

Pluto in relationship to the Moon in any aspect always leads to an intensification of the moods and the potential for emotional manipulation or acting out: tantrums, emotional withdrawal, feigning illness or emotional crisis used to gain attention. In some cases the person will create genuine illness or manifestations of extremity via self-harm or suicidal behavior in order to express their extreme frustration or to illicit the extreme response they fantasize would allay such frustration.

Another potential reaction to the extremity of emotional range is denial. The prior emotional shocks may have been so hurtful that the person learns to shut down prior to any feeling or natural connection arising with the idea that it is better to risk no contact than one in which the outcome is profound disappointment or let down. Such a reaction creates a conflict between the natural sensitivity, vulnerability and empathic capacity of this placement and the rigid or dissociative stance that they are adopting in order to control their powerful feelings. The by-product of this conflict can be behaviors whereby the person uses attack as the best form of defense. They might learn to manipulate or control others, pushing them to their emotional limits or unconsciously seeking their emotional vulnerabilities in order to exploit them, and by so doing protect their own. Or they might take the approach of becoming invaluable to another person by discovering and exploiting the other person's weakness, acting as the *de facto* counselor (or caretaker) without revealing their own vulnerability. Then they can be emotionally significant to another person without risk of being overexposed or having their own dynamics revealed. This close emotional context with others can become its own form of protectionism, denying the person's deepest feelings while establishing seemingly irreplaceable significance in the emotional lives of others.

To the extent that unresolved anger is a legacy of the childhood experience then such anger will eventually spill out into their close relationships. This might take the form of rages or tantrums, of overt attempts to control or dominate the other, or through the expression of silent and sulking moods in which they fill the shared space, subtly dominating the emotional atmosphere. Emotions are deeply felt with this placement and the intention is to get to the bottom (Pluto) of every mood and feeling (Moon) in order to understand the nature of the conscious emotional body, the ego nature. When this insight becomes stabilized within an emotionally secure person the potential for great psychological depth and extraordinary emotional sensitivity is revealed.

Another prior-life issue potential signified by this Pluto position (and also by Pluto in the 10th house or Capricorn or the nodes of the Moon and their rulers in the 4th or 10th houses) concerns gender discomfort. This discomfort might arise due to recent gender-switching from the past life to the current life such that they carry strong body memories or imprints of being the opposite gender. This discomfort might also express due to significant prior-life experiences that have their origin in gender conflicts, such as the cultural practice of the abandonment of female children, or the rejection of the emotionally sensitive male child as an inappropriate heir. Jeffrey Green sees the Moon, with its dark and light sides, as the representative of the anima/animus principle, which illustrates that every man has an inner feminine aspect (anima) and every woman an internal male (animus). So we might see individuals with the Cancer/4th house Pluto expressing some kind of imbalance in regards to gender, or rejecting conventional gender definitions as limiting, due to past-life experience.

Some 4th house Pluto people are born into families that support the growing evolutionary developmental edge of emotional self-reliance and are very supportive to the individual. Some families, while dysfunctional, do not seem to impact the individual as negatively as one might expect if they have already begun to internalize the lessons inherent to this placement prior to this life. Yet even in these situations emotionally difficult memories from prior lives can be triggered in the current life during periods of stress or introspection, or when the very nature of the prior-life memories is triggered in an echo-like fashion. In this case the compounding effect can be intense and overwhelming emotionally. As Hawkins writes:

> Although the suffering of loss is triggered by a specific event, the painful emotions of attachment have actually arisen from multiple sources over time, and there may be more of it below the surface than was first expected. Thus,

each loss actually represents all loss, for the experience is of loss itself and not just the specific event that brought it up to awareness. A helpful source of strength during the processing out of painful emotions is to identify with all of humanity and realize that suffering is universal and innate to the phenomenon of being human and the evolution of the ego.[9]

The polarity point here in the 10th house/Capricorn reflects the need for emotional maturation and self-determination. The essence of Capricorn as an archetype is the owning up to responsibility. The essential issue here is an emotional one – the need to take responsibility for all the emotional dynamics and scenes of the past as part of the karma of the individual. Rudolf Steiner calls this revelation a "sacred moment" when we can say:

I will put aside the transitory effect of life; I will view my sufferings in such a way that I feel how the wise man in me has been attracted by them with a magic power. I realize that I have imposed upon myself certain experiences of pain without which I would not have overcome some of my shortcomings.[10]

This inner "wise man" is the epitome of the Capricorn archetype that in its mature form urges the child to grow up into its own genuine power. Steiner's insight teaches us that from the point of empowerment we better understand our place in the Cosmos. We are not victims of some capricious fate but are instead participatory beings that co-create the world we inhabit with our karma and what we hold in mind. By embodying the Capricorn polarity, the child inside the Cancer archetype matures, learning not to blame others for their feelings or emotional problems. They see others as people with their own issues; supporting players in the human drama through which we are, by grace, given a precious opportunity to see our own dynamics and begin the great work of liberation from them.

Pluto in the 5th House/Leo

The Leo archetype stands as the supreme expression of the ego of the individual. Here the developing ego reaches its fulfillment through a focus on creativity and self-actualization. Pluto in the fire signs or houses tends to feel it has some kind of special destiny, but nowhere more so than with Pluto in Leo or the 5th house. In contrast to the instinctual sense of discovery with Pluto in Aries/1st house, the Pluto in Leo/5th house person experiences a conscious sense of creative purpose, a direct knowingness, with all the sense of entitlement that such knowledge can bring.

This feeling of specialness is intrinsic and operates from birth. The intensity of the feeling generates a powerful need for attention, to be recognized as special and unique, with consequences for the parent who fails to maintain this feat of endurance. The need in the person with this placement is compulsive and very difficult to satisfy. These individuals may test the parent with an endless pursuit of love and recognition, emotionally manipulating situations to make sure the primary focus remains on themselves. Parental attention directed towards others can provoke a highly defensive reaction. There is no guarantee that these feelings will not accompany the individual into adulthood.

The need to be in charge, and the intense narcissistic self-focus is an evolutionary necessity with this placement. There may have been lifetimes where their own developmental issues were problematically side-lined, or central concerns of theirs were overlooked. It now becomes imperative that this is not the case and the drive from deep within is to generate recognition for their powerful creative urges and desires. The position of the South Node of the Moon and its ruler will indicate the degree of aggression of the self-impulse just as it will indicate issues pertaining to any past restrictions that the soul is seeking to overcome. The critical issue is to identify the creative impulse as it was left off in the past (understood via the South Node of the Moon and its ruler) and to encourage its evolution via the North Node of the Moon and the polarity point of Pluto.

All people with Pluto in the 5th house or Leo have the need to advance some key aspect of their creative nature. The delusory potential in this is in believing their personal self to be the sole cause of the creative impulse, an inflationary tendency which distorts the true picture. The capacity for diva mentality arises. The image of the rock god reached its zenith/nadir (depending on your point of view) within the Pluto in Leo generation.

As it evolves, the 5th house Pluto/ Leo soul begins to recognize the reality of creativity as an expression of the joy and abundance of divinity within. Life expresses itself through the field of reality in which we are self-conscious centers of co-creative experience. The obvious "sin" of Pride, in the sense of *hamartia* (literally sin as "missing the mark") is that it is predicated upon the central premise that the ego is the author of experience. This avoidance of the true source of the Self can lead to over-identification with the creative role or purpose and blind the person to the way their personality or egoic needs corrupt the original intention. Conversely if the Leo energy is blocked in some way, via Saturnine restrictions in the early home-life or through disappointment or lack of feedback (remember that in prior lives many of these individuals have struggled to express themselves in the ways that now require emphasis) then an exaggerated sense of powerlessness is experienced as it seems to them that no one cares about their gifts.

An extreme grievance about the world's lack of recognition somehow dooming you to mediocrity is just as problematic an identification as thinking that somehow, like Canute that you can control the tides.[11] As Thomas Moore writes about creative people in *Dark Nights of the Soul*:

> I notice that two issues torture these people. First is the quality of their work. Generally they overvalue what they have done and are reluctant to edit, change, and educate themselves in their art. They tend to be inflated and self-important. I can understand that to be creative in the first place you have to have a large sense of self. But an unrealistic assessment of the work can make you uncertain. You don't know if your efforts are good or bad and you may question yourself constantly. But at the same time you may think of yourself as a genius.[12]

Some individuals with Pluto in Leo or the 5th house, a Pluto-Sun aspect or an emphasized Leo signature (such as the South

Node of the Moon or ruler) will have subconscious memories of being treated as special, either due to aristocratic or artistic heritage. This can lead to unconscious expectations that things will be the same again and can cause pain or discomfort if they are not. It will lead some to manipulate others in order to get the required affirming response from them. They might achieve this through taking the victim stance or perhaps by using an illness to gain attention.

Some with this placement may take on an aggressive pursuit of money or success, then pressuring others around them to behave in the right way to maintain their vicarious relationship to such riches. In public workshops, Jeffrey Green has emphasized the manner in which the Leo archetype can operate like the apex of a pyramid, the Leo Sun shining like the Pharaoh with its subjects below it in ranked hierarchies of privilege.

In order to maintain the endless feedback it craves the Leo type can utilize emotional gambles and ultimatums in an attempt to get the attention they desire – threatening to rock the boat or to spoil the party – and causing quite a scene in the process. In a marriage such risk-taking may express as the illicit affair. If the partner is perceived as insufficiently appreciative of the Leo person then that lack of attention fuels the search for it elsewhere. This can become the basis for a karma of using others to satisfy temporary dissatisfaction and then dropping them – a recipe for dishonesty and manipulation.

The occurrence of this kind of affair in prior lives can also provide the basis for problematic karma with children in this life whereby prior-life affairs have resulted in illicit or hidden children. This can in turn manifest as problematic relationships within the family in this life or in the adoption of step-children, or by active involvement with non-biological children who are linked to them by the karma of these past acts.

From the center of identification with their own creative purpose and their ongoing struggle to actualize this purpose these individuals will tend naturally to promote such awareness in others. This can be an enormously positive and rewarding experience for others who in that moment feel the sun shine brightly upon them. However the sun may not shine unconditionally should the Pluto in Leo/5th house person decide that the recipients have delayed in the appropriate appreciative response. In friendship this might be experienced as an irritation. But in work or family situations, and especially with the Pluto in Leo individuals' children, this can become more problematic. What was initially expressed as encouragement can quickly turn into controlling behavior that, although initiated with the intention of promoting the other's creative cause, is hijacked by frustration and excessive intensity. The potential exists for the child of the Pluto in Leo/5th house parent to feel this as extreme disappointment and/or invasiveness.

The need in the Leo/5th house Pluto individual to promote their own creativity is so strong they must also promote it in others. To the extent that they subconsciously fear (Pluto) their own capacity to do so they will fall prey to over-intensity with others, possibly even rejecting children or friends as being too backward or lacking in creative ambition relative to their own. If they feel their creative mission is blocked or thwarted they are capable of strong negativity towards others, including their own children, as enjoying an opportunity that they themselves are unable to attain. Nathan Schwartz-Salant describes this insightfully:

> It has been suggested that idealization plays a crucial role in the formation of the narcissistic person…According to this theory, the child has been the target of lofty and grandiose parenting ideals. Through largely unconscious communications from parental figures he or she has been given the 'charge' to fulfill unlived ambitions, which are actually the archaic forms of parental failures of individuation. It is clear that if the child is treated as 'special', difficulties will arise from so concentrated a form of attention, since the basic requirement is to overachieve. But the matter is far worse. The narcissistic person has simultaneously been given a completely opposite message – namely, the devastating message of envy. The message is transmitted as follows: 'You are wonderful and I hate you for it. You have it all, and since I don't, I despise you for what I do not have.' Here, having 'it all' refers to more consciously idealized qualities espoused by the parents.[13]

The problem is this: to the extent that we are driven by our urge to creatively actualize and we are unable to satisfy that urge,

then we are prone to leak our failure as a powerful mix of unresolved fantasies for others – either as criticism, control or even subconscious envy of their, as yet, unadulterated opportunity and potential. This can be very toxic for those we're in relationship with,
especially our children.

The evolutionary intention expressed by the Aquarius/11th
house polarity point is to develop objective awareness in order to
counteract the excessive subjective focus of this placement. The individual needs to consider the social usefulness and needs of the
collective when expressing their own creative impulse. Some may
find themselves blocked in achieving their intended goals until this
realignment takes place. This can happen when the person realizes
that the central concern of life must include the perspective and
needs of others.

This same Aquarian objectivity might balance family life. The
Pluto in Leo individual needs to become friends with their children
and family, respecting them for who they are in and of themselves
rather than indulging fantasies about what they could or ought to
be. Non-dualistic spirituality teachers like David Hawkins point to
the (Aquarian) insight that the self is the author of one's actions, but
not the source. This insight can lead to feelings of liberation. The
recognition of a higher order of meaning actually increases the creative potential and joy of this placement. Many of the problems the
Pluto in Leo/5th house person has relate to the unresolved lessons
of the Cancer archetype (i.e. the need to locate the source of happiness and security from within). The successful expression of the
Leo archetype depends upon discrimination between the personal
ego expression, the nature of the individuality, the I and the Self.

The evolutionary intention expressed via the Aquarian polarity point is to come to a more detached understanding of some
of the traumatic experiences that may have blocked, distorted or
shaped the drive towards individual self-expression. The Aquarian
insight functions as a laser, cutting through the central illusion of
being special. Hawkins describes it thus:

> First the student thinks he is special and great. Then he
> learns from the teacher that this is the ego and pride. So
> the student thinks the teacher is great and special, after
> all if he has a special teacher he is still unique and special

due to his association with the teacher and the student is off the hook to admit his own pride. Then a good teacher will make clear that "all Glory be to God", this forces the student to project somewhere else. Here the group itself allows for a final stronghold and one can hear "We are special." This is indeed a sacrifice for many, to be willing to be like any other pencil and at the same time to allow God to do the writing is what surrender is. As St. Benedict reminds us "All are welcomed as Christ": all are seen as Divinity with no personal distinction or specialness. All are respected and loved equally.[14]

Pluto in the 6th house/Virgo

In tracing the development of subjectivity from Aries to Leo we have noted the power of the instinctual body, the consolidation of our essential needs, our learning and communication skills, the development of the emotional body and ego from our early home-life to the burgeoning desire for the creative actualization of the self. In Leo, the creative power of the self reaches a zenith creating a pyramidal reality-structure where the powerful individual is the centre of their world passing down instructions to others to follow. This royal or feudal model forms the basis for personal relationships and collective relationships and it is not hard to trace its influence into the fabric of our politics, media and society today.

If in Leo the creative power of the subjective self reaches its apogee, then in Virgo we see a transition point or sharp contrast. The need arises to return to level ground, and to re-evaluate the self through a fundamental re-examination. The Pluto in Virgo/6th house archetype seeks a reassessment of the self's drive to continually authenticate itself and instead seeks to deconstruct the self, to place it at the service of others, or of useful work. In this way a profound humility is sought as the ego bows to larger forces and to a proper assessment of self and environment.

The transitional nature of the Virgo archetype can be seen through its position within the archetypal Zodiac with Aries on the Ascendant. At 150° from Aries, Virgo is associated with the principle of the quincunx aspect. This aspect is of crucial importance to understanding Virgo since it is denotes *crisis*. Crisis is the experience that can occur when we are faced with seemingly forced or fated internal or external transitions. In Virgo we meet the waxing quincunx, the first of two (Scorpio is the second). The nature of the crisis symbolized by Virgo is one of the will. The Virgo archetype brings an adjustment to the feeling of supremacy of the personal will expressed through Leo (the trine) so that the will can make the powerful transition needed in order to accept the other, as expressed by Libra (the opposition).

In Virgo the question shifts from "how can I be special?" to "how can I be useful?" The issue of right work is emphasized as the self desires to fit into a larger whole, to offer something functional to the collective. With the impulse to understand an inflated sense of self-importance as essentially delusional these individuals may have experienced many humbling moments in this and other lifetimes as part of a necessary purification. This by its nature can constitute an inner crisis, especially when the individual (mistakenly) turns humbling into humiliating, and the personal crisis becomes traumatic.

What is the purpose of the crisis? Let's consider the mental properties of the Virgo archetype. Virgo's constant self-questioning is intended to get to the bottom line (Pluto) level of understanding. Self-analysis is intended as part of an overall examination of self-motivation with the desired outcome being a new discrimination, an increased possibility of understanding the nature of our motivations and behaviors in order to fulfill the remit of being useful, of contributing to a greater whole.

With Pluto in Gemini/3rd house, Mercury acts in a Yang fashion in order to bring about the import and export of endless new ideas and information. In the Yin function of Mercury with Pluto in Virgo/6th house the intention is to discriminate from the data already collected as to which is the most useful. The desire is for a spring-cleaning of the inner and outer library or hard drive in order to toss out what is inauthentic, and what is no longer useful or necessary. The danger is that the very process of mental self-analysis becomes the end product instead of merely leading up to it. The trap is that this person never reaches a conclusion and instead endlessly moves through the data in a repetitive loop of critical thinking that ultimately leads nowhere.

In Virgo the intention is to become self-critical to the extent that it provides the backdrop for a new understanding of the self and its interaction with others. But the self-criticism risks developing into a habitual pattern of negative thinking that endlessly chatters away in the background, subtly undermining any attempts to actually galvanize the experience of the self into a new direction or new way of being. This kind of criticism leads to immobility. In this fashion the very process designed to assist reification of the self-concept becomes instead a way of damaging that concept to the point of disabling it.

This problem can lead to a loss of perspective for the Pluto in Virgo/6th house person because the psychological and mental stress of re-evaluation can be so intense that they cannot remember the original intention for entering the re-evaluation in the first place. All they are left with is a long list or complaints, the critical mass of their attempt to identify the problem. Under the weight and pressure of this negative evaluation of self and surroundings, this person can find it hard to get in touch with a constructive sense of purpose. This problematic cycle can only be overcome by returning to the intention behind the crisis of self-analysis, which is to re-orientate the self to a more objective sense of itself in the relational world and the collective structures of humanity.

On an emotional level, feelings of lack dominate the Pluto in Virgo/6th house person and comparisons between self and others result in a constant feeling of inferiority. This operates across generations so that the success and empowerment of the Pluto in Leo generation, while problematic, also results in the Pluto in Virgo generation feeling inferior by comparison. Over time the feeling of inferiority becomes the basis of a perceived sense of lack. This in turn lays the groundwork for a psychology of meaninglessness that can take hold of the Pluto in Virgo/6th house person in challenging moments. Any event in which they feel compared to others and find themselves lacking, or any perceived mistake on their part (whether noted by themselves or pointed out by another) can trigger a downward spiral of negative thinking that results in a feeling of meaninglessness.

Such futility can also stem from an emotional response to collective events. One danger for the Pluto in Virgo/6th house person is an over-identification with the disenfranchised to the extent that a form of emotional paralysis begins to occur. The list of complaints they have about the world is so large that it seems insurmountable. It feels to them like nothing can be done, that the scale of the problem is too big. And the belittling of the self leads to this person feeling like an ineffectual and seemingly meaningless human being (the complete deflation of Leo grandiosity). In this way a psychological pattern of futility and an emotional experience of despair becomes all-consuming with full Plutonian obsession and intensity.

Many people with Pluto in Virgo or the 6th house incarnate with memories of not feeling good enough, or the pervasive feeling of having done something wrong. These memories often come from having tried to live up to a high moral standard and found wanting as the result of not being able to reach a too-high standard of perfection. The feeling of something lacking, something wrong inside them becomes the basis of not feeling good enough to achieve their vision of a good life and a worthwhile contribution. This becomes a self-fulfilling prophecy as the very failure to live up to their potential becomes the basis for further guilt. Some people with this placement perpetually fluctuate between cycles of crisis and guilt, effectively paralyzing themselves from taking any kind of step forward.

A more subtle version of this dynamic expresses as denial and making excuses. Many Pluto in Virgo people deny that they want what they do for fear of failing to be able to achieve it. Then they make endless excuses for why they can't move forward.

Others with this placement work ceaselessly, as if such constant busyness will keep any existential anxiety or discomfort at bay. In extremes, the individual may take on board responsibility after responsibility as if nothing could stop them from doing what is right, even though inside they feel only exhaustion and emptiness.

Other compulsive behaviors used to circumvent an internal feeling of lack might include endless distractions like reading trashy novels, television, shopping, perpetual cleaning, obsessive cycles of thought, superstitions, drink and drugs or compulsive sexual behavior. Physical illness that arises as a result of self-denial, exhaustion and emotional blockage can force the individual to stop and confront the circumstances of their personal reality. At these moments, crisis actually becomes a catalyst for bringing the issue to a head. Positively responded to, the crisis can transform life for the better; unheeded it becomes more fuel for the internal guilt machine.

A key source of the internal guilt with Pluto in Virgo/6th house is that many of these individuals have unconscious memories of lifetimes with strong monotheistic religious conditioning, particularly that of Christianity, Judaism and Islam, the "religions of the book." While the genuine teaching of God's love can be beautiful, what we're looking at in this case are the numerous spiritual teachings that are critical about the body, sexuality, the emotions and the feminine. These affronts to one's earth-bound humanity have led many people to internalize guilt at their "original sin" – a permeating sense of guilt that does not even arise from a valid incident. This sense of injected or inherited guilt is problematic, because there is no easy way to make reparation for it since it comes from no real event. Therefore is has the capacity to grow unchecked in the consciousness.

Such teachings have had a tendency to emphasize the transcendent aspect of God in such a way as cause one to compare the "unworthy human" to the glory of the godhead. This can contribute to long-standing internal shame on a subtle body level within the Pluto in Virgo consciousness.

This person might also externally project their internal criticism. This person may appear to be critical of everyone or everything as if nothing is good enough. In fact this is a reflection of how they relate to themselves on a deep level. This all comes from a feeling of wanting to live up to an unattainable standard of perfection. The desire for purification, often stemming from unconscious memories of religious vows and aspirations, leads to the potential for inner or outer criticism as an expression of the stress of not reaching that state. The reality is that such perfection is not possible in a static sense.

The internal struggle this person faces as they find themselves out of the comfort zone of the prior self-development (Aries to Leo) and not yet entering into the social world (Libra to Pisces) can lead to a feeling of core aloneness. In some individuals this experience is so traumatic and overwhelming that it leads to suicide or self-harm.

The 12th house/Pisces polarity point suggests the need to apply forgiveness and acceptance and realize that creation is already perfect in its transitoriness: the rose seen as perfect in decay just as much as in full bloom. In this way the Pisces polarity alludes to a forgiving perception of both the universe and the self. In forgiving the self, the release from shame alters and reveals the true beauty of life underneath.

The Pisces polarity point refers to a need to simplify the person's life, in particular the mental life. The interior thought-processes in Virgo can tend toward an endless covering of the same self-defeating ground. There is a need to close the ongoing case of the inner trial and to learn to act (Virgo, as an earth sign) practically in a step-by-step fashion on the verdict reached. The more power one gives to the mind, the stronger negative thinking can become. In some instances the best practice is to simply stop paying attention. The Pisces polarity holds the eternal truth that below the surface of the ocean, the water is still. Thinking stops as the self begins to make peace with its own existence instead of perpetuating an endless frenzy of inner activity as a defense against that existence. The essential issue then is the surrender of the contents of consciousness in order to experience the context of divinity and the reality of love (Pisces) that underlies creation.

Pluto in the 7th house/Libra

The cardinality of Pluto in Libra alerts us that a new evolutionary cycle is underway. Following the transitional archetype of the 6th house/Virgo, the key issue with Pluto in the 7th house or Libra becomes understanding the self through the mirror of others. Consequently there is a need to initiate a variety of relationships in order to learn about the nature of the self as it is experienced within numerous social contexts. Through meeting different sorts of people the person with this Pluto placement begins to learn about themselves via comparison: I am like this person and not like this other person. In order to facilitate this there has been an on-going lesson in how to listen to others, how to understand where other people are really coming from versus the projected idea we have of them or the way we imagine others might fulfill our needs. This placement requires the development of empathy: the need to evaluate experience from another's point of view.

The process of purification represented by the preceding archetype of Virgo emphasizes a balancing of the subjective glorification of personal creative power in the Leo archetype so that the potential to meet others on an equal basis in Libra might occur. To the extent that the prior process of purification was not stringent enough, pre-existing narcissistic desires and wounds will potentially cloud the Pluto in the 7th house/Libra person's pattern of relating and leave them overly dominant, overly concerned with their personal power and potentially aggressive in the pursuit of the satisfaction of their needs. To the extent that the Virgo archetype was expressed more as masochistic humiliation than humility, the potential is for the individual to become overtly disempowered and needy, carrying a sense of not being good enough for other people into the relationships they form.

While the scales of Libra indicate balance, since this is a new evolutionary cycle *balance is often more a goal that is being aspired to than it is a reality*. In fact more often than not the Pluto in the 7th house/Libra individual is likely to manifest extremes within their relationships, or even cycles of extremity in how they form relationships. They might have periods of time where they experience themselves as overly isolated and other times when they are in danger of losing themselves in a whirl of social activity.

While the need to form new relationships is an imperative part of the soul intention to grow, the pitfall of many Pluto in Libra/7th house relationships is that the person may be destabilized by the myriad opinions of, and reactions from, others. People with this placement are at times vulnerable to being overwhelmed by other people's needs or desires to the detriment of fulfilling their own. With the Libra archetype the Venus rulership is in a yang form, an outgoing aspect of its expression, which stands in stark contrast to the yin form of Venus evidenced in the Taurus archetype. With Taurus the Venus focus is inner, on personal survival and the capacity to identify and meet personal needs. In contrast, the external focus of the Libra archetype puts one in danger of affording excessive meaning to others.

This issue of co-dependency can be thought of as a culturally supported contagion. Through the proliferation of the Hollywood romance, and in the financial and social/religious attempts to preserve a conservative view of marriage, we live in a culture that gives higher value to romantic love and the dyad as the only legitimate form of intimacy. It is surprisingly common in our culture for married people to have almost no friends or outside interests. This places enormous pressure on the marriage or long-term partnership to meet all of the needs of each partner.

Co-dependency stems ultimately from an incapacity or fear of being alone. This fear is often evidenced in the Pluto in Libra/7th house individual and also in those with Pluto in stressful aspect to Venus. On one level, the fear of being alone is a death anxiety: the experience of the other (or their desire or love) is a shield to one's existential vulnerability. To become aware of one's humanity is to feel one's naked vulnerability in the face of the scale of the Cosmos and its seeming indifference to one's humanity. In the face of this, people often cling to things, patterns of addiction, and other people.

In the seminal work *We: Understanding the Psychology of Romantic Love*, Jungian Robert Johnson points out that since medieval times and the practices of chivalric and courtly love we have maintained an ideal about relationships which leaves us prone to the naivety and desperation of our projections.[15] The Knight that the young woman dreams of is not going to show up, or if he does it will be with the discovery that he also farts in bed, or acts just like her tyrannical father, or behaves in ways that further undermine her fantasy. At some point, no matter what, the reality of our projection is challenged by the reality of the other. It is this moment that Johnson argues cogently is the only possible beginning of real love. The intentional act of loving, the choice to meet the other, warts and all, is critical to our understanding of the Pluto in Libra/7th house placement.

Many relationships never evolve beyond the meeting of the need in mutual projection. We meet someone who fits our image of the perfect partner and we are fortunate that we meet their image of the perfect mate and we then become glued by that fit of imagery. This is necessary glue it could be argued, a tool for bonding. However if this is all there is, it is sticky! We see time and again the failure of the glamorized Hollywood marriage, the actress wife falling in love with her co-star or the actor husband unable to remain faithful. Such people represent the epitome of this issue. They are living in a world where all the people around them support the fantasy that they *are* the role that they are playing as a couple and they become hooked in the romance of that, lost in the projection.

There is a powerful compulsion in the Pluto in Libra/7th house person to project needs or expectations onto others which can then lead to issues of overt or covert manipulation of the relationship in order to maintain an ideal fantasy or expectation of how it ought to be. It is hard to underestimate the extent to which human beings want the world, and other people in the world, to conform to their expectations. Acknowledging this T.S. Eliot writes in *Four Quartets*, "Go, go, go, said the bird: human kind Cannot bear very much reality."[16] To bear the reality of another human carries the potential of loving them for who they actually are versus engaging with them in a superficial kind of psychic mutual masturbation.

In his book *Choice Theory: A New Psychology of Personal Freedom*, William Glasser makes the critical point that apart from extreme poverty or biological illness the great majority of human suffering stems from problematic relationships. He offers an analysis of what constitutes the most serious problem within relationships:

> The simple operational premise of the external control psychology the world uses is: Punish the people who are doing wrong, so they will do what we say is right; then reward them, so they keep doing what we want them to

do. This premise dominates the thinking of most people on earth. What makes this psychology so prevalent is that those who have the power – agents of government, parents, teachers, business managers, and religious leaders, who also define what's right or wrong – totally support it. And the people they control, having so little control over their own lives, find some security in accepting the control of these powerful people.[17]

This dynamic is signified by Capricorn, the natural square to Libra, which creates a permeating sense of control issues within human relationships. The man beaten down by humiliating work conditions then beats down his wife and children. The woman who feels undervalued in her job criticizes and shames her partner or her children. Glasser creates a simple but enlightening list of how we create control problems in our relationships:

1) You wanted someone else to do what he or she refused to do. Usually, in a variety of ways, some blatant, some devious, you were trying to force him or her to do what you wanted.
2) Someone else was trying to make you do something you didn't want to do.
3) Both you and someone else were trying to make each other do what neither wanted to do.
4) You were trying to force yourself to do something you found very painful or even impossible to do.[18]

It is a rare person indeed who after careful consideration of the above points cannot raise their hand and say that they have been in painful situations with others in some (or most likely all) of the above ways.

As we consider the natural square from Cancer, we find Libra the focal point of a T-Square formed by the opposition of Capricorn to Cancer. Capricorn antagonizes Libra, and the Cancer square points to the unresolved security needs from our upbringing. This leaves us masking our vulnerabilities with a compensatory control and then we create pain and problems in our relationships. This is true to some extent of anyone in relationship, but as the Pluto in the 7th house/Libra individual has had the intention to initiate many relationships both in this and in recent prior lives, there may be an emphasized tendency to have manifested problems with a number of people. So this placement suggests pre-existing relationship karma.

One possible pattern for the person with this placement is that of unresolved endings with other people, whereby the Pluto in the 7th house/Libra person has left a relationship without proper closure with their partner, who subsequently feels unclear and abandoned. Conversely they may have been left by a partner before they felt ready for that relationship to end. Such endings often happen when the Pluto in Libra/7th house person feels they have fulfilled the needs they had prior to forming the relationship and there is, as such, no further need to continue. This may (or likely may not) coincide with the other feeling the same way. To the extent that the problem of intimacy has not been clearly understood, some people may manifest a trail of past partners, all of whom never experienced the sense of being cared for as an intentional choice.

Another manifestation is a co-dependency whereby people have clung to each other to assuage the demands of the world or of their individual life path. Often this dynamic entails one dominant and one submissive partner, the dominant partner resisting intimacy by controlling and the submissive partner denying their personal power through ceding control. In certain extreme cases such dependency requires forced separation – often the death of a partner – in order to begin the reorientation back to individual growth.

The specific nature of the prior life relationship patterns can be explored through an analysis of the South Node of the Moon, its ruler, aspects to the ruler and any planets squaring the nodal axis. Additional information can be found through analysis of the natal Venus placement, aspects to the Venus placement and the 7th house cusp.

When Venus is retrograde the issue of problematic prior relationships is emphasized and there will often be an explicit evolutionary intention to meet people again with whom the person had difficult prior-life endings in relationships with.

The polarity point of Aries/1st house suggests the need to maintain individual purpose and the freedom of the self to grow at its own pace, with its own predilections and preferences. This polarity point relates to the courage to just be, to not surrender one's individual evolutionary journey, one's soul path of growth, in exchange for fulfilling the needs or expectations of others.

In a psychosynthesis training I attended, a teacher presented us with a beautiful image of a healthy long-term relationship. The idea was that instead of the image of two people holding hands and looking into each other's eyes, we can envisage those two people turning and facing the world together, still holding hands (maintaining contact) but journeying forth into their communities, their creative and working lives, side by side. This ideal assumes the courage for the relationship to be one of mutual growth, including the purely individual growth that is central to this process (1st house/Aries).

Pluto in the 8th house/Scorpio

In the 2nd house/Taurus the soul is learning to identify its own needs and resources from within and tends to create a limited field of awareness in order to highlight them most effectively. By contrast, the 8th house/Scorpio wants to challenge its pre-existing sense of identity, its needs, talents and resources. In essence Pluto in its own house and sign represents a deep confrontation with the parameters of what we are and what we are not. The journey of experience via relationships initiated with Pluto in the 7th house/Libra leads us to the edges of our potential, what we already are and know about ourselves. By the power of Pluto being in its own house, the potential of what we might become is revealed. As such the 8th house Pluto individual tends to seek out symbolic forms of power in order to osmose some of that power into themselves by assimilating the qualities that attracted them in the first place. These attractions may include powerful people or systems of knowledge, money, death, ritual, occult or religious imagery, sexuality or ordinarily taboo forms of experience or interaction.

The paradox of this search for power lies in the attraction and repulsion experience central to the Pluto complex. Intense attractions are formed that then expose pre-existing limitations, which lead to repulsion. For example, I am attracted to a body of knowledge, e.g. Evolutionary Astrology, because it holds the promise of helping me understand myself in a new and exciting way. Then I find that in my study of it, limitations are revealed about my previous understanding of myself. I then struggle until I have mastered this new form, all the while with a sense of disempowerment about my present state of consciousness. In frustration I may decide to reject Evolutionary Astrology as irrelevant, or belittle myself by comparison to what I am not. I have come to a place in my development where I desire change and metamorphosis, but I've arrived at that impulse through a realization that my present state is not alright, or not enough. I have the choice to either generate enough energy to break through this impasse, or fall back frustrated and give up.

The Pluto in Scorpio/8th house person will experience the cutting edge of this dilemma of metamorphosis – that in changing they grow, but that in order to change they must experience dissatisfaction or even revulsion at where they currently are. Such dissatisfaction is all too easily transferred onto the symbol, person or object of interest that elicits their attraction.

The essence of this dilemma is rooted in the discrepancy between the desires of the ego and the soul, which in this placement can become locked in an extraordinary struggle. The soul desires empowerment and expansion through new forms of knowledge and new ways of deeply relating to others and to the world. The ego requires security through familiarity, seeking to defend its own comfort zone from the powerful urge to transform past prior limitations. This central choice between ego and soul is heightened with this placement. The individual with Pluto in Scorpio/8th house has experienced cycles within this and prior lives that alternate between power and powerlessness. They have experienced power via their absorption of symbols of power and then powerlessness in the face of those same symbols, an apparent paradox depending on the level of integration.

In another example of this dynamic, this person may have a strong personal and sexual attraction to someone. If the person responds to their advances, they feel powerful. But rejection leaves them feeling powerless. Such cyclic empowerment and disempowerment serves to push the personality up against its previous definitions of itself and force itself onto the cutting edge of change. In this regard a crucial issue with Scorpio/8th house is to discriminate in personal relationships, so that there is recognition of when another is just not right for them, or is manipulative or destructive. There is an opportunity to distinguish between powerlessness as something that is a necessary corollary to having loved as opposed to powerlessness as the result of being used by another to get what they want. In a similar fashion there is a learning curve around personal power when another is intensely attracted to the 8th house Pluto person. How will they use this power?

When it comes to intimate relationships, the potential for resistance (a critical concept in understanding the nature of Pluto) is enormous. Resistance may come if they cannot let go of the other person. It is especially hard to let go if that person has become "everything" to them. The way another person can "make them feel" is just as addictive. When such 8th house attractions become very intense the power felt from the other person can take this person to the limits of what their previous sense of identity may have been.

This pressure on personal boundaries is experienced as an attractive proposition for the person who seeks transformation. But it is repulsive to the part of the psyche that is content where it is and not wanting to change.

Such pushing of the boundaries of personal identity forms the basis for obsession and compulsion. Just as something or someone is resisted, so the deeper unconscious desire for change leads to obsession or unconscious compulsive behavior. Sigmund Freud became aware of an intense attraction/repulsion felt between him and Carl Jung. On a trip to America where they were both to lecture, Freud fainted when they were discussing the discovery of a preserved ancient human in a peat bog. He justified this to his followers as his unconscious sensitivity to Jung's death wish towards him. This has a certain degree of truth but we might more simply say that two such powerful men were bound to want, despite the attraction, to go their own way. Jung was not prepared to just follow and accept all of his mentor's teachings, and in breaking away he expressed the urge to individuate. The simple image of the ancient human lying in the ground can be understood not just as an image of Freud's corpse but as an image representing the potential understanding contained in the archetypal layers of the Psyche, which Freud reduced to sublimated Eros or Thanatos, desire or death urges. This was Freud's attempt to name the Pluto complex – attraction (Eros) and repulsion (Thanatos or death). We can see this as an essential struggle within human nature as it deals with powerful soul impulses while also desperately clinging to whatever personal or egoic security it already has.

In his 1984 book *A Criminal History of Mankind*, Colin Wilson charts the evolution of man's inhumanity to man (the only animal that kills its fellow creature *en masse* and for pleasure) as indicative of man's relation to the evolution of consciousness. He sees in the compulsion/repetition of certain criminal impulses in mankind an expression (however distorted) of the urge to individuate and to experience a transformation of personal power.[19] The case of Edward Gein (August 27, 1906 11:30 pm, North Lacrosse, WI) was adapted for films such as *Silence of the Lambs* and *The Texas Chainsaw Massacre*. Gein murdered two women, using their skins and body parts (along with others from corpses he had disinterred) to create a sort of mannequin for him to employ in a macabre exploration of the relationship with his deceased mother. His chart has a prominent Pluto signature opposite the Moon and T-square to Saturn. Pluto is on the Ascendant and not in the 8th house – though his Saturn (the resolution point of the T-square with Pluto-Moon) is the ruler of the 8th house. And we see in Gein's statement "I had a compulsion to do it" the power of that Pluto energy.

The compulsion bespoke an urge to liberate himself from the object of attraction/repulsion, the figure of his dominant mother. Inspired by pornography and literature on Nazi medical experimentation during the Holocaust, Gein conceived and executed a plan to recreate her, literally wearing her on himself, murdering women of similar age and looks to his mother in order to achieve this end. He took deep psychological compulsions (Pluto) about his mother (Moon) and enacted them literally (Saturn) through the shaping of the skin.

Pluto is the source of compulsion in the Zodiac, stemming from deep psychological needs that the personality struggles to articulate or contain. This energy is processed through conflict with the object that inspires a will-to-power and a concomitant fear or weakness. Gein expressed this energy via serial homicide although the conflict might be just as evident in the case of a young monk struggling in reconciling physical and emotional needs as he seeks to sublimate his desires in emulation of Christ. Whatever is most important to us, we struggle with the most. When applied to others this idea forms the basis of the cliché: we hurt most the ones we love.

Since the potential for hurt in personal relationships is so great, the issue of discrimination regarding relationship choices and power dynamics is critically important. Many people spend a good deal of time blaming their lover or their spouse for their personal misery. This dynamic is in many ways a Pluto/8th house problem. Partnered people have merged their resources and identities, yet to the extent that they are scared of their own personal power, or are unsure how to handle their own needs, they expend considerable personal energy blaming their significant others for their own suffering. I am reminded of one client whose partially-deaf mother was reluctant to ever ask anyone to speak up in social situations so that she could hear them, with the consequence that she began to withdraw from social interaction. When her husband spoke with others she would berate him for hours afterwards for not including her, and yet she never wanted him to mention her issue with hearing and never took responsibility for sharing it herself. In refusing to acknowledge her own needs she doomed herself to regular interpersonal struggles and suffering, frequently adding her increasingly frustrated husband to her list of wrongdoers. He adapted in his own way by playing golf every day and developing his own separate social circle, again adding to his wife's sense of isolation and increasing her capacity to blame him for that.

Unresolved attachments from prior lives create another kind of relationship challenge for people with this placement. This can include intense sexual attractions or sexual manipulation. Often these types of relationship stem from difficult prior-life relationship endings and the unresolved negative feelings the participants have toward each other. Such negative feelings may permeate the current relationship with seemingly "irrational" outbursts that on analysis may reveal the nature of the prior-life damage (see the work of past life regression therapists Patricia Walsh or Hans Ten Dam). If unrecognized, these feelings can lead to re-traumatization or severance of the present relationship. These feelings may include violent outbursts, murderous or suicidal preoccupation, as powerful negativity and hurt accumulated over lifetimes makes its way into seemingly ordinary domestic disputes in the present. To the extent that one person feels hurt, abused, manipulated or abandoned, they feel they must compulsively hurt, abuse, manipulate or abandon the other. These scenes can play out over and over again. When linked to strong sexual feelings, a sort of passionate negativity results and abusive karma is perpetuated. In this regard we can observe that not all sexual activity is loving, and plenty of people mistake anger and hatred for loving intimacy.

The polarity point of Taurus/2nd house refers to the continuing need to develop the inner self relationship, the capacity to identify and satisfy personal needs of one's own volition. No matter how loving one's partner, or how intense one's relationship is to symbolic forms of power, no one other person or thing is going to make us happy, or satisfy our every desire. In fact the sooner the illusion of personal happiness existing outside of the self is punctured the greater the chance of leading a fulfilling life. In learning to meet one's own needs from within much of the basis for compulsion in relationships with others is removed.

The 8th house side of this polarity is over-emphasized when someone commits suicide because their lover has absconded. This kind of retaliatory suicide is very common – it reveals the compulsion of the 8th house as it overrides the survival instinct of the 2nd house, the message being, "if you will not meet my needs then neither will I."

A more insidious form of suicide that we might term "passive suicide," occurs when someone overeats, abuses substances or simply drives their car off the side of the road one day because they were not paying attention. In these actions the person expresses the loss of a sense of personal meaning which overrides their survival impulse or personal needs (2nd house polarity). Developing the sense of larger personal meaning really begins with the 8th house or Scorpio, for here powerful forces are sensed as working within the cosmos and the person begins to seek a relationship to these forces in order to obtain that power. The difficulty lies in the fact that as these forces are sensed and aspired toward they also generate considerable personal resistance. In our weakness, selfishness and narcissism (love of the incomplete self, love of the wounding) we can often feel incapable of the total surrender required of us to achieve balance.

Pluto in the 9th house/Sagittarius

With Pluto in the 9th house/Sagittarius the sense of larger forces in the cosmos (which began with the Scorpio archetype) is heightened. These individuals have been and are manifesting an evolutionary desire to understand themselves within the context of the greater cosmos. Through travel, philosophy, various faiths and metaphysical studies they seek to learn about themselves and their place in the world around them. This can equate with conventional religion or homespun philosophy and adventure. As these people begin to truly think for themselves, they might study various different forms of thought as expressed through cultural, religious and spiritual teachings. They are beginning to develop their personal intuitive connection with larger cosmic forces and as they reach higher states of the spiritual condition these people often become natural proponents of teachings that include the spiritual potential of all living beings.

In the previous Scorpio/8th house archetype, we see people who have experienced intense personal relationships and cycles of power and powerlessness begin to develop an ability for self-analysis and penetrating analytical insight into others which we might call a natural psychological capacity. In the next stage of development, Pluto in Sagittarius/9th house individuals may have incarnated into multiple different cultures within many different time periods in order to satisfy their need to understand the world through a variety of cultural, philosophical and religious frameworks. As such these people can display a remarkable natural intuitive capacity, and may appear to think differently from the prevailing cultural norms in which they have grown up in the current life. This can become the basis for a problematic sense of cultural alienation from the prevailing worldview of the present culture, presenting many issues with education and readjustment. In some 9th house Pluto individuals this alienation never really abates and they may become rootless, some physically wandering the earth in order to satisfy this restlessness and others intellectually voyaging on a perpetual journey of discovery. For some the alienation is unbearable; perhaps it was too intense or experienced too early in life without developmental support. These people can then all too easily drift into a borderland mentality that includes experiences of homelessness, criminality or simply falling off the map in some way.

With Pluto in Gemini and the 3rd house there is a compulsive need for data about the immediate environment, to classify the world and to engage with it conceptually. In contrast the compulsion for the Pluto in Sagittarius/9th house person is the search for meaning, the seeking of a personal and universal truth. The focus with this placement is on an intuitive perception of the whole of life, rather than a focus on the data received from within the immediate environment. Gemini labels the objects of the phenomenal world; Sagittarius seeks to understand why said objects exist and to what larger end.

Some Pluto in Sagittarius/9th house individuals are natural loners, for whom the seeking of a personal vision has overtaken more conventional needs for security or achievement. For many of these people the experience of alienation from the current environment, while initially painful, is necessary in evolutionary terms in order to return them to their personal journey or vision quest. In this way the memories of different cultures and the ways those cultures related to the cosmos at large are triggered as the individual steps back from their current cultural *milieu*. Often such memories precipitate a process of realignment with forms of knowledge or religious teachings from other times and places.

In Plato's Socratic dialogues (e.g. *Meno*) the Greek word *anamnesis* is used to equate true learning with the faculty of deep memory. Some Pluto in Sagittarius/9th house people display a highly developed intuitive capability permitting them to recall sequences of prior-life experiences and/or memories from the place between lives –the deep memory. Access to this knowledge can prove problematic for a number of reasons. First, it can further heighten the already present feelings of alienation as "outsiders" from the current scientific/materialist culture of the West struggle to understand or validate it. Second, it makes it harder for the intuitively gifted individual to discriminate between reality and the taints of their own narcissistic wounding and/or personal prejudice. Third, even if a process of discrimination is applied and the person feels the insights are valid it can be difficult to communicate this information to others, which may be received non-verbally or through symbolism. The question of how to meaningfully pass this information on to others can become an emotionally-charged issue for this person, for as always in Plutonic matters, emotional attachment is a powerful magnet that can cause destabilization.

Through these powerful feelings of emotional attachment some people with this placement become preoccupied with the current expression of their need for understanding. For example, an interest in Buddhism can become obsessive as the individual attempts to (subtly or not) coerce others into accepting the teaching, or struggles to relate to others who are not into the same path. While wishing to share one's thoughts and interests with others is understandable, this person exalts this need into a fever pitch, culminating in the potential for cultish identification with certain figures, teachings or world-views and the possibility for fundamentalism of all kinds. The unmet need stems from the insecurity of the individual on an existential level who then seeks certainty on a cosmological level to compensate for their feelings of vulnerability in the world. To believe that their path is the One True Path serves as a great comfort to people who feel deeply insecure and this can lead to misguided attempts to convert the world to their viewpoint.

The polarity point of Gemini/3rd house suggests a need in this person to facilitate the understanding that there are multiple approaches to truth and that different people in different (inner and outer) places live and find meaning in diverse ways. The polarity point functions via verbal and written confrontations with others who question the solid foundation of the Sagittarius/9th house individual's world-view. To the extent that this world-view is compulsively adhered to in order to as assuage anxiety, the person may become emotionally fixated on the teaching. As the subject of their insecurity is broached the person may entrench themselves ever further into the perspective they have decided is the "one correct way" to approach meaning in life. At this point they become evermore brutal in their denunciation of alternatives.

This pattern forms the potential source of cultural and religious conflicts, the irony being that some of the worst conflicts in history stem from viewpoints that are actually very similar. Some of the most severe religious conflicts have occurred between Catholicism and Protestantism, off-shoots of the same revelation, or between the Red and Yellow Hats in Tibetan Buddhism. The political extremes of communism and fascism (as embodied by Stalin and Hitler) seem nearly identical from our twenty-first century perspective. One of the greatest conflicts in the modern world is between Islam and Christianity, two religions that acknowledge essentially the same God revealed through the same lineage of Prophets, except for the fact that one emphasizes one prophet over another!

As they are questioned about their faith or approach to life, some with this placement may begin to exaggerate their level of understanding or capacities in order to compensate for the insecurity that such questions bring up. In this way, although they profess to follow their path in order to seek truth, they themselves begin to weave an inner lie in order to magnify their own standing so that they can respond more strongly to the questioning voices that challenge them via the polarity point in 3rd house/Gemini. In his lucid exposition of the guru problem *Feet of Clay*, the eminent psychotherapist Anthony Storr raises the issue of the feedback loop that such exaggerated intensity might require:

> Intensity of conviction is necessary if a guru is to attract disciples. This is not to say that all gurus believe everything they preach; but an initial conviction of having special insight is probably necessary if a new sect is to be born. Many people go through conversion experiences and hold strong religious or other convictions without being impelled to preach or to convert others, but gurus require disciples just as disciples require gurus. We must consider the possibility that the conviction expressed by gurus is less absolute than it appears in that their apparent confidence needs boosting by the response of followers.[20]

I am not suggesting that there are no enlightened or pure teachers out there who quite naturally attract people to them through the purity of their enlightened insight. In the East this tradition is firmly established. Yet there are also many people of less-developed consciousness who profess to be more enlightened than they are. The importance of perspective in these matters can hardly be over-emphasized. In a number of important books including *Power Versus Force*, Dr. David Hawkins has argued than man's incapacity to distinguish between leaders and visionaries of integrity and those who have fallen or utilize coercion has cost mankind untold suffering, including the loss of tens of millions of lives in the twentieth century alone.[21]

If we accept the idea of divinity, a loving God or a beneficent Buddha nature we can see that even if one's teacher is in a "fallen" state, if the aspirant is sincere in their devotion then the enlightened entity or state (e.g. God) will witness that sincerity. The intention is often as (or more) spiritually relevant than outcome. While this ameliorates some concerns, there is nonetheless an extremely serious philosophical and spiritual issue for the 9th house aspirant. Many of the most sincere people are capable of misguiding themselves and therefore others to the most devastating extent, not to mention those few with evil intent who simply desire the downfall of others to aggrandize themselves or to express their own nihilism. Many great thinkers have attested to the reality of evil and we may observe that as some seekers turn ever more toward the light, the resulting brightness illuminates many of their personal shadow issues just as it may attract certain occult cosmic forces that do not want to see the light grow unchecked.

A further paradox with the energy of the seeker at it applies to this placement is that to be constantly *seeking* precludes *finding*. This feeds the attraction/repulsion dynamic of the Pluto complex. This person may be seeking so desperately because they feel so agitated or repulsed by where they actually are in their spiritual development. It is helpful for the person in this state to remember the axiom "no matter you go, there you are." Often times we journey far only to arrive back where we started, and it is in dealing with our existential agitation, our shame and self-repulsion that we might begin to enlighten from within instead of perpetually seeking without. The person with the strong future-orientated, seeker energy of Sagittarius needs to be aware of this tendency to perpetual questing because often the object of the quest has been under their nose all along. This is the insight developed so beautifully throughout T.S. Eliot's *The Four Quartets* as this famous extract from *Little Gidding* attests:

> With the drawing of this Love and the voice of this
>   Calling
> We shall not cease from exploration
> And the end of all our exploring
> Will be to arrive where we started
> And know the place for the first time.[22]

Pluto in the 10th house/Capricorn

When Pluto is in any house or sign it emphasizes the planetary ruling archetype, in this case Saturn. To understand Pluto in Capricorn is to understand the full range of Saturn's possibilities, and as such it can help illuminate the nature of powerful Saturn aspects in our chart, Saturn transits (such as the critical Saturn returns) and progressions.

As we traverse the archetypes from Pluto's point of view we are essentially laying bare the potential of all twelve archetypes, the building blocks of our entire astrological symbolism, the symbolic manifestation of all of consciousness. In this way we see that the entire complex symphony that the birth chart comprises is built from only twelve notes, the complexity and the beauty emerging from the connections between the notes and the manner in which they are interlaced, forming endless variations of melody and rhythm. Such structural understanding is critical to any comprehension of Capricorn and/or Pluto in the 10th house.

Saturn relates to the way we structure our consciousness. People with Pluto in the 10th house/Capricorn have been learning about such a framework and the way that this manifests in both the internal and external worlds. As a result these individuals have been seeking to understand the nature of judgment: both how they themselves make judgments (and on what basis) and how others with whom they relate make judgments about them.

In order to make judgments one must have a world view. When the previous archetype of Pluto in Sagittarius/9th house is fully embodied, the person develops a consistent cosmological understanding or world view. The basis for exploration of the Capricorn/10th house issue of judgment depends on the beliefs that were established in the preceding archetype. The criteria adopted for understanding one's personal experience will now be tested through family experience, social groupings, tribe and society at large, all of which are their own expression of structures of consciousness – interwoven patterns of value judgments and conditioning factors.

Saturn relates to conditioning and with Pluto in Capricorn/10th house the impulse to understand the nature of conditioning is pressurized and emotionally intensive. The desire is to form a meaningful role within society and to express personal power based on self-determination and self-discipline in order to achieve these goals. Some will have begun to develop this empowerment, and may have memories of prior lives in which they enjoyed power and status within their communities. The danger with these memories is the extent to which they produce a subconscious sense of entitlement which dominates the way they behave in the world in this life, leading to the potential for manipulation or control used to achieve their ends. In this way prior conditioning leads to expectations that may or may not be fulfilled in the current life. If these expectations are not fulfilled the reaction may tend toward attempting to force the issue, misappropriating resources and power to compensate. Or there may be a tendency towards depression or a struggle with a sense of futility to the extent that this person isn't able to achieve that feeling of power in the same way again.

Futility or pervasive pessimism will also occur within those individuals who have not yet learned to develop the self-discipline and perseverance necessary to climb the ladder within given social constructs of meaning. They may have unconscious memories of prior lives where they also felt defeated by the system or a sense of mistreatment from others as they may have been judged as lacking in some way. These memories can add up to a difficult burden to carry: a residual subconscious guilt that they have failed to live up to their evolutionary intentions. They will see this reflected in the pressure of expectations from themselves, their family or their societal group. In extreme cases, this guilt can form the basis of pathological morbidity and nihilism.

A central issue for the person with this Pluto placement is to accept responsibility for one's action and to therefore begin to mature emotionally and psychologically. There is a need to accept that one's own thoughts, desires and actions have accumulated as one's individual karma, the momentum of one's prior actions leading to the reality of one's current circumstance.

The existential thinker Heidegger describes this with the concept of "thrownness," which suggests that once one accepts that to not act is also an action, one is "thrown into situations" without being able to reflect on them first, for to reflect on them (not act) is also something that can be interpreted as an action.[23] One therefore must rely on instinctual interpretations, and go with the flow. Taking this further, the sense of involuntary volition into one's current life – the idea that we did not consciously decide to be born, is not true. To be born actually represents the consequences of all one's previous actions (both external and internal) and as such we are the authors of our own fate.

Out of this the question might be asked, "Can we become bold enough to transform our fate into our destiny?"[24] This is the intended evolutionary goal of this placement. Unfortunately, it is not a foregone conclusion that everyone with this placement or an emphasized Saturn signature in their chart will achieve that end.

One challenge with the Capricorn/10th house placement is that to the extent that we place our own power outside of ourselves then we position ourselves as victims of circumstance. The really critical time when we are unable to be in full control of our own fate/destiny is childhood, when we are necessarily at our most dependent. To the extent that excessive judgment or mistreatment occurs at the vulnerable developmental stages of childhood then significant problems with personal power and expression can result in adulthood.

Many people with Pluto in the 10th house/Capricorn experience some degree of coldness, judgment or artificially high standards imposed on them during childhood from which they internalize guilt proportional to their perceived failure to live up to those standards. Freud's concept of the super-ego refers to the internalized standard of right or wrong, a code that is learned in childhood which has as many variables as there are households with children. These conditioning factors are being sought out as part of the evolutionary impetus to understand the nature of how we make judgments and how consciousness is structured. The easiest and most immersive way to learn about an issue in evolutionary terms is to be born into it, to live in a situation that embodies what we are seeking to learn about. The problem that arises here is what we might call the goldfish factor – to the extent that we are trapped in the fish bowl, it is very hard to see out of it. We may as well try to see our own eye.

Some people with Pluto in Capricorn/10th house are just trying to understand the structures of society and as such have chosen certain conditioning situations in order to learn. Once in the challenging situation, the evolutionary purpose is often obscured and cyclic experiences of power and powerlessness become something that weighs on this person who has (at least partially) forgotten their original intention. Some others with difficult parental relationships or a tendency towards a psychology of futility have had so many prior experiences of negative judgments, cold treatment or disempowerment at the hands of those in power (be it parents or leaders of society) that they have lost the thread of the evolutionary intention all together.

A direct issue for the person with a Capricorn/10th house Pluto is the meaning of work. Some people will live their lives almost entirely through their work. The workaholic syndrome relates to the earth triad in a number of different ways. With the 2nd house/ Taurus there can be a fear of not having enough and the underlying anxiety about biological security dominates the compulsive need to work and to earn. With the 6th house/Virgo there is an urge to be compulsively busy in order to block out inner emptiness and working is a convenient culturally sanctioned method to achieve this end, not to mention an important part of the Virgo need to be useful and be of service. Contrastingly, the 10th house/Capricorn person contrives the urge to work as part of an overall need for power and status. Work has a driven quality relative to how much the person identifies with their power and status and fears losing them. Interestingly these work-focused types of Capricorn/10th house Pluto individuals may inadvertently raise their children in the same cold environment that they found themselves in by being absent from their children's lives. Among men in the industrialized West the "absent father" syndrome is a major subject for therapeutic analysis.

The Capricorn archetype also relates to a collective karma. We can calculate the nodes for every planet, not just the moon. And for everyone alive right now the South Nodes of Jupiter, Saturn and Pluto are in Capricorn. The ways in which we collectively structure our society (Saturn) according to our beliefs (Jupiter) and explore our most transformative and in-depth psychological processes (Pluto) are currently shaped by the conditioning factors of Capricorn. This reveals the importance of this archetype in forming our current collective understanding of power and its role in shaping our civilization. Unfortunately, as human history attests, power has been routinely abused, so much so that P.D. Ouspensky considered history to be nothing other than the history of crime.[25] During the twentieth century alone examples to support this idea might include the Holocaust, the Stalinist purges, the Maoist cultural revolution in China, and the current violent fight to control oil production. There has barely been a period in history free of war, famine or vast migrations of a displaced and vulnerable populace.

Some people with Pluto in the 10th house/Capricorn will have been victims of such mass destructive events and this will leave them more prone to the struggle for meaning and the potential futility of feeling of being burdened by past losses. Others may have sided with the oppressors in prior lives and may struggle in this life to find healthy expression of their will to power because of layers of unconscious shame and guilt from that past. Interestingly both prior-life victim and perpetrator will carry a powerful sense of loss and to some extent share the same current struggle to regain a balanced sense of personal power.

Many cultural anthropologists have found that cultures with a high incidence of rape share one or more of the following: a high investment in the military; gender-segregated activities and upbringing; distant male sky gods; and a recent history (within the previous century or so) of large-scale collective trauma (war, famine and/or forced migration of the mass populace)[26]. Cultures that use power in a forceful, destructive way then combine sexuality or Eros with the power impulse, resulting in rape becoming a common occurrence. Take for instance the frequency of sexual assault within violent conflicts, from rape to state-sanctioned prostitution.[27] In cultures that distort their understanding of power by equating it with coercive power *over* others, there is no safe space for the expression of the feminine qualities of beauty, creativity, joy and intimacy. This his-story, this legacy of patriarchy weighs upon us all, and finds its origin in the Saturn/Capricorn archetype.

The polarity point of Cancer/4th house signifies the necessity of a re-identification with the experience of nurture and personal emotional belonging. For balance, the Capricorn/10th house Pluto person must foster security and well-being from within without needing power and status to bolster self-regard. This person needs to recognize that family and the emotional life deserve their own time and focus and that allowing this time can balance the other concerns of life.

With the North Nodes of Jupiter, Saturn and Pluto all currently in Cancer, the Cancer polarity point is especially important for all of us. In his book *A Sacred Place To Dwell*, Henryk Skolimowski, a

Polish professor of Ecological Philosophy, argues that we need a new inclusive spirituality and that it must include a reverence for the earth and a sense of the earth as our home.[28] The idea of the earth as an interconnected system was proposed as a scientific reality by James Lovelock with the metaphor that everything that lives on this earth is part of a family.[29] This idea isn't new, and many indigenous cultures held such a view. One beautiful expression of this can be seen in the Buddhist teachings on compassion, which hold that since we have all lived before, everyone is family, and anyone could potentially be your mother from a past life, so we must take care of all. It is this sense of being at home on the planet that needs radical expression at this time. To the extent that we can make peace with our own emotions, we have a chance to live in peace with each other.

Pluto in the 11ᵗʰ house/Aquarius

We try to avoid our individuality, but that is a big problem. Individuality sometimes comes out of ego, like wanting to be an emperor, a king, or a millionaire. But individuality can also come from personal inspiration. It depends on the level of one's journey, on how far you have been able to shed your ego. We all have our own style and our own particular nature. We can't avoid it. The enlightened expression of yourself is in accord with your inherent nature. - Chogyam Trungpa[30]

It can be useful to consider Pluto in Aquarius/11ᵗʰ house as a reaction to Pluto in Capricorn/10ᵗʰ house. This individual has been seeking to understand and then liberate themselves from all the sources of conditioning they have experienced in this and in other lifetimes. With this placement there is a need to renew the concept of the self through a unique sense of identity, as free as possible from externally-imposed familial or societal constructs. Pluto intensifies the need for this rebellion signified by the Aquarian archetype. The desire here is for a radical act of separation from the karmic past – from who they have been, or from how others have seen them. In this way the Uranian/Aquarian archetype is always in conflict with Saturn/Capricorn. Aquarius seeks to liberate from conditioning while Capricorn seeks to build and accept it.

The Aquarius/11ᵗʰ house Pluto individual has a powerful need to detach from the external environment and social groupings in order to see those interactions with a new perspective. As an example of the potential gifts of this experience we can consider the story behind the writing of *Ulysses*, James Joyce's great novel. Joyce wrote the novel while living in Paris, a self-imposed exile he undertook in order to achieve the necessary distance and perspective to be able to write objectively about his home city. Sometimes we have to step out of our familiar routines to understand the patterns that play out in our lives.

To separate from the karmic past and liberate the identity into a new life is not easy and because the Pluto complex operates as a need for security through what is familiar we encounter in this placement a radicalism that for most people will engender considerable insecurity. When the evolutionary intent is radical the capacity for resistance is enormous. A predominant fear with this placement is that by taking the steps toward individuation away from the prevalent conditioning factors of one's personal life, one will become isolated. This fear is far from being baseless paranoia since many people do experience long periods of emotional and cultural isolation when they step out of the mainstream. Yet by holding back the evolutionary intention just to play along with the established norms, this person begins to feel increasingly hollow inside. Such emptiness is the basis of another kind of loneliness that eats away at you even while you are surrounded by family, colleagues and friends.

Throughout history we can see examples of people being ostracized, bullied and killed for daring to express a viewpoint deemed heretical by the consensus. Many brilliant scholars have been punished for seeing the world differently, even though their visionary ideas are now accepted as commonplace. If the idea that the earth is round challenges consensus, and you're the first to point it out, you're up against massive opposition. Many brilliant souls have been burned or tortured for daring to have an individual experience or view of God that did not fit the guidelines handed down by the Church.

This problem of the consensus fighting back against those who dare to break free of its constraints is one of the reasons why we can associate the archetype of Uranus/Aquarius and the 11th house with traumatic memories. The short-term memory or conventional mind we use to label information is signified by Gemini. The Virgo archetype describes how we sort through this information and structure it meaningfully (e.g. for an examination). The Sagittarius archetype corresponds to the philosophical system or larger order of meaning in which to place this data into context. In the Uranus/Aquarius archetype we have the higher octave of Mercury – thought, memory, and communication operating on a higher level. So we can relate the Uranus archetype to the long-term memory, which includes past-life experience.

In *Uranus: Freedom from the Known,* Jeffrey Green describes Uranus as liberator but also as a prior-life trauma signature in the birth chart.[31] I've been able to corroborate this assertion in my own practice and I work with the idea that when Uranus, a planet in the 11th house or a planet in Aquarius is in a major stressful aspect (conjunction, square, sesqui-quadrate, quincunx or opposition) to other significant parts of the chart it constitutes a trauma signature. I will explore this in detail in Chapter 3. By trauma I am referring to a difficult experience held in the long-term memory, that part of the unconscious mind that on some level remembers everything that ever happened to us. This is the kind of memory accessible at times in dreams, meditation, vision questing or through hypnotherapy. For the person with this Pluto placement, many of these memories involve experiences that have come about through judgment, punishment or violent response from the collective as a result of the individual's need to break free.

On a collective level Western civilization has for centuries paid lip service to freedom while struggling to actually provide it to the majority of its citizens. Greek democratic ideals were forged in a culture that denied women a political voice and which had most of its menial tasks done by slaves. Many people have past life experiences of slavery, disempowerment and brutality stored in their long-term unconscious memories.

The nature of the South Node of the Moon, aspects to the node and its ruler and the Uranus placement itself will reveal some of the traumatic issues within the consciousness of the 11th house Pluto person. For this person, these issues are now in need of recognition. Because to the extent that they remain unconscious, they many act as stumbling blocks to the evolutionary intention to resolve that past. As these issues are understood and released this person's intention to liberate is facilitated.

There is a need for the 11th house Pluto individual to form alliances with people of like mind through friendship or through groups that offer support while the individual learns to express the new views. The importance of like-minded friends and groups can't be overstated when considering the support necessary to contradict bedrock prior conditioning influences such as familial and educational systems. The problem with such counter-cultural groups is that they can become their own sources of oppressive conditioning where perversely one may become judged for the failure to conform to the alternative outlook of the subculture.

Aquarius as an archetype is ruled by Uranus in modern astrology yet in classical astrology, its ruler is Saturn. The Saturn co-rulership symbolizes the problem with structure that such alternative societies or counter-cultural/utopian groups struggle with. Many alternative groups fail because of lack of basic structure. Others fail because the issue of structure becomes so great that it unconsciously dominates and people within the group are paradoxically made to follow rules of conformity or "forced" to be liberated. The freedom movements of the 1960s including the Civil Rights movement and the Women's Rights movement are ripe with examples of failed organizations that struggled unsuccessfully with structure issues.[32]

The constant struggle between liberated insight (Uranus) and the need for meaningful structure and organization (Saturn) is an archetypal one.

A further shadow with this placement occurs when certain old ideas or teachings are re-hashed as if they were brand new. We can see this currently in various "new deal" and "back to basics" political campaigns in which past ideas are flouted as a current radical trend. Consider the re-use of the phrase "tea party" in modern American politics in 2010. The past is recycled as radical chic in a labored and unoriginal attempt to deal with current problems. When Pluto is hand-in-hand with Uranus (Aquarius/11th house) we see the capacity to recycle the past in old clothes just as we distort the future with our present concerns, all as an expression of our need to understand our present conditioning and the way we experience our current life situation.

Needless to say many of the groups that this person might gravitate towards in order to express their alternative viewpoints have ideas that are just as problematic as the ones they are trying to escape. In his book *The Dedalus Book of the 1960s: Turn Off Your Mind*, an engaging gallop through the dark side of the 1960's (the decade which saw the Pluto-Uranus conjunction in Virgo), Gary Lachman makes clear that while many people were genuinely seeking a liberated experience of peace and love a great many others were preying on the naivety and lack of boundaries of those same seekers.[33] Many aspects of the Haight-Ashbury scene in the flower-power heyday were more dangerous and violent than the conditioned world such people were seeking to escape, as drug dealers and sex offenders congregated on the influx of youthful bodies entering San Francisco. We see in the paradoxical confluence of Leary's simplistic message of hope and Manson's acting out of the extreme dark side of the story a dance of the two sides of human potential, both men later sharing adjacent incarceration cells at the courtesy of the Federal government. As we seek liberation, we release potential chaos and the Dionysian wave that results can engulf and destroy people.

Nietzsche warns us that, "Insanity in individuals is something rare - but in groups, parties, nations and epochs, it is the rule."[34] He is pointing to what can happen to the unconscious power impulse particularly as it strikes within group consciousness. This may unfold more subtly if the group disavows power all together, yet it will likely still be present. The key with Pluto in this placement is the urge to individuate, to become the person that one always wanted to be, free of past traumatic influences and conditioning factors. To the extent that a group supports this process it is useful, but the point at which it begins to block this process signals a problem.

To the extent that the individual with this placement fails to act on the impulse to free themselves from the accumulated prior conditioning then there will be extreme alienation and disassociation from their present life circumstances. This can manifest as posttraumatic shock or PTSD whereby life is experienced as a series of hollow interlocking moments from which the person feels a core personal alienation.

The polarity point of the 5th house/Leo expresses the need for this person to creatively self-actualize in order to express the potential to move beyond the disassociation produced by trauma into a more creative period of recovery. To the extent that the individual has subsumed their identity within a group (many therapeutic groups attract their fair share of wounded birds) then the polarity point of the 5th house/Leo speaks of the need to get in touch with the purely selfish impulse to evolve and to celebrate the creative potential of the individual self apart from the cover of any particular collective movement. If the individual has experienced core alienation from the present society (through a rejection of its conditioning or through a traumatized incapacity to relate to its rules) then the 5th house/Leo polarity point speaks of the need to find a creative medium with which to re-engage and relate to people within the given culture. This is about seeking a balance between individuated creative expression (Aquarius-Leo) and self-development that serves the whole (Leo-Aquarius). To cut one-self off from either the personal or the collective energy is to shut out a considerable part of what is important in life.

Pluto in the 12th house/Pisces

Pisces and the 12th house represent the culmination of the Zodiac and as such this archetypal complex blends the potentials of the other signs. Yet its underlying symbolism corresponds to the origins of consciousness. The central issue facing the individual with Pluto in the 12th house/Pisces is how to relate to creation as a whole; how to align the individual consciousness with a transcendent belief system that allows for an experience of surrender to and/or participation with the whole of life.

There is a need with this placement to identify and dissolve the barriers that exist between individuality and the collective unconscious in order to align the personal energy with collective or transcendent energies. This in turn effects a replenishment of the self. The Pluto placement itself and aspects to it, the South Node of the Moon, and the ruler of the South Node will indicate the way the dynamic of surrender/resistance has occurred in the past. These signatures will show the kind of barriers that the person has erected between themselves and transpersonal energies. The reason for these barriers pertains to the Pluto complex: to the extent that identification with the personal self produces security, the continuity of the personal self will be rigidly adhered to. Yet the evolutionary intention here – which generates enormous pressure from within – is to step beyond the personal self and into the world of transpersonal forces. The potential feeling of a loss of control generates subconscious insecurities and becomes the basis for all sorts of fears, phobias and personal ritualized or magical thinking.

The fear of transpersonal experience can be likened to a fear of death of the personal self. As Ernest Becker makes clear in *Denial of Death*, death anxiety is a primary concern underlying a whole host of seemingly unrelated problems.[35] Not least of these is man's attempt to overcome his death anxiety by hoping to achieve immortality through artistic and cultural projects that will outlive him. As one seeks status (a large house, an SUV, great works of creativity etc.) one seeks to transcend this inherent limitation, the chaos and vulnerability of life and the insecurity it engenders. There is nothing wrong with seeking a larger significance through one's brief life. The shadow is that if we are doing this only to hide from our fear of death we may become subconsciously very destructive.

The desire for profit, profligate materialism, or even religious or cultural fundamentalism may take over as we seek to replace our unconscious insecurity with something indelible and secure. As a motivator, this drive for immortality is responsible for myriad human blunders, including cryogenics, excess spending by those with wealth to extend life for a few months (while the great majority of the rest of the world die for lack of basic procedures), and the political and environmental complexity surrounding our current oil addiction.

While sublimating the personal ego into a larger cultural or creative project is one way to achieve a kind of significance beyond death, the evolutionary intention with this placement (as the culmination of the archetypal journey through the Zodiac) is to experience direct contact with transpersonal forces, to undergo personal existential and spiritual experiences that create new meaning and purpose in life. To the extent that the fear of losing control or the fear of death predominate, the individual may cling to whatever represents individual power in order to maintain a sense of order and control within their lives.

One aspect of the Pisces/12th house Pluto experience can be likened to being on a cliff top. The solid rock and earth underneath represent the known past, all the ways the individual has self-expressed and internalized a sense of who they are. The solidity of this ground represents existing personal and cultural identities that the person has become used to and comfortable with. Then before them stretches the beauty and power of the ocean, moving away at the bottom of the cliff drop. This ocean represents transpersonal psychic and spiritual forces – the Heavens of the Abrahamic religions, the *dharma kaya* or enlightened mind of the Buddhists, the Atman of Hinduism, the ocean of pure potential, the field of energy that is the ground of our being. The Pisces/12th house Pluto individual is invited to leap into the ocean. Even for those who are attracted by this idea the drop will seem long, the change from one way of living to another appears challenging. To the extent that the fear of losing control (the projection of a death anxiety onto the ocean of being) predominates in the consciousness of the person on the cliff they will cling to whatever solid objects they can find, determined not to fall.

Yet the evolutionary pressure to engage with the force that is the ocean is continuous. To offset this pressure the individual may elevate the meaning of the rock to which they are clinging, thereby seeing everything in life through the lens of that rock in order to avoid facing the seething hugeness of the ocean below. The rock may take the form of a primary relationship, a core idea or concept, a physical attribute, a sense of humor, a sub-group within the given culture, a pervasive cynicism or even the rational mind itself. Whatever the nature of the metaphoric rock and however those close to the person relate to it, the underlying intention is to preserve the individuality in the face of the evolutionary pressure to surrender it at the cliff-face of a higher order of reality.

If the evolutionary impulse to experience the ocean meets such resistance then the potential for inner cycles of meaninglessness and despair can result. These occur in part because the individual needs to experience larger forces and to integrate their personal identity within a world in which they experience transcendence and a higher order of meaning.

With the Saturn/Capricorn archetype, the identity reaches an awareness of its own mortality and the impact of space and time. For instance, after the first Saturn return many people find that they are not able to waste time like they did in their teenage years and early twenties because time feels too precious. With Pisces the potential exists for this stable identity to surrender to the reality of the soul, the higher self, a transcendent and immortal Being of which individual consciousness is merely an aspect. If surrender is allowed to happen, the person can experience a rejuvenation of the psyche whereby space and time are seen as playgrounds of the spirit. Hence there occurs a creative renaissance which reinvigorates and re-contextualizes the persona. So the evolutionary intention is to ultimately lead this person to a new experience of energy and integration and if it is resisted a sense of ennui and despair can result. Paradoxically this same existential depression can lead the individual back into searching for a source of higher or deeper meaning and the evolutionary intention is once again taken up.

As cycles of meaninglessness compel the person resisting the evolutionary impulse then they are left facing a difficult situation. They may act out a variety of scenarios hoping to discover themselves through playing the various parts each self-created drama demands. The problem becomes one of personal identity in that this "acting" can lead to progressive disconnection from a congruent personal reality into experiences of breakdown, madness and profound depression. In other cases the metaphoric rock that is fetishized to counter anxiety in the face of the transcendent impulse has so much time and energy invested into it that it becomes a source of great power and success for the individual. This can make it all the more difficult for the person to put down the rock and fall into the ocean.

In *Neptune, the 12ᵗʰ House and Pisces* Maurice Fernandez has shown that many people with emphasized Pisces/12ᵗʰ house signatures become a conduit for the collective: either as politicians, actors or musicians, or in public life, they channel the collective energy. In some cases this derives from an investment in their own sense of meaning. In others the energy emerges from the collective unconscious which they consciously (or unconsciously) access. Paradoxically because of genuine resistance to surrender some achieve worldly success or recognition, just as others receive energy from the archetypal forces to which they have surrendered.

There is no easy way to resolve the Pisces dilemma but we can see that some people's public life is an expression of who they really feel they are, indicating a surrender to an archetype, or openness to life energy. Whereas others feel hampered or restricted by their public identity, aware that they have constricted some part of their development in order to play a role.

Another challenge with Pluto in Pisces/12ᵗʰ house relates to dreams, desires and ultimate aspirations. Let's return to the defense of playing out various dream realities as protecting the self from a crisis of meaning. This kind of defense includes the risk of really losing the thread of personal identity. Yet we encounter an archetypal dilemma in this placement: which desires are meant to be acted out and which desires are only meant to be fantasies enacted in dream life (day or night)? In the book *Serial Killers*, Donald Seaman and Colin Wilson demonstrate that the cold, unloving childhoods that make up the classic serial killer profile (with patterns of extended bedwetting, lack of school friends and cruelty to animals) lead to an extraordinary fantasy life, fuelled by sexual frustration and anger at perceived lack of success. The authors note the curiously passive identities of their case studies, commonly exhibiting vanity and a sense of victimization that expects reward without commensurate effort. Their crimes then become an acting out of what they should have (power, sexual mastery etc.) that the fantasy life has preserved. That same fantasy life (reflecting on the event afterwards) then fuels the compulsion to commit more crimes.

This cycle is critical in almost all of these types of killers. And while everyone has a fantasy life it is useful to study the extremes of human behavior in order to gain a clear understanding of the "normal" majority. A person's fantasy life forms a critical part of their development and allows for the expression of otherwise forbidden desires. In a healthy person the many compensations of successful integration into society and personal relationships ameliorate the more peculiar or destructive fantasies. But for the criminal, this line is crossed. We may say it is obvious in the case of the serial killer that their fantasy life should have remained fantasy but the compulsion within them is typically too great, and they feel forced to act. Some are so aware of this that they become almost willfully careless in order to facilitate their capture. Others request the death penalty as they know they cannot change. Their compulsions stem from their reliance on the inner fantasy life to compensate for the failures of their actual life, their problematic personal relationships and lack of sexual empowerment.

Many people with Pluto in the 12th house/Pisces have powerful fantasies about their personal identity or creative or sexual potential which exert pressure on their imaginations and emotional lives. Some fantasies are occasioned by lifetimes in which they have experienced heavy religious conditioning as to the perfect standard of behavior to which they should aspire. Such religious conditioning is a product of their evolutionary intention to align with a transcendent belief system, which in many monasteries and convents goes hand-in-hand with other teaching. For example, an individual with a sincere desire to embrace a transcendent reality enters a monastery looking for God and encounters instead long sermons on the nature of Original sin and man's depravity. Some with this placement have had prior-life experiences of being imprisoned or incarcerated in some form and have compensated by retreating into a powerful fantasy life. Distinguishing which fantasies serve the evolutionary impulse to engage with larger forces of meaning from those which are regressive and representative of insecurity is a critical process for this person.

Many people with Pluto in Pisces/12th house find that previous exposure to religious or spiritual teachings has developed their intuition to a high level of acuity, permitting them to experience an innate knowledge as to what is right and what is wrong – a moral compass. This becomes distorted when the dream reality that they create to escape anxiety is bought into and celebrated as being real. Many such creations are so successful it would be hard to know that they were based on an inner fiction.

Some of these individuals feel they have fallen below their own strict moral sense, they feel they have let themselves down. In extreme cases these individuals have experienced lifetimes of persecution and criticism as representative of their own inner guilt and corresponding desire to atone for what they feel they have done wrong. To the extent that the punishment they attract becomes divorced from any sense of wrong-doing it can simply invoke masochistic tendencies and becomes, instead of a meaningful atonement, simply a chaotic force that destabilizes their lives.

Others with this placement become sacrificial heroes/heroines trying to save everyone around them as their identification with goodness or the idea of salvation leads them into exhausting and ultimately draining cycles of behavior. The antidote is always the same – to achieve surrender and to swim regularly in the (metaphoric) ocean to refresh the psyche.

Ultimately the evolutionary intention here is surrender. Some will not bend and will persistently glorify the personal ego before admitting the transcendent source of the self. Others will hesitantly make small steps toward the unknown and then recreate patterns of familiar behavior and identification in order to offset the "threat" of the transpersonal. Still others will cyclically reinvent themselves through the dissolution and re-emergence of the self. As they re-emerge, other aspects of the personality crystallize, requiring further dissolution. This can be an ongoing cyclic renewal of meaning or, conversely, an endlessly futile loop of personal failure and emptiness. If the ego is identified as the only source of consciousness then there can never be consistent happiness or fulfillment. The evolutionary pressure of Pluto in the final Zodiacal archetype demands that we look beyond the parapet of the ego's castle and take in the starry Cosmos.

If, in the exact passing moment of each instant, there is a complete willingness to totally surrender to it, one can suddenly, in a flash, transcend the ego, and the way opens for Realization wherein the Light of God as Self reveals the Source of all Existence and reality. If the ego has neither past, present, nor future to focus on, it falls silent. It is replaced by the Silence of the Presence, and thus, the way to sudden enlightenment is available at all times. It occurs naturally when the fascination with the story of the 'me' of the past, present and future is relinquished. The illusion of the 'Now' is replaced by the reality of 'Always.'
- Dr. David R. Hawkins[36]

The 6th house/Virgo polarity point operates here as the necessity of consistent self-questioning as to the nature of one's dreams and one's potential for self-delusion while also maintaining one's openness to the non-linear realms. It also refers to certain daily or step-by-step techniques, such as meditation, prayer, mantra, and the kind of self-analysis that can facilitate a readiness for the influx of transpersonal energies. These methods provide a counter point to the more subtle inner transformation that this Pluto placement is facilitating. The mental analysis of the earthy Virgo archetype keeps the process grounded.

This Virgo polarity also pertains to the idea of spirit grounded into service, and the call to bring the transcendent to earth and harness it for practical use. The Virgo polarity is a counter force to the tendency for excessive introspection or navel gazing that can consume some people as they seek to develop a spiritual awareness. Balance is found if spiritual development proceeds alongside a relationship to the world and the idea of service to humanity as a whole.

Chapter 2

The Moon's Nodes

Although we are most familiar with the Lunar Nodes, every planet has two nodes. The nodes are simply abstract points in space formed by the passage of any planetary body above and below the line of the ecliptic *(see figure 1)*. The ecliptic is formed by the apparent motion of the Sun through the sky, along which we encounter the twelve archetypes of the Zodiac.

In a future book I will explore the meaning of the planetary nodes. For now let's turn our attention to the moon's nodes.

The foundation of Evolutionary Astrology rests on the understanding that Pluto and the nodal axis of the Moon work in tandem to create a picture of the past orientation of the individual, their evolutionary intentions and goals. To understand how Pluto and the Nodes work together it helps to start by considering the level of consciousness that they symbolize. Pluto represents the deep unconscious material, while the Nodes represent material that is more clearly in one's conscious awareness.

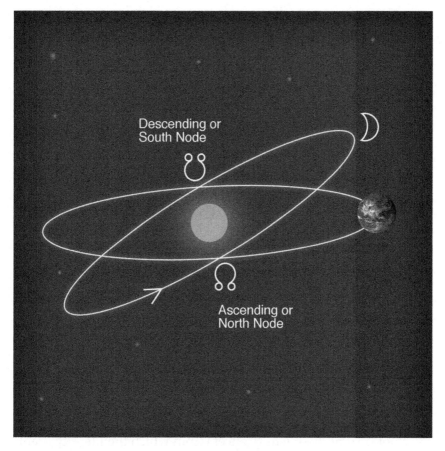

Figure 2. *The nodes relative to the ecliptic.*

The Water signs viewed as a trinity present a threefold representation of the nature of the Self within Evolutionary Astrology:

The Cancer Archetype (including the Moon and the 4th house) corresponds to the conditioned self, or the emotional body – patterning of the current life. This archetype illustrates the nature of the experiences of early home-life, relationships with primary care-givers and the psychological make-up of the personality. This ego identity is summarized by our name, our nationality, the personal story of our background and the minutiae of our formative life experiences.

The Scorpio Archetype (including Pluto and the 8th house) corresponds to a deeper self, the deepest unconscious motivations of the self. Here we find the level we might call soul which is distinct from the Moon, which is a more ego-based conditioned self. Scorpio represents the *fundamental concerns* and issues of the soul as it is evolving over multiple life times. This level of experience may be primarily unconscious, and is the deepest level in which we can experience our individuality.

The Pisces Archetype (including Neptune and the 12th house) corresponds to both the collective conscious and unconscious – the 'sea' from which all forms arise. Pisces represents the experience of divinity, the luminous emptiness, the godhead, Atman or ocean of being from which everything emerges. To experience this reality is to undergo a temporary suspension of the sense of a *separate personal self*, entering instead a state of *non-dual awareness* where there is no longer a distinction between the knower and the known.

When we consider the relationship between these three archetypes, we see that from the sea of the spirit (Pisces) arises the individualizing wave of the soul or subtle mind (Scorpio) which desires individual expression. This desire then manifests the conditioned self, the emotional body or lens (Cancer) from which the identity is able to process reality directly within space and time.

Using the language of the planets, the soul (Pluto) manifests the dual nature of desire: both the desire to separate via individual expression (manifesting through the Moon, or conditioned self) and the desire to return to source (Neptune or Spirit).

The Role of the Moon's Nodes

Since the Moon represents the specific lens of identity that allows the film of the unconscious and prior karma (Pluto) to play out in life, then the nodes of the Moon represent *the evolutionary potential of the ego*. Neptune represents the pure white light of consciousness shining through and animating the story.

The nodes are not real bodies. They are abstract points in space which are representative of the arc of the movement of any planet – the line it *has traced* and the line it *will trace* in the sky relative to the Zodiac. In essence they represent the history of that planet's movement before it reached the line of the Zodiac and the projected future movement as the planet rises above the line of the Zodiac. As such, we can add meaning to this movement by saying that the South Node of the Moon represents the *history* of the Moon (or conditioned self) and the North Node of the Moon represents its *intended future* or evolutionary intention.

Starting With Pluto

The symbolism itself gives rise to the astrological method of first analyzing the Pluto placement in the birth chart, and then analyzing the South Node of the Moon in order to fully understand the soul's journey, past, present and future. Pluto denotes the fundamental issues and motivations of the deeper self and the South Node of the Moon represents the prior-life ego structures that have attempted to fulfill that purpose.

Our prior-life egos can be seen through the history of the Moon. As the Pluto placement represents our deepest attachment, the past selves can be understood to have incarnated in order to express that deeper purpose.

We can go further by looking at the ruler of the South Node of the Moon, which represents another expression of how a person managed to facilitate the deeper (Pluto) purpose and how these issues played out for the prior-life personalities. Through the nodes, critical information can be discerned as to why a person was born into particular circumstances in this life. The nodes can show us where they have picked up from where they left off.

In this way we look at each chart grounded by an in-depth understanding of what has occurred before. Through the Pluto placement and the nodal axis of the Moon details can be ascertained as to the unconscious dynamics and prior karma that influences a person coming into this life. However we are not attempting through our analysis to create a prior-life diary complete with times, dates, and physical realities. Fundamental to the nature of the Moon is the subjective experience. What we *can* understand are the core archetypal themes that have motivated an individual on a deep level over a long period of time. The true potential here is to delineate the soul's purpose over many lifetimes and deduct crucial information that reveals meaning in the current life.

What About Reincarnation?

Without giving an extensive overview on the question of reincarnation, I can share a number of observations that I've made from personal experience about the idea of the soul learning over many lifetimes in order to become closer to its source. For instance, some of my clients have (not always intentionally) experienced the recall of prior lives during and after our sessions. The fact that the material arises at all within our sessions indicates a therapeutic need to explore this issue.

One client (the subject of a case study later in this chapter) had past life recall even though she did not intend to and had no previous belief or interest in the subject. Nevertheless there existed an internal psychic pressure that sought to be expressed in our session.

While such events are therapeutically relevant in my healing work, they do not necessarily prove the existence of reincarnation as fact. The Perennial Philosophy – with its emphasis on long cycles of soul evolution – informs this book.[1] However, whether reincarnation is adhered to as fact or not, the simple experiential reality of people in therapy and in regression work is valid in and of itself. Even without conscious interest in the subject many people experience prior life recall and I stand by them as they process. This reliving of past lives is indicative of their subjective importance, even if not their literal truth.

While some books of genuine intellectual rigor (*Exploring Reincarnation* by Hans ten Dam for instance) strongly suggest the historical truth of prior lives, we may still adopt an agnostic attitude to prior-life recall and be effective astrologers, therapists and counselors.[2] There are many alternative explanations to past-life recall, the most elegant of which involves Jung's idea of the collective unconscious from which we draw archetypal forms to enrich our personal unconscious and creative lives. Remembrance of prior lives could be drawn from this collective matrix and might therefore indicate archetypal issues or complex unresolved stories within the unconscious that present useful material for study and resolution

Although this book makes no ultimate metaphysical claims for the basis of past lives as historical fact, for the sake of simplicity such experiences will be referred to as prior lives without recourse at every juncture to explain the theoretical or metaphysical complexities of the issue.

Pre and Peri-Natal Experience

Pluto also symbolizes archetypal themes occurring within the womb and during birth. Stanislav Grof's work with LSD-influenced psychotherapy and holotropic breathing shed light on this profound level of formative experience before, during and after the birth process via his observation of thousands of people. Through the paintings, drawings and writings of his clients, Grof identified four archetypal levels of experience, which he termed "basic perinatal matrices." In his books *The Holotropic Mind* and *Psychology of the Future*, Grof demonstrates the manner in which biological stages of the birth process catalyze certain themes in the psyche of the embryo.[3] These can in turn be accessed by the aforementioned regression methods. In one example, as the baby enters the birth canal it may experience an intense struggle that resonates with an archetypal conflict between good and evil. Unconsciously, as this struggle progresses the infant make take on the form of a great hero fighting, or even the form of Christ on the cross, or other examples of the sacrificial god-form as the infant experiences the mythic intensity of the birth process fully.

Grof suggests that some infants get stuck at a particular stage in the process and as a result may find these unresolved unconscious dilemmas restricting their adult lives. Grof and others have found that these uncomfortable symptoms can be ameliorated by reliving the birth within a therapeutic context. Relating the symbolism of Evolutionary Astrology into these ideas, Pluto corresponds to the kinds of archetypes that would prove most powerful, compulsive, resistant or transformative prior to and during birth.

The Moon has a long tradition in astrology as representative of the mother archetype, which needs to be re-languaged as "primary caregiver," since we know that mothering does not only always emanate from the biological mother. But for the sake of understanding the birth experience, considering the Moon as symbolizing the biological mother serves as a bridge to connect our understanding of the relatedness of the Moon's nodes to the birthing process.

From this perspective the South Node of the Moon and its ruler symbolize very early childhood identity on a pre-verbal level as it exists before the current-life Moon imprint has had chance to mature into the emerging infant ego. It follows then that prior-life experience and the karma and evolutionary desires resulting from them, determine the nature of birth and the conditions of early childhood.

The Terminology of Evolutionary Astrology

Evolutionary Astrology takes its name in part from its focus on what is termed the *Evolutionary Axis*, which refers to the Pluto placement, and the nodes of the Moon and their respective rulers. We look to this axis of experience to understand the evolution of the soul.

Another term we'll refer to in this book is the *polarity point* of Pluto. This is the point directly opposite the placement of the natal Pluto. The polarity point, its sign and house, are considered for the balancing influence it can bring to the issues symbolized by the natal Pluto.

In the next chapter I will introduce a way to add the higher mind (symbolized by Uranus) to the *Evolutionary Axis* as another aspect of the soul.

Orbs

Since the Evolutionary Axis refers to the broad brush strokes of the soul's evolution through time, the orbs we can use for major aspects such as conjunction and squares to Pluto or the nodal axis of the Moon can be wider than we might use in other astrological methods. I have found that aspects to the Evolutionary Axis can be experienced clearly within orbs of 12°, and may even prove relevant at an orb of up to 15°. Richard Tarnas' work gives us insight into why this might be.

In *Cosmos and Psyche*, Tarnas uses an orb of 15° to explore the diachronic cycles of history (cycles linked by a similar astrological aspect e.g. the Jupiter-Uranus conjunction of 2010-11 links with 1968-9 when that same aspect previously occurred). When analyzing the data, those wider orbs emerged as relevant to an understanding of historical broad cultural brush strokes. We find a parallel with the *Evolutionary Axis* in that it also refers to the broad issues, in this case at the personal level of one soul evolving over aeons of time.

Try using this slightly wider orb with your clients when working with the Evolutionary Axis and see what you find.

Five Elements

As the soul seeks expression through an identity in order to explore the nature of its desires, the Moon serves as a lens for the personality to orientate in space and time. This is akin to the teaching of the five elements in Chinese medicine, which represent underlying currents of energy that form the bedrock of the "ten thousand things" – the Taoist term for the many possibilities of the world.

To experience life's multitude of possibilities we need an identity in a specific space-time context, and a particular cultural background (Moon). Yet underneath the surface are the elemental concerns and driving energies of Pluto – the deepest urges of the soul.

Just as the yin/yang symbolism of Chinese medicine underlies its five elements theory, expressing duality, so too does the soul have a dual desire nature which we can understand in the context of Evolutionary Astrology. The soul desires to individuate and find meaning in its individual self-expression and conversely to remove the sense of separateness of the identity by returning to the source from which it emanated.

This source (Neptune) to which all things yearn to return is like the Tao itself, the underlying Way or "action that is no action" holding all the experiences of soul and ego in context.

Transference as a Doorway to Karmic Experience

Through understanding the archetypal themes that have preoccupied the evolving Self on a unconscious level (Pluto) and by making those desires more conscious, we may facilitate their successful expression through the vehicle of the natal chart. By understanding the South Node of the Moon we see the types of prior selves or personal concerns that colored the expression of the central purpose. Through the ruler of the South Node and aspects to the both the

South Node and its ruler we can identify potential obstacles to the evolution of the soul's purpose (Pluto) on an individual level (the South Node of the Moon).

In recognizing that such prior-life experiences form the basis of the birth process itself and the conditions of very early childhood, we begin to obtain a therapeutic insight that informs much of my current work. Which is that prior-life karma informs early childhood relationships (what psychologists term "object relations" and therefore the early transference material that depth psychology wishes to engage with). So in effect, the way adults project transference onto a lover or a therapist echoes the way they transferred onto their parents as a very young child. Yet more radically, that same experience of transference is a direct route into the nature of the prior-life karmic experience.

In practical terms this presents a revolutionary therapeutic potential: in addressing the transference issues between my client and me we are addressing the core karma that the person brought into their life and played out in their early childhood. This is a direct line into what James Hillman refers to in *Suicide and the Soul* as the sharing of karma between counselor and client.[4] This is both radically simple and profoundly complex. The case study at the end of this chapter will bring to light some of these complexities.

Preferential Relationships

We can also see this karmic inheritance playing out in the ways in which we relate to our parents. We can observe that different children from the same family can each have a completely different subjective experience of a parent. Consider the following hypothetical example.

A mother returns to work after a period of home parenting. Her eldest child is seven and the youngest is five and both are in school. The children are all biologically healthy boys and part of a loving family. While the five year old reacts to the new separation from the mother just fine, the seven year old – just now in his first Saturn square – is terrified and begins to act out with bed-wetting and rage.

Let's say the seven year old has a karmic history, observable in the chart, of betrayal and prior-life abandonment trauma. And as one possibility let's consider that he was kidnapped from his family in a past life and sold into slavery. This *unconscious* prior-life complex is triggered by the current mother's new absence and begins to *unconsciously* influence the boy's not-yet-fully-formed identity. Our five-year-old has a completely different karmic history and therefore a completely difference experience of the mother's absence.

The idea of a *tabula rasa* – that each individual is born a "blank slate" ready for life's experience to be written onto it is, as any sensitive parent knows, complete nonsense. Even the child of a few hours old has a unique presence and the infant of just a few days old seems to have the most distinct character.

The instinctual understanding many parents have of the unique nature of their child, is actually that of his or her own karmic imprint.

Karma & Free Will

Karma is a Sanskrit word meaning action, or deed, understood as that which causes the entire cycle of cause and effect. I use it throughout this text as a useful shorthand for the accumulated actions, thoughts, desires and experiences of one's soul throughout all of time. It is therefore the critical indicator of the magnetism of the soul, the type of quality it emanates.

In the teachings of David Hawkins, the current reality of each person is arranged around the karma of the individual just like a magnet polarizes iron filings, evincing the power of that magnetism as patterns of experience that the individual manifests.

We are not only subject to our karma, however. With free will we have the freedom to make choices in the moment that affect our karma. What we hold in mind at all times holds the key to understanding all future karma we will manifest, and to how we respond to the karma that is now unfolding.

This freedom we have in every moment is a critical evolutionary possibility that we can tap into at any time. In any given moment, choice is possible. With the conscious awareness provided by understanding the Evolutionary Axis, we're faced with the responsibility to choose how we react to life. We might make the decision to wallow in the despair of past karma in relationships (feeling like a victim) or we might take responsibility for our role and our karma and embrace our power to change.

In this way Evolutionary Astrology offers a model for personal analysis that stands in sharp contrast to the fate-based deterministic astrologies of our cultural heritage.

Taking responsibility is an act of will that makes possible the surrender of the past karma. I use surrender here to mean offering up the contents of consciousness to the underlying power of the field, which Hawkins calls the "underlying context of everything," the essence of which is divinity manifest throughout all possibilities of experience that can be held in consciousness.

In using the term karma throughout this work we should take care not to confuse it with the frequently negative connotation it has in modern slang. Karma does not just mean that you reap what you sow. Karma is the culmination of what we are and have been both externally and internally. It can be "good" or "bad" in our relative experience but if we're paying attention, profound healing can occur when we own our karma, taking existential responsibility for everything we are and have been.

Hawkins teaches that "every hair on our head is counted," that the multi-dimensional field that is the power of Always (not just now) contains a trace of everything. Every thought, deed, desire, fantasy, heroic or pathetic thing we have ever done literally (or imagined ourselves doing) is noticed. Just as importantly the *intention* behind every inner or outer experience is also noticed by the all-embracing totality of the Always. When one truly grasps this insight into karma, and the profundity of its existence throughout all of space and time it can be shocking.

Pluto in relationship to the nodes of the Moon is the route to understanding this level of experience through the natal chart.

The Pitfalls of a Cookbook

In order to increase our understanding of the lunar nodes we will explore each of them separately through the archetypes by remembering first our earlier proviso that *this is a poet's cookbook*. Use these sections only as initial observations, as starting points for your analysis. Attempts at a definitive classification of every possible configuration would serve to defeat our goal of realizing the full potential of Evolutionary Astrology. Imagine learning the twelve archetypes as if they were twelve notes of a musical scale, then learning to listen to and play them in tandem, throughout their endless combinations. To create a structural part of the method through rules or examples is crucial to developing our initial understanding. But take the following examples as a starting point for intuitive reflection and *not as a prescriptive catalogue*. If we narrow our focus too soon when trying to understand a birth chart, we are prone to missing the totality of the symphony by being too caught up in each individual note.

So with that, it's time to dive in. We'll start by exploring the potential of the nodes through the 12 archetypes. We'll consider squares to the nodal axis of the Moon and also the ways in which Pluto (or other planets) conjunct the nodes can influence the overall picture. The descriptions of the nodes of the Moon that follow tend to emphasize psychological dynamics that the placements might relate to. There are many other ways to approach the nodes – for example as the South Node of the Moon relates to prior-life experience it can assist in ascertaining information as to the kind of epochs in history or specific cultures in which a person's prior lives took place. But for now we'll make an understanding of the psychological dynamics and archetypal themes our primary interest.

You may notice some similarities between these nodal signatures and our earlier exploration of Pluto through the archetypes. This similarity exists because we are always exploring the same twelve archetypes – we're just changing the lens through which we view them. With the nodes of the Moon as our lens, we're considering the past and present experience on the level of the conditioned self (a conscious and accessible part of our identity) whereas when we used Pluto as the lens, we were considering the primarily unconscious forces and desires of the soul.

A mature understanding of all twelve archetypes permits us to enjoy their interaction with each other. Like seasoned musicians we might discern the different chords and modal signatures, which in turn will enable us to improvise within them harmoniously.

The Lunar Nodes Aries/Libra Axis

South Node in 1ˢᵗ House/Aries

With the South Node of the Moon in the 1ˢᵗ house/Aries the individual has tended towards a need for independence in order to have the freedom to express their will. This is primarily an instinctual process. The need for space occurs in order to have free reign to experience the strength of their will and in doing so, discover their desires and then act on them.

Any restrictions of their desire or ability to express their will can cause intense frustration and the potential for aggressive action taken in order to preserve their freedom. By thinking about the natural squares that occur from the 4ᵗʰ and 10ᵗʰ houses, and the Cancer/Capricorn archetypes, we can understand more about where these restrictions may stem from. (*Note: Additional information may be gleaned from any planetary aspects that also occur in the birth chart.*)

The Natural Squares

The natural **4ᵗʰ house/Cancer** square to 1ˢᵗ House/Aries suggests the potential for restriction by way of anxiety that arises due to the need to *establish security through familiarity*. This security need clashes (square) with the need for freedom and perpetual self-discovery that the South Node in 1ˢᵗ house/Aries person requires.

This may take the form of conflicts with the family, whose needs restrict the individual's required self-expression. It may also show up as problems in childhood that create internalized patterns of anxiety which emotionally disable the person from their desired self-expression. In this latter situation, displaced childhood needs are carried unconsciously into later life and play out as the person attempts to self-assert or when they enter close relationships.

In the **10ᵗʰ house/Capricorn** square we find the potential for restriction through *conditioning influences* imposed upon from outside, whether from the family, society or civilization at large. The person must conform to certain rules in order to remain part the given societal infrastructure, e.g. a school or a job. Such rules become blocks to the natural desires that arise within the individual on an instinctual level.

To the extent that outside conditioning influences are repressive, they can become internalized as "introjects," or internalized messages of "thou shalt not." This can be likened to the influence of what Freud named the "super-ego" – the idea that the "id," the instinctual will, needs to conform to in order to exist within society. Without these conditioning influences there is the potential for anarchy and unchecked aggression from the individual, yet if these conditioning factors are excessive they often become internalized as a form of persecutory anxiety, or the feeling that whatever one does is wrong. This then becomes the basis for rage, which if suppressed, leads to depression.

North Node in the 7th/Libra

With the North Node of the Moon in the 7th house/Libra the evolutionary intention has been to open up to new ways of relating to others. To the extent that unchecked expression of the instinctually narcissistic will (1st house/Aries) has become limiting for the individual, the desire to experience life through the mirror of other people increases. Input from others then serves to expand the individual's perspective of previous experiences gained through the 1st house/Aries past.

Just as relationships are desired and needed here, they may also bring up fears about the loss of previously hard-won independence. To the extent that there are planets on the South Node or planets squaring the nodal axis (or even planets in stressful aspect to the South Node ruler) the tendency to struggle with abandoning the old pattern of willfulness will be more pronounced.

South Node in 7ᵗʰ House/Libra

With the South Node of the Moon in the 7ᵗʰ house/Libra the pre-existing mode of behavior has been to learn about the self through relationship. Reality has tended to be experienced on a compare-and-contrast basis, forming relationships with many people, both like and unlike themselves. They may have experienced learning through contrast to others who were not like themselves, and conversely experienced resonance with those who were of like mind.

Because of the past patterning, relationships can become so important to the person that they dedicate all their time to them, either through prolonged interaction with others or through excessive reflection on their meaningfulness. Both of these processes can become exhausting. As a result of such an intense focus on other people the individual can become depleted and have periods of withdrawal from any social interaction. This rhythm can become a pattern as cycles of overt involvement with others are followed by periods of withdrawal. These extremes can become the basis for a core insecurity or instability in the self.

The Natural Squares

The natural **square to 4ᵗʰ house/Cancer** suggests that, to the extent that stresses in the early home life create anxiety, relationships may become the safe haven to which the person emotionally clings. This can generate huge pressure on the relationship as it assumes an inflated importance through the conflation of unmet infant-parent needs which then are expected to be met by partners or friends. Such displaced childhood needs can saturate this person's adult relationships, becoming the basis for co-dependency. The partner is turned into a parent as the "child" in the individual clings to the object of their safety. Co-dependency in turn becomes the basis for excessive proximity to the other.

In our culture many couples are celebrated for the fact that they never spend a night apart from each other, as if this is the epitome of love. In fact excessive proximity is liable to generate emotional distortion. Certain characteristics of the people involved become magnified, unbalancing the capacity of the individual to make sense of reality. A lack time spent apart leads to imbalance.

The natural square to 10th house/Capricorn suggests that the conditioning factors within any given external structure, family or society can also create stress within the relationship experiences being sought. We have already seen how our society tends towards sentimentalizing excessive contact between people leading to loss of perspective within long-term relationships. Yet imagine living in a society in which falling in love and eloping is punishable by being tracked down and publicly executed for having disregarded the prevalent religious and cultural arrangements. This still happens in many parts of the world today. An entire tradition of Chinese lyric poetry was based on the suicide notes of doomed lovers, which expressed the impossibility of being together juxtaposed with the reality of their love.

Conditioning factors can wreak havoc on the nature of human relations and stressful aspects from Saturn (or planets in the 10th house) to the nodes can indicate such problematic influences.

North Node in the 1st house/Aries

The North Node of the Moon in the 1st house/Aries symbolizes the need to embrace the path of self-actualization in order to offset any imbalances created by placing excessive meaning on the shared reality of relationships. This represents a desire to have the courage to develop individually without reliance on another and without imbalanced cycles of excessive activity followed by exhausted withdrawal.

Whether the person wants or needs relationship is not in question. But the focus must shift from how past relationships were experienced as restrictive. This person now needs the freedom to undertake a journey of becoming – a perpetual renewal of the self through consistent action based on one's desire. This requires a shift towards a healthy degree of self-assertion with the realization that it is not being nasty to other people to say "no" sometimes, or to draw a line in the sand when something critical to self-development is at stake. This placement calls for the courage to be oneself. There is a need to release any residual fear that by not pandering to others one will be abandoned, empty, or meaningless in some way.

The Lunar Nodes Taurus/Scorpio Axis

S. Node in 2nd house/Taurus

With the South Node of the Moon in the 2nd house/Taurus the person has tended to internalize and compress their inner nature in order to consolidate their resources on both an internal and external level. This has often occurred because of survival pressures or concerns that have forced the individual to turn inward in order to identify their strongest resources. Desire is strong and highly internalized to withstand external pressures and allow the greatest protection from the environment. The danger is such that the survival mode that they have adopted becomes a limitation in its own right and they experience themselves as stuck on some fundamental level.

The Natural Squares

One aspect of the stuckness relates to the **natural square from the 5th house/Leo**. In consolidating one's resources to develop inner re-silience (Taurus) this person potentially loses creativity and joy in life (Leo). This in turn can restrict their capacity to creatively actu-alize. Living in survival mode results in tunnel vision whereby the psyche is not able to find inspiration or sufficient energy to fuel the inner creative needs of the personality.

One way this can manifest is through having children (Leo) in difficult material or emotional circumstances (Taurus) in which the parent(s) become so depleted that they are unable to nourish the creative, playful part of themselves, thus depriving the child of that aspect of their attention. In some situations this can indicate a prior (or current) struggle with either resources or values that results in the abandonment of the child and a resultant shutting down of the emotional life. Recent history provides us with many possible sce-narios that could lead to such a complex, including that children born out of wedlock were often taken away and sometimes the sin-gle mother also ended up in an asylum of some kind.

In the **natural square to the 11th house/Aquarius** we can see that an element of personal and collective trauma is involved with the formation of the survival mode approach to life. The trauma signatures within the Uranus/11th house/Aquarius archetype are explored in depth in the following chapter, but for now we will assume their correspondence.

For example, the loss of a child example from above is a traumatic one, but the stress indicated by the 11th house/Aquarius square aspect implies the potential for serious personal or collective traumas that force the person to develop internal resources in order to ensure physical survival. This can include memories of times in which they were unable to do so.

Vast collective disasters, war, famine, and earth changes kill and displace millions. People are at times reduced to eating grass or living among the rubble of their lost residences and communities. These disasters can trigger long-term complexes wherein the person is blind to all but the imperative of continuing physical existence. This process can become a habit embedded deep within consciousness – an imprint that continues long after the actual events that triggered the response have passed. The danger becomes that a long time after the event (potentially lifetimes after) the individual is still unconsciously acting as if the same conditions were present.

North Node of the Moon in 8th house/Scorpio

With the North Node of the Moon in 8th house/Scorpio the evolutionary need is to be challenged by others, or by an inner realization of the need for transformation, in order to break through the limits the person has experienced or created for themselves. This person will attract significant others who are not prepared to accept their tunnel vision and who will invite or confront them to open up and to embrace life in a transformed way.

Planets conjunct the South Node of the Moon or in stressful aspect to the South Node or its ruler will indicate the level of resistance to the new message coming through the 8th house/Scorpio other. This soul has an intention to transcend powers accrued in the past, risking powerlessness as they emerge from their protective shell in order to meet others. There might also be an intention to embrace a new path or direction that leads to transformation.

South Node in 8th house/Scorpio

With the South Node of the Moon in the 8th house/Scorpio the individual has tended to ally themselves with powerful people and/or systems of knowledge, thereby challenging their own power through such allegiances. Regarding systems of knowledge, I make a differentiation here from the Sagittarius "quest" for knowledge. In the Scorpio archetype, the intention is not necessarily a search for meaning, but rather to claim or try on the power inherent or implied in a powerful belief system.

This signature is an indication of previous struggle with the desires of the soul and a conscious understanding (on a personality level) of their primacy. The level of this understanding is based on the evolutionary stage of the individual. For some the struggle related to material power. For others, occult or symbolic forms of power were the issue. And yet others had experiences of gnosis.

While the individual has experienced the power of larger cosmic forces both internally and externally, they have also undergone cycles of powerlessness as they are not able to relate to or express such power. This may take the form of lack of money or authority on the material level, or psychological experiences of devastation as prior forms that facilitated conscious expansion seem to disappear, leaving the individual bereft.

The Natural Squares

The **natural square to the 5th house/Leo** symbolizes this cyclic sense of disempowerment. To the extent that the person has desired to creatively actualize and empower themselves (Leo) they have periodically experienced powerlessness (Scorpio) as they expose their pre-existing limitations and the resulting frustration that can bring.

At the core of the Scorpio archetype is a piercing uneasiness that is born out of the residue of all previously failed attempts at the actualization of personal power. To the extent that this influence remains unconscious then their relationships and creative life are cyclically darkened by it. This is one of the reasons why this archetype relates to hiding – the occluded quality these people can express as they seek to maintain a protective veneer over the vulnerable and potentially self-destructive side of their nature. Any person with an emphasized Scorpio signature (such as South Node in the 8th house/Scorpio) might engage in manipulative behavior in order to protect or hide their vulnerability.

The natural square to 11th house/Aquarius symbolizes the fact that many people with the South Node of the Moon in the 8th house/ Scorpio have experienced traumatic shock or loss in the past. The legacy of this unhealed trauma may show up in many forms. One common theme is that of the betrayal of trust. For instance, this person may have trusted someone with their deepest feelings, only to have them betray that trust. Or this person might experience people turning against them as a result of feeling manipulated.

Because of such experiences, these individuals have a highly-developed psychological awareness of the motivations of self and others. Prior betrayals have incubated in them a capacity for stringent character analysis in order to test others in an effort to avoid further let-downs.

Many people with South Node in the 8th house/Scorpio have formed very deep soul connections with others in prior lives and while some of these may have unresolved issues relating to abandonment and betrayal, some have been more positive and supportive of the individual's evolutionary growth. Many people with this placement will manifest relationships in the current life in order to clear past karma relating to the way prior relationships ended. Some will connect again with people who have helped facilitate progress in the past.

North Node of the Moon in 2nd house/Taurus

With the North Node of the Moon in the 2nd house/Taurus, the evolutionary intention is to develop a consistent set of *inner values* that lead to self-reliance so that they are no longer as dependent on deep relationships from the past as a way to actualize their goals. The newly developed internal values serve to create an alternative foundation for the psyche so that it is not so prone to manipulation, betrayal and loss. In order to achieve this, many people will need to withdraw from their external environment for periods of quiet focus so that they can identify resources that come purely from within.

The loss of seemingly essential relationships or symbolic forms of power (social standing, money, key psychological identifications) serve to isolate the individual for periods of time so that they can learn to rebuild a solid foundation of self-worth from within.

Some critical issues that arise with this placement include how to take care of the self, how to make enough money, and how to generate energy and meaning from inside themselves without relying on the shared resources of others or of institutions.

There is also a need here to question the meaning and value accorded to sexual experience. People with the South Node of the Moon in the 8th house/Scorpio have often experienced intense initiatory sexual experiences that have led to powerful feelings of merging with others. This stands in contrast to the experience of those with the South Node of the Moon in the 2nd house/Taurus, who are more grounded in the body and the physical experience of sex but not as comfortable with deep merger and emotional complexity.

People with the South Node of the Moon in the 8th house/Scorpio have an overdependence on using the intimate link with another to access their own soul nature. There is a compulsion to experience union with another, rather than acknowledge the full extent of power that already exists within themselves. Self-reliance comes through the regular practice of relating to their body and their own internal needs in an on-going and attentive fashion.

The Lunar Nodes Gemini/Sagittarius Axis

South Node in 3rd house/Gemini

Individuals with South Node of the Moon in the 3rd house/Gemini have manifested previous identities that are intellectually curious about the world around them. This person may have been born into different cultures with different languages and customs that they have wanted to learn about as part of a consciousness-enriching quest to gather information and experience.

In those who also have planets conjunct the South Node (or another strong emphasis by aspect to the South Node ruler or to a Gemini planet) may have gifts with languages or great fluidity within specific cultures signified by those planets. They carry these gifts into this life and remain very familiar and comfortable with the cultural experiences indicated. In some cases the person may not feel comfortable with their first language and may gravitate towards a different language or a different cultural expression. These attractions conversely betray a certain alienation from their current culture of origin. With the nodes in 3rd house/Gemini, 9th house/Sagittarius there is a general openness to the migration of ideas across cultures and of travel in general as a current life opportunity to continue the journeys of past times.

The Natural Squares

The **natural square to the 6th house/Virgo** indicates a crisis of discrimination. Experience and data has been collected, but what remains to be done with it? One danger here is that the search for knowledge and experience has become an end in itself with which the person has begun to feel overloaded.

The tension inherent in the 6th house/Virgo involvement points to developing filters so that data is sorted *before* it is stored, so that the memory is not flooded with random unsorted material and then unable to process important new information.

Another potential problem here is that some of the information (Gemini) the person receives or internalizes is critical or persecutory (Virgo). This may arise out of a past experience of sibling bullying or abuse, or a prior-life clash of cultures with people who have very different sets of values.

For example, nomadic peoples, travelers and hunter-gatherers are indicated by this nodal placement. As more settled cultures developed the land around nomadic peoples, they were exposed to outside cultural influences such as hierarchical power structures and monotheistic religion. The tension resulting from the exposure to more restrictive societal constructs is symbolized by the natural square to 6th house/Virgo. Gemini is an essentially polytheistic expansive archetype, but through certain cultural or religious teachings that critique man's relationship to nature (Virgo) this normally expansive quality becomes more restricted.

The **natural square to 12th house/Pisces** symbolizes the potential disillusionment of the South Node Gemini person who comes up against the fundamental limitations of the mind. Two essential points arise here. The first is that there is simply not enough time to visit every country and learn every language, to read every book or watch every movie. No matter how much energy is put into the acquisition of information, there is a limit to what can be taken in.

The internet has further increased the availability of information, making it that much more difficult for the 3rd house/Gemini person to keep their desire for new information in check. At the time this book was written, it is estimated that 250 billion emails are sent every day. It is now extremely easy for people to exhaust themselves daily to the point of disillusionment by their quest for new information. Often pursued in a frantic and scattered way, we see a kind of infantilism arise – a mental childishness that can too easily detach the mind from the body.

This problem is exemplified by pornography addiction, in which the detachment from mind and body can become problematic in this person's real, in-person relationships. The 12th house/Pisces illusion is no match for the real experience. The square symbolizes the tension between the two and the challenge in discerning the virtual from the real.

The second essential point symbolized by the 12th house/Pisces natural square is that fundamentally the mind can only ever *label* reality, it cannot *know* it. This is something that many spiritual traditions have long taught: that the map is not the territory, and the menu is not the meal. Spiritual reality (Pisces) can only be experienced through the discriminating purity (Virgo) of the intu-ition (Sagittarius). In the highest expression of Gemini we see the proper role of the classification function of the mind, which is to achieve a degree of symbolic understanding of the world in order to orientate towards it. To make the accumulation of labels a goal in and of itself leads to feelings of profound disappointment and meaninglessness.

North Node of the Moon in 9th house/Sagittarius

The North Node of the Moon in the 9th house/Sagittarius actualizes an intention to create or adopt a belief system that is large enough to give some degree of structure and meaning to the endless data that has been amassed. A philosophy or world-view can be adopt-ed in order to give shape and context to the information collected.

For example, the Kabbalistic system utilizes a symbolic Tree of Life to describe multiple worlds on multiple levels, all of which have associations – letters of the Hebrew alphabet and many other symbolisms. Kabbalists joke that God created Kabbalah to over-whelm the mind of the intellectual in order to break them down with the immensity of the mental challenge, so that they would come forward transformed and humble. This approach of intellec-tual exhaustion via overload contrasts with the Zen Buddhist ap-proach that cuts through the mind-trap by starving it to death with simplicity.

The person with this nodal placement has the future intention to develop the powers of the intuition in the personality so that they can start to see the bigger-picture and begin to find meaning among the chaos of information.

South Node in 9th house/Sagittarius

With the South Node of the Moon in the 9th house/Sagittarius the person has developed a foundation of intuitive capacity from which they can order their experience or just *know* things about themselves and the world around them. It is common for such people to have had prior lifetimes in which they explored many different cultures, this time with a particular orientation to the dominant philosophical and religious practices of the cultures into which they are born.

This person has already developed the capacity to consider themself part of a larger cosmological whole – a perception linked to their evolutionary condition or focus. For some there may be a primary religious orientation to life in which reality is dictated from the teachings, or they may have a homespun philosophical set of rules for life. In others we see a personal search for meaning throughout many different religious or cosmological teachings or ideas in which the person is in a process of selecting what feels right for them. For others, spiritual teachings become the basis for direct experiences of intuitive revelation which in turn provide the foundation of the identity.

The Natural Squares

In the **natural square from the 6th house/Virgo** we see tension regarding the issue of discrimination. The individual might question which philosophy or framework best helps them express their personal truth. Many monotheistic religions have teachings about man's inherent sinfulness or imperfection which can become the basis for a kind of injected guilt, which, when internalized, leads to a person feeling bad about themself without having ever done anything wrong.

A further problem created by organized religion is the tendency to invalidate the personal connection with spirit by insisting that it be mediated through priestly hierarchies. Problems arise when the individual has experiences of personal intuition or revelation (Sagittarius) and is persecuted or criticized (Virgo) for this. Many people with this placement have had their personal intuitive or spiritual experiences invalidated or demonized.

Another problem emerges with the possibility of past-life memories of natural indigenous cultures (Sagittarius) in which the person experienced a collective identification with nature, and a collective understanding of the body as holy and as natural as any other creature or form. Such a view can be contrasted with the religious teachings that have been forced upon indigenous peoples by zealous missionaries and more "developed" cultures. These teachings include a belief in our inherent sinfulness and the need to turn to God to purify (Virgo) the spirit.

Collectively, this experience represents a profound schism that has shaped western civilization, a split whose unconscious roots have led to many of the ecological issues that we face in the twenty-first century.

The **natural square from the 12th house/Pisces** represents another form of tension as to the ultimate meaning of individual experience and of the relationship of the personal vision to the whole field of consciousness. Many people with South Node of the Moon in the 9th house/Sagittarius struggle to articulate their intuitive conception of meaning and then feel isolated or ostracized within this struggle. The way this operates on a collective level illustrates the dilemma.

Many indigenous peoples of the Americas were devastated when the concept of the ownership of land was introduced, suddenly seeing their sacred pilgrimage routes and landscape temples fenced off from them. Many people and communities disintegrated, sometimes turning to drink or drugs to stave off feelings of meaninglessness. This is now true in epidemic proportions in many major urban centers in western countries where the very cultures that oppressed the indigenous people encounter their own struggle with meaning – which becomes masked in various forms of escapism and wish-fulfillment. Pisces represents both a deep connection with the source as well as the longing to escape meaninglessness.

North Node of the Moon in 3rd house/Gemini

With the North Node in the 3rd house/Gemini the evolutionary intention is to develop the faculties to explore and expand on their intuitive perceptions through dialogue with others. In this way a person who has tended to experience an overall grasp on reality through their own personal vision begins to learn about the relativity of "truth" as it is experienced through the lives of others.

Truth is then understood to be essentially subjective – one person's truth is not universal for everyone.

Fundamentalism can arise when people cling, because of insecurity, to their vision of truth as if it were the only one. Of course many conflicts in the world today involve this type of clash between religion and worldview, each side consciously and unconsciously invested in their own approach, oftentimes to the point of valuing their positions and abstractions over human life. This kind of fundamentalism is symbolized by the Sagittarius/9th house archetype.

Through interactive dialogue, with both sides speaking and listening, and by learning different languages and cultural mores, the person with the North Node in the 3rd house/Gemini learns to value the many varied forms through which people experience personal and collective meaning.

The Lunar Nodes Cancer/Capricorn Axis

South Node in 4th house/Cancer

With the South Node of the Moon in the 4th house/Cancer the individual has sought to develop an internal sense of security, a secure ego with which to meet the vicissitudes of life. As such, prior-life family experiences gain an emphasized importance as the crucible for the development of the personality. To the extent that the South Node of the Moon, or the Moon (as its ruler), is stressed within the chart (by conjunction, square or quincunx to other planets) we see the level at which the attempt at developing a secure personal reality has been thwarted.

The capacity exists for carrying old patterns of insecurity into the current life experience. Early childhood in this life is an indicator of the kinds of unresolved prior-life issues that have played out in the past.

This placement can indicate a central karmic issue with the current-life mother or care-giver, whereby that individual has played a crucial role (not necessarily as the mother) in the prior-life experiences that shaped this person's current emotional approach to life.

Another key issue with this placement regards present and past life gender roles and identities that have been experienced as restrictive. This individual may have switched genders in this life after a series of lifetimes predominantly as one gender. Across multiple prior lives we will all have experienced being both genders, but here the emphasis in the chart suggests that the gender change is an issue and that it may cause a problem of some kind.

The Natural Squares

The natural square from the 1st house/Aries points towards situations in which prior-life family experiences restricted the development of the independent will and have since become the source of built-up resentment and frustration within the emotional body. That the individual may experience restrictive parenting or gender-role identification in the current life is an echo of past restrictions of the will, or of the movements of the individual in the past. This can become the foundation for anger, triggered by current life experiences of restriction and heightened by multiple lifetimes of feeling hampered in their personal expression.

If the blockage to emotional development is very severe it can lead to arrested development, an immaturity born of having one's self-assertion consistently compromised or rejected. This chronic lack of personal freedom can lead to bursts of rage as the individual aggressively seeks to overcome the inadequacies of their environment. Even as the individual may appear to be seeking freedom at all costs they may still remain very vulnerable because inside themselves they are still very child-like and paradoxically still want safety and relationship even though they appear to rage or want to break free.

The **natural square from the 7th house/Libra** shows the potential tension caused by unresolved childhood material as it expresses in adult relationships. The family remains the root cause of the adult tension here. We might see a family that disapproves of the 4th House/Cancer person's relationship. Or we might find a family that is too inadequate emotionally or materially to equip the individual with the necessary tools for successful adult relationships. I've found repeatedly in my practice that when there are repetitive patterns of relationship failure in an individual's life this is almost always the result of the unconscious patterns of relating that were established in the early home-life.

To the extent that the child's core need for security and love is not met then the person will unconsciously seek out people to meet those needs as an adult. To the extent that both adults fail to understand that unconscious process, the tendency exists for the transference of the early childhood material to disrupt the relationship.

The power of transference of early childhood feelings onto later relationships is so powerful that it can manifest literally as an unconscious aspect within the partner being triggered into behaving just as the parent did. This is the phenomenon of counter-transference, a redirection of the partner's feelings back to us in response to our transference. For example, a young woman who is bullied by her father as a child might as an adult find herself silenced in any stressful or important situation, which can in turn be so frustrating to her partners that they shout at her, confirming her fear that every partner she attracts is just like her bullying father.

North Node of the Moon in 10th house/Capricorn

The North Node in the 10th house/Capricorn represents the evolutionary need to mature and to take responsibility for the emotional life and the nature of adult and familial relationships. In taking responsibility for the emotional experiences of childhood, even though these experiences might have been difficult, the person takes responsibility for their karmic inheritance and creates a foundation for more liberated adult relationships and personal freedom. In this way the person begins to recognize that the inner child is an archetype present in every person, and that by taking care of the child within them they can transform their personal experience and relationships.

The inner parent is the part of us that can be responsible for our emotional body and that creates the necessary inner security for successful adult experiences. So while it might be inappropriate to carry a doll into an important business meeting it might be very appropriate to check in emotionally with the five-year-old inside us and identify how safe they feel in that situation.

The North Node in the 10th house/Capricorn also refers to the need to go out into the world and establish status and meaning outside of the family. This includes exploring the nature of gender roles within society so the individual can define for themselves what it means to be a particular gender in a particular society, adapting to those conditioning influences as part of their search for self-expression.

South Node in 10th house/Capricorn

With the South Node of the Moon in the 10th house/Capricorn the individual has been developing a sense of responsibility for their actions and exploring the nature of judgments – both those they have made and those that others have made *of* them. Prior-life experiences often include exposure to heavy outside conditioning influences as the person struggles to comprehend the structure of families, societies and other systems of power and status. Such prior conditioning is symbolized through the Saturn placement, its aspects and aspects to the South Node of the Moon.

Stressful aspects to Saturn or the South Node of the Moon in this placement indicate experiences of negative judgment and restrictive conditioning, perhaps through cold familial situations where duty and deference to formal expressions of bonding are emphasized above affection and spontaneity. This placement can also indicate experiences in highly formalized and hierarchical cultures in which power and status are highly valued. The individual may have vacillated between embodying such status and being ordered around or controlled by others with relatively higher status. Such experiences create an acute awareness of *social standing*.

This placement also indicates a karmic backstory with the individual's father, who may have shared some of these imbalanced past-life experiences within highly ordered societies.

The Natural Squares

The natural square from the 1st house/Aries suggests tension arising out of the over-emphasis on duty and status (Capricorn) which has left the individual's need for personal freedom and self-expression unfulfilled. This becomes the basis for rage if such needs are imprisoned for too long. As rage is expressed it can become violent, damaging the social standing of the individual, maybe leaving them still more disempowered or even incarcerated. This in turn creates a psychology of futility and despair. The individual has memories of being overwhelmed with their own need for freedom and yet feels there is no way for their intensity of expression to attain meaningful embodiment.

With some individuals the South Node of the Moon in the 10th house/Capricorn refers to experiences within tyrannical families or dictatorial cultures in which their needs for personal freedom were all but destroyed. Some people may have experienced vast collective diaspora or displacement, war or famine as the product of mass controls within hierarchical and/or abusive systems. These memories generate depression, much of which is actually related to their historically repressed anger at the loss of their personal freedom to simply be.

The natural square from 7th house/Libra points to the fact that just as prior conditioning influences can negatively impact on their individual freedom (Capricorn square Aries), these influences can also be the basis for repression within relationships (Capricorn square Libra). One example is the instance of arranged marriages, which may or may not take into account the best interests of the individual. Even in the case where families or dynasties arrange unions that will best perpetuate their cause, the individuals involved may become overwhelmed by the pressures of the political and social interests of their families or the world around them.

Loveless arrangements plant the seeds for depression. As the individual gives up on personal happiness in relationship, they may give up on personal happiness all together. This can result in such coldness and emotional armoring over time that they succumb to imposing similarly restrictive influences upon their own children. In this way entire lineages can be born out of frustration and the repression of personal needs.

In other situations the individual may have become so damaged by personal and cultural repression that when they do enter a loving relationship by choice they carry an intensely damaged inner child, whose needs have been sufficiently repressed that they unconsciously dominate the relationship.

North Node of the Moon in 4th house/Cancer

With the North Node of the Moon in the 4th house/Cancer the evolutionary intention is to recover the inner child and to allow the sensitive and expressive emotional nature to flow again unimpeded. This involves a process of identifying the positive qualities of responsibility and realigning the experience of the family and societal structures from the past with the warmth and love that was missing.

There is a return to the child, a return to the archetypally feminine experiences of nurturing, touch and personal safety. And by archetypally feminine, I am referring to those states that are an essential aspect of both genders. In learning to create and experience a safe personal reality in which to experience vulnerability and softness, the individual is able to reintegrate elements of themselves from which they were estranged in the conditioned past. In this way judgment returns as a tool that the discriminating consciousness can use to evolve, free of its punitive connotations of guilt and condemnation.

To the extent that events in the past have necessitated authentic guilt – a genuine sense of having done wrong from deep within the person – then they can be processed now consciously within the emotional body, rather than existing in a split-off state as an aspect that feels too shameful to be owned.

The Lunar Nodes Leo/Aquarius Axis

South Node in 5th house/Leo

With the South Node of the Moon in the 5th house/Leo the individual has tended towards a consciously narcissistic development of their creativity and self-expression. Aspects to the South Node of the Moon and to the Sun will reveal the nature of this prior development. With the Sun, the integrative energy of the current life, as the ruler of the South Node of the Moon, the individual's will-to-be has undergone substantial development in the past.

Often the person with this placement will have an internal experience of feeling special or knowing that they have some talent or capacity that they are seeking to bring into being once more. To the extent that they are capable of discovering and expressing these inner gifts, the individual will tend towards generosity and a benevolent outlook. To the extent that these gifts are frustrated (either because of an internal struggle to articulate their form or an external struggle to find an appreciative audience) then the individual will tend towards bitterness and will struggle to overcome a selfish preoccupation.

The Natural Squares

The natural square from the 2nd house/Taurus suggests that this person's self-expression can be frustrated. This individual (in prior lives and in the current life) may have struggled (or be struggling) to find the resources to express their inner image of themselves. This may show up simply as the lack of money – not being able to afford the training that their specialized gifts require to be properly developed. It can also show up as being born into families that are struggling to survive and have no time for the grandiose needs of this narcissistic and creative child.

Conversely the family may have money and buy the child everything they demand, but are lack the capacity to offer personal validation or the real understanding that is also wanted. This becomes its own problem for such a spoilt, talented, insecure individual. Such situations form the basis for a narcissistic personality defense, whereby the creativity of the child comes up against the enormous pressure to shine projected by the parent. And yet to the extent that the parent has repressed *their own creativity* the child encounters the unconscious envy and emotional resistance of the parent from which they feel they must protect themselves.

Defenses are then based on an internal lack of resources, a failure of self-sufficiency in which the individual is always seeking the emotional validation they felt was lacking. Yet they do not believe in the truth of any validation they do receive, and form a self-destructive psychology in which they feel defeated before they even begin. Without a degree of self-sufficiency (Taurus) the individual may struggle to turn their high levels of creativity (Leo) into meaningful form.

The natural square from the 8th house/Scorpio points to another aspect of this struggle. To the extent that the individual feels restricted by available resources the temptation arises to manipulate people and situations in order to gain the recognition that they feel they deserve. This can take the form of misappropriating other people's resources: physically, financially, emotionally or creatively. They may take ideas from others without acknowledging their indebtedness, or become heavily invested in others to the extent that they are insecure personally, feeling abandoned when this investment does not lead to the requisite outcome.

There may be a karma of dishonesty, of having used or been used by others to the extent that the passionate need to express their creativity was allied with core insecurity about their capacity to do so. This can lead some people into seeking power through certain occult, the breaking of taboos, or of carrying secrets as a form of power over others in order to satisfy their own sense of entitlement.

Some people with the South Node of the Moon in the 5th house/Leo have memories of aristocratic lifetimes or other experiences of status and as such, they may be used to treating others as mere mirrors that reflect their own glory. This can lead to feeling let down or betrayed by others when they fail to fulfill expectations. This also becomes the basis for loneliness and a perpetuation of the very lack of recognition they have always feared.

The stress of this square indicates that these narcissistic defenses can best be undone via genuinely committed relationships with others. In loving another being, the individual begins to realize the validity of the other's responses and needs, and the fractured mirror of their own past relationships becomes clearer through this acknowledgment.

North Node of the Moon in 11th house/Aquarius

With the North Node of the Moon in the 11th house/Aquarius the evolutionary intention is to develop a sense of shared collective meaning in order to counterbalance the individual developments of the past. The individual needs to step back and objectively assess the nature of the prior-life development in order to ascertain how to serve the larger needs of the whole in the current life. In this way certain unconscious memories of status and power are transformed.

For example, consider a person with the karma of aristocratic memories who is now born into an ordinary home and family. Through the development of their artistic gifts this person again achieves the feeling of being special, but through the media of art in which they delight in others' appreciation. In this way the love and creativity developed in relative privilege in the past is now channeled into the everyday miracle of living a creative life, even as the trappings of that life are ordinary.

The sense of being extraordinary needs to be developed into an expression that serves the larger cause of humanity. In that way balance can be achieved. The objective realization of the North Node of the Moon is that the person is *not actually that special*; or that if they are, so is everyone else. They need to step out of their ivory tower, overcome their selfish preoccupations of the past and engage with the collective journey of humanity.

The North Node in the 11th house/Aquarius indicates the need for conscious awareness of prior-life development, both to overcome past blocks and to find new meaning in the archetypal depths of the psyche, a meaning beyond mere personal self-expression.

South Node in 11th house/Aquarius

With the South Node of the Moon in the 11th house/Aquarius the individual has tended towards stepping back from the collective in order to experience their difference and to develop a more objective awareness of their true nature and capacities. To the extent that there are stressful aspects to the South Node of the Moon or to its ruler Uranus, these experiences will have been traumatic, or the individual's need for understanding has been triggered by traumatic experience (see chapter 3). Such experiences of trauma are the basis for splitting off parts of the psyche in order to protect the integrity of the whole. This leaves a residual post-traumatic stress that can be carried over from a prior life without even having a significant current-life trauma to trigger it.

The traumatic component of past experience can exaggerate the necessary detachment that arises in this placement, leading instead to dissociative states and psychological dissolution. Many people with the South Node in the 11th house/Aquarius have experimented with alternative forms of social interaction and/or community living, involving the formation of deep friendships that contrast with the family of origin. Many people with this placement will have had experiences of feeling different, of living on the edges of the mainstream.

The Natural Squares

The natural square from the 2nd house/Taurus reveals the degree of the severity of traumatic memories of rejection and the ways in which such experiences threaten the person's relationship to their own needs and values. Survivors of traumatic experiences struggle to identify and meet their own needs in the ways that they were able to prior to the trauma. Even those who choose to live outside the prevailing trends or structures of a given society frequently undergo material struggle, as the process of resource allocation gains power through mass consensus.

For example, people in the 1960's who, under the auspice of the Pluto-Uranus conjunction of that era, sought to embrace alternative lifestyles, struggled to achieve sufficient material, emotional and psychological security for their vision. Many later succumbed to the prevalent social trends, (re)entering the "rat race" for cash and material security. Even the murderous actions of Charles Manson and his notorious Family were motivated by Manson's delusion that he should be a rich and famous Hollywood scenester.

The natural square from the 8th house/Scorpio represents an archetypal power struggle. To the extent that this person's needs are not met and their vision of life is not supported they may abuse power to gain what they desire. Furthermore, feelings of powerlessness resulting from traumatic experience frequently leave people feeling at the whim of larger forces, vulnerable and imperiled. Core trauma has an impact on a soul level and the fragmentation that the trauma-explosion creates can feel as though one is losing parts of oneself. They can feel that parts of themselves are left behind, or blown out of the body as a result of the impact.

One key source of personal trauma with this placement is that of being betrayed or abandoned by those to whom one is most allied on a soul level. This is the most brutal aspect of the Scorpio archetype, often involving the internalization of a secret self-hatred and fear that has arisen from the experiences of past betrayals. Some with this placement detach themselves (11th house/Aquarius) so as never to risk the feeling of betrayal again. Others who have learned to step back and detach from themselves in order to experience their own true capacities – free from personal delusion (a fundamental process in the Aquarius archetype) – then gain the capacity to form a more conscious relationship with their own soul (Scorpio).

North Node of the Moon in 5th house/Leo

With the North Node in the 5th house/Leo the evolutionary intention is to develop the creative potential of the self from the foundation of self-awareness that has been garnered from the past. If the past has involved traumatic experiences that have shaped the identity this goal becomes all the more important. The North Node then indicates a return to the self in order to overcome the prior fragmentation.

To enjoy a personal self that is fulfilled and celebrated is a part of the universal plan for being alive. In order to grow in evolutionary terms there is no need to abandon the self. In fact, to do so confers a substantial disadvantage. When we are traumatized, fragmented or ungrounded we are unable to tune into the energy which is the foundational point of our spirit and our essence.

Caroline Myss wrote perceptively in *Anatomy of the Spirit* that in order to heal one must have caught up with all the disparate parts of oneself. She holds that at every developmental stage in life where we fail to self-actualize, we leave parts of our energy body stuck at that particular time. When we add the idea of reincarnation, this concept takes on greater significance. To heal and to grow we must have enough of ourselves and our energy available in the present to be able to move forward with purpose. If too much of our energy is wrapped up in the past, it's more difficult to move ahead. The North Node of the Moon in the 5th house/Leo symbolizes this necessary return to the self.

The Lunar Nodes Virgo/Pisces Axis

South Node in 6th house/Virgo

With the South Node of the Moon in the 6th house/Virgo the individual has tended in the past towards experiences and inner self-analysis designed to puncture the bubble of personal superiority and narcissism. At some point we all believe that we are special simply by dint of the experiential fact of our own subjectivity. We dream our dreams, we view every event primarily from our own perspective and we see ourselves as the hero or heroine of our inner drama. This is not necessarily problematic, but the central emphasis on life as being primarily for or about *the self* is delusional (as the Pisces polarity will show us). The Virgo archetype exists to subvert this delusion in order to create a basis for relationship predicated upon equality.

The individual with this placement tends towards a high level of mental activity which is focused on exploring how the person views themself and how they might improve on past performance. Much of this improvement takes the form of being less self-centered and/or self-preoccupied. An obvious problem that arises here is that the inner process of analysis can itself become preoccupying, leading to a different kind of self-obsession (to the extent that prevalent ego dynamics have been insufficiently understood).

The person with this placement has a highly-developed sense of service to others so the issue of right and appropriate work may assume primary importance. Many with this placement will avoid work that does not feel useful on a collective level. Due to their desire to overturn what is perceived to have been a selfish orientation to life (noted because of the preceding sign, Leo – see Chapter 1), some of these people set up and endure humbling or even humiliating experiences in order to reverse the pecking order. The desire to be the master becomes the desire to be the servant in order to experience parity and restore balance, so that in the following archetype (Libra) others can be met truly as equals.

In many cases this leads to the shadow of not feeling good enough, a sense of lack about themselves, or an inner void that they find difficult to fill. This arises as the result of having ripped the heart out of their personal sense of self in order to clean it of its egocentric delusion.

The Natural Squares

The natural square from the 3rd house/Gemini symbolizes an issue with regard to all the data that the individual is amassing about themselves through past thoughts and actions. A central challenge here is discrimination. This person needs to ask, "What is the truly critical information I am gathering about myself and what is simply too much detail, or too narrow a focus that might disrupt me from achieving my goal of insight?"

Many with this placement have experienced hearing severely negative messages from others regarding their behavior and/or inner nature, taking the form of criticism and persecution. These experiences reflect the soul's growing desire for humility. The ego-centricity of the prior Leo archetype has been understood but the desire to compensate can become humiliating. The negative words that others speak enter the stream of the individual's inner dialogue, resulting in negative self-analysis that tends towards self-laceration. With some, this process can reach a hallucinatory intensity whereby the negativity they are exposed to is so intense that they lose all other sense of reference and internalize the persecutory view of their nature as if it were the unassailable truth. This can become the basis for a primarily masochistic relationship to self and world.

The natural square from the 9th house/Sagittarius relates to the issue of self-value and internal dialogue or messages. The desired intention of the Virgo archetype is to return to a greater truth about the self. But in regard to the assumed masochistic psychology (which is fuelled by internalized criticism) the person actually enters a distortion equally as great as the narcissistic one in the Leo archetype. They exaggerate (Sagittarius) how shameful and bad they are, an inverse of the Leonine over-investment in self-worth. However this belief is as narcissistic in an inverse direction as believing that one is great and special.

People caught in the Virgo trap can treat themselves worse than they would ever treat anyone else. In fact, even though they may hold the belief that God loves his children, these individuals, caught in the hypnotic power of introjected guilt and criticism, can believe that they are so "special" that they are the only one living being who does not deserve God's love. Western monotheism emphasizes a judgmental Creator. Through the Christian teaching of original sin we are judged from birth as fundamentally wanting. Within the collective unconscious and through prior-life experience people with a strong Virgo signature are acutely sensitive to this message.

North Node of the Moon in 12th house/Pisces

With the North Node in the 12th house/Pisces the evolutionary intention is to embrace forgiveness for the seemingly endless shortcomings of the self, allowing surrender to life and to one's flawed humanity. In realizing that creation itself is in a process of perpetual becoming, reality is in effect itself evolving. No static fixed perfection exists. No distant God is waiting to judge us for the mistakes of our ancestors, and no hell exists to punish us other than the one we create for ourselves. Instead the experience of Pisces teaches that we are all human, and we all make mistakes. The right use of Virgo discernment is that in working on our lives step-by-step we can move closer to our true potential. There is no rush. *A Course in Miracles* suggests that space and time only exist for us to realize the truth of who we really are.

The teaching from the Buddhist Heart Sutra "Samsara is Nirvana" expresses the essence of the Pisces polarity to Virgo. The Cosmos presents a perfect opportunity to grow. That the circumstances of our life are the perfect expression of our karma and the ideal opportunity for our evolution is symbolized beautifully within the natal chart. Even without an explicitly spiritual outlook this nodal placement indicates the healing perspective to be gained by the individual through recognizing that their search can have an ending, and that the on-going inner dialogue can reach a conclusion, which is transcendence and concomitant self-acceptance.

South Node in 12th house/Pisces

With the South Node of the Moon in the 12th house/Pisces the person has tended toward experiences of isolation and contemplation in order to surrender their existence to some kind of higher order of meaning and/or transcendent experience/belief. There is often a high degree of sensitivity as the person has learned to open themselves to more subtle influences within prior lives. This sensitivity can reach a problematic level whereby the person experiences a loss of self, or a sacrifice of their life or personal identity. Such states can be the consequence of experiences of slavery or of voluntary or involuntary seclusion or imprisonment.

The loss of self may take the form of susceptibility to escape through fantasy, inner dramas, delusions or even psychosis. The person's inner fantasy life intrudes on their capacity for orientation to "ordinary" reality. The past experiences of isolation may leave the person with hindered or extremely selective ways of relating to others. One's identification with religious symbolism or messages may be strong enough at times that it causes some to lose their personal identity, although this loss of self may actually be a comfort to many with this placement.

The Natural Squares

The natural square from the 3rd house/Gemini relates to problems the individual may have in communicating their experiences or in relating conceptually to the world around them. Non-ordinary states are hard to explain verbally because they are non-linear in nature whereas the nature of the mind and language is to classify and order reality in a primarily linear fashion. The poets are those who endeavor to intensify and stretch language through metaphor and musicality in order to present an experience of the subtle world. But not everyone is a poet and even the best poets struggle to find words in the face of the All. Many spiritual teachers remain silent, the better to emphasize the linear confines of language.

To the extent that the self has lost its worldly anchor, being subject to excessive fantasy, delusion or psychosis, then the problem of orientation to mundane reality becomes intensified. People who have been in prison for a long time often struggle when they are

returned to the outside world. There are examples of past prison in-
mates who, once free, commit petty crimes in order to be returned
to the familiar surroundings they feel more comfortable inhabiting.
For them, the outside world has become too difficult to adapt to.

Other people with this placement lose the ability to classify
their experience in any way that is comprehensible to them. What
some religious people might see as a "second birth" is for others a
birth into a world of strange voices, accompanied by the conviction
that their mind will never be a comfortable or friendly place again.
This is the impact of a breakdown of meaning. There may be strong
fears with this placement of madness, inner chaos and/or despair.

The natural square from the 9th house/Sagittarius suggests
that to the extent there has occurred a loss of self there will also
be a loss of meaning. The South Node in the 12th house/Pisces can
relate to religious or spiritual disillusionment that can leave the individual lost at sea, struggling with meaninglessness and despair.
Such disillusionments are among the most painful experiences that
a human being can endure, often resulting in a profound loss of
faith, the repercussions of which reverberate over many lifetimes.
If the individual has sacrificed themselves for causes that no longer seem relevant or meaningful they may experience grief and
feelings of having wasted what was most precious to them. This
feeling lingers and corrupts future possibilities, overwhelming the
potential for new directions with pessimism and hopelessness in
a vicious cycle. As new avenues are darkened by the projection of
past failures, the present loss of meaning endures simply through
lack of other options.

Conversely if prior experiences of surrender and transcendence have given meaning to this person, then the influence of the
9th house/Sagittarius can bring great comfort. But alongside this
comfort stands another kind of problem – that of over-identification
with the particular teaching in which meaning was found, leading
to an exaggeration of its importance. We can find here the tendency
towards wanting to convince or convert others to the same path
and the potential for a fundamentalist approach to belief. All this
stems from the conviction that the existential anxieties of the past
have been assuaged through a path that must be rigidly adhered to
for fear of falling back into despair.

North Node of the Moon in 6th house/Virgo

The North Node of the Moon in the 6th house/Virgo reveals an evolutionary intention towards service and meaningful work, either as expressions of the meaning found in the past or to counteract past experiences of the loss of self.

The Jungian analyst Marie Louise von Franz emphasized that work remedies the chronic immaturity of the "eternal youth" within us all, who takes great flights into spirit and imagination but tends like Icarus to fly too far too soon, thus falling into death. Meaningful work and the dedication to serve others is the counterpoint to spiritual development. Out of this realization the great vehicle of Mahayana Buddhism was born. The yogis and realized ones of this tradition perceived that seeking enlightenment purely for oneself was a trap. They created the Bodhisattva Vow as a dedication to remain in service until all sentient beings gained the enlightened condition – surely one of the purest and most beautiful ideals ever envisioned.

Furthermore the North Node in the 6th house/Virgo indicates the need for powerful and honest inner analysis as a way of avoiding the pitfalls of becoming lost in one's own fantasies or delusions. In this way one can apply step-by-step techniques to bring the person who has lost themselves back to a meaningful relationship with the world around them. For instance, one can employ on-going methods that support the past insights and sensitivity developed through the South Node, such as journaling, meditation/contemplation, healthy diet, exercise and self-remembering. All of this is the epitome of the higher expression of the Virgo archetype – to undertake an integrated effort to improve oneself as an expression of one's true potential.

The Paradox of Polarity in the Nodal Axis

This discussion of the Moon's nodal axis is intended only as a starting point in order to facilitate consideration of the issues and potentials involved. It is necessarily partial and brief. There may well be significant meanings of the nodes of the Moon in an individual chart for which these introductory guidelines are *far from adequate*. They are given here to ignite contemplation and learning through the experience of looking at charts to see how the *Evolutionary Axis* might work within a person's life. Nothing should be relied on more than the synchronizing of people's natal charts with their lived experiences. The reality of an individual's life must take precedence over any abstract thesis gleaned from the chart.

That said, students of mine have expressed a need for an explanation of the analytical method to facilitate their learning. As they begin to grasp the components of an archetype in order to apply them to the nodes of the Moon, they often struggle when having to blend such seemingly polarized archetypes. So for example, when I present a chart with the South Node of the Moon in the 1st house in Libra, I often hear cries of frustration from students who have just begun to integrate and understand the independence (Aries) – relationship (Libra) axis only to now have to somehow blend these two archetypes together.

So how do we understand the chart when the polarities are expressed in this fashion: **South Node of the Moon in the 1st house, but in Libra** (the 7th house)? The psychoanalyst D.W. Winnicot (renowned for his work with children, author of *Playing and Reality*) claimed that the signature of maturity is the capacity to handle paradox.[5] When we are first learning something new, by definition our understanding of the subject is somewhat immature and it is easier to think in terms of black and white rather than all the shades in between. But life and the evolutionary journey of the soul tends to present a more colorful picture.

When we find that the nodal axis is polarized in this way we notice a paradox in the issue of independence versus relationship. The *specific way* that this paradox has played out will be found in the Pluto placement, through the nodal rulers and aspects made to all of the above. Yet in holding on to the idea that paradox has formed a critical part of the past development, we can already gain insight into how to blend two seemingly opposed qualities.

So how might this specific paradox play out? We could start by saying that the person has initiated (1st house) many relationships (Libra) in prior lives but has tended to maintain an independence (1st house) from the partner or significant others (Libra). Another dynamic we might observe is that the individual may have initiated relationships (Libra) that in some key way were always destined to end, therefore preserving once again the cherished independence (1st house). This could take a variety of forms, e.g. fundamental incompatibility or problematic behavior that serves to put a time limit on the connection.

Another example could see relationships (Libra) that are conducted like a war, full of aggression and conflict (1st house). Or one in which the independence of the past (1st house) saw an on-going yet frustrated desire to initiate relationship (Libra). Conversely, prior lives in committed relationship (Libra) may have included profound resentment and desire for freedom (1st House).

In this way you can see that one aspect of the archetype represents an *external condition* and another aspect of it relates to the *internal desires or aspirations*. This paradox could refer to a situation in which the individual has manifested a diversity of relationships (South Node in Libra) purely on the basis of sexual instinct (South Node in the 1st house) only to leave those partners when the desires are satiated.

The diversity of human experience dictates that there exist many more possibilities than the above examples and we must take into account the other critical placements in the birth chart, which expand our understanding of the issues even further. These examples are intended simply to give you a feel for the potential of blending the archetypes.

Further paradoxes may manifest if the ruler of the South Node of the Moon is in the sign opposite to the South Node.

Technicalities

Skipped Steps

A fundamental issue arises with the nodes of the Moon when planets square that axis. This kind of planetary placement represents a core issue that has been thus far unresolved, a "skipped step" in the process of moving from the patterns described by the South Node of the Moon towards the evolutionary intentions symbolized by the North Node of the Moon. The planet in square represents issues that have interrupted the progression of development. It's likely that the person has taken a step towards the North Node intention and then fallen back into old South Node patterns. Due to the importance of the planets squaring the nodal axis, we'll take a look at these skipped steps next and follow with the rulers of the nodes, and finally, planets conjunct the nodal axis.

The Orbs

We can use a relatively wide orb when considering any aspect to the *Evolutionary Axis*. I consider a strong aspect to be within 12 degrees and I encourage you to start to think of an aspect as potentially operative up to 15 degrees of orb with the idea that the wider orb encompasses the broadest brush strokes of the evolution of the soul. Test the wider orbs with your charts and clients and see what you find.

Skipped steps represent issues that are obstacles to the evolution of the individual. They might either remain completely unresolved or they may seem to have been resolved but really aren't, proving to be much more complex or troubling.

Which Node Comes First?

Give yourself a moment to digest this next image. I find that when I'm teaching the following concept, a visual aid works best. Use the diagram and chart below for reference.

The node that has most recently transited the planet squaring the node is the one through which the issues *represented by the squaring planet* need to be resolved. Due to the retrograde motion of the

Moon's nodes this can seem complex to calculate. For a simple visual aid, imagine yourself standing on the planet that is square the
nodes. Now look into the center of the birth chart. Which node is on
your left? That is the node that represents the point of integration.

Try it with the following chart example (fig. 3), which has the
moon square the nodes. Looking at the chart below, imagine yourself standing on *the Moon* and look towards the center of the
wheel. Now look to your left. Which node is **to the left** of the Moon?

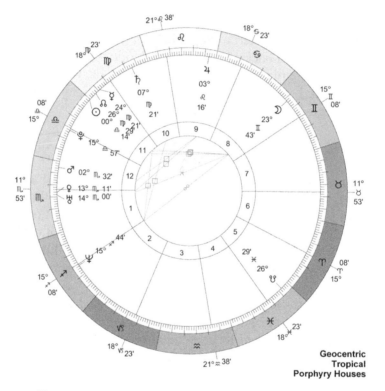

Figure 3. *Which node is the resolution point for the moon?*

If you guessed the *South* Node, you're correct! The moon
here is square the nodes and resolves via the South Node.

How the Skipped Step Integrates

> **North Node:** If the skipped step integrates through the **North Node of the Moon** then the intention is to develop the evolutionary potential of the North Node of the Moon while taking responsibility for the unresolved material signified by the skipped step.

> **South Node:** If the skipped step integrates through the **South Node of the Moon** then the intention is to go back into the past in order to rediscover the cause of the problem or a lost aspect of the issue. Going back into the past then becomes a way of moving forward and ultimately accessing the evolutionary potential of the North Node of the Moon.

Skipped steps will often imply unresolved issues that were partly developed in the past but remain incomplete or not fully realized. Even the North Node may have been partly developed in the past, but in a manner that remains problematic or unresolved. Thus *both nodes of the Moon and their rulers* need to be taken into account when analyzing the prior-life dynamics.

Skipped steps often represent challenging issues or unresolved psychological material and can be very difficult for people to come to terms with. Due to the planetary function of the Moon being representative of the conditioned self – the emotional body and core emotional complexes of the personality – the Moon's nodal axis reveals vital information pertaining to the evolution of the self.

Squares to the Planetary Nodes

Our analysis of skipped steps applies only to the nodal axis of the Moon. That being said, squares to the nodal axis of the *other planets* also suggest the potential for unresolved material. This remains an infrequently-explored area of astrological literature and practice. Since the other planetary nodes are not a part of the *Evolutionary Axis* we do not apply the same wide orbs. Possible interpretations of the other planetary nodes will be explored in a future book.

The Meaning of Planets
Square the Moon's Nodes

The Sun

The Sun as a skipped step indicates that a central part of the current life energy and purpose (the Sun) is to resolve the issues symbolized by the square to the nodal axis, through house and sign and through the node it resolves through. This placement indicates the current life as the critical one for the resolution of the unresolved material. This material is experienced in this life as part of the core nature of the individuality and sense of personal meaning. This placement has echoes of the symbolism of the hero's journey (Joseph Campbell The Hero With a Thousand Faces) and can involve the individual having to create or maintain a personal vision in isolation or in conflict with others around them in their life. As such it represents a challenge to individuate.

The Moon

When the Moon (or a planet in the 4th house or in Cancer) squares the Moon's nodes we can anticipate unresolved issues with the family of origin, with the formation of the personality and with the emotional body. There may be specific unresolved material involving the mother or primary caregiver. There will be an inherent insecurity in the personality via a tendency to project the experience of security or happiness outside the self onto the family, or significant others.

This placement may indicate unresolved gender issues. There may be dissatisfaction with gender roles, with issues stemming from the patriarchal bias of our culture and the resulting suppression of the feminine. Or there may be a recent gender switch between this incarnation and the previous one, resulting in a strong identification with the opposite gender.

Mercury

When Mercury (or when a planet in the 3rd house/Gemini or the 6th house/Virgo) squares the Moon's nodes we are alerted to the possibility of unresolved issues in the *mental life* of the individual. This can include overly rigid thinking or excessively restless curiosity that lacks discrimination as to the kind of material the mind is taking on board.

This placement may represent an issue with internalized messages or introjects of a critical nature that undermine the strength of the personality. Such internalized guilt, emphasized in the 6th house/Virgo archetype, can become the basis for internal shame and/or a masochistic tendency.

This placement may indicate a range of communication issues – for example an issue with trusting the opinions of others. Lies or conflicting views as to the nature of the truth may have had profound consequences in prior lives.

Venus

When Venus (or a planet in the 2nd house/Taurus or the 7th house/Libra) squares the Moon's nodes we are looking at unresolved material pertaining to how a person relates to themselves and therefore the way they relate to others. The range of possibilities can extend from extremes of isolation to excessive social activity that leads to a loss of identity through exhaustion.

This placement can indicate an issue with *projected* meaning, or not seeing the true reality of others due to our transference onto them. We might transfer unresolved issues onto our partners and friends, co-opting them to play roles in our own inner drama.

This placement can also refer to a life-threatening situation whereby the self has become highly anxious, causing great difficulty in relating to its own needs. It can indicate a situation whereby the person needs to learn to be alone, to love and accept themself before being able to meet others on an equal footing.

Mars

When Mars (or a planet in the 1st house including the Ascendant or Aries) squares the Moon's nodes the nature of the unresolved material pertains to the nature of desire and the instinctual will. The range of possibilities here includes unresolved anger, unresolved sexual feelings and physical or sexual violence. Anger with or from others could be threatening to stability just as hidden anger could also be at play, its passive toxicity being part of the problem.

This placement can signify situations whereby the will has become co-opted in some fashion and the person is overly compliant or "lost." We could also see a situation in which excessive dominance has distorted the soul's original intention.

This placement can indicate an unmet need for independence which can then be a source of suppressed anger. But the unmet need can also express as a source of paradox in relationship, whereby the freedom to grow with another is desired but a subconscious fear of entrapment prevents this need being fulfilled meaningfully.

Jupiter

When Jupiter (or a planet in the 9th house or in Sagittarius) squares the Moon's nodes the nature of the unresolved material relates to the person's beliefs, the teachers or teachings that they have followed (from homespun philosophies to the great spiritual traditions) and their relationship to faith.

This skipped step can indicate an issue with honesty, either through a conflict of how the "truth" has been perceived, or through an inner lie – the nature of the inner lie often stemming from internal exaggeration at the expense of the true picture of the nature of the self. This untruth can become the basis for a crisis of self or, if exposed publicly, can also change the level of trust someone has placed on you, thereby *changing the belief system* they have about you.

This placement can signify a crisis of faith or a conflict within the self about an understanding of the truth, or an issue with a teaching they have followed. This crisis of faith becomes a fundamental doubt in the capacity of the person to understand their place in the greater scheme of things. This can therefore indicate an issue with alienation.

Saturn

When Saturn (or a planet in the 10th house or Capricorn) squares the Moon's nodes the nature of the unresolved material relates to the conditioning that the individual has been exposed to, either through the family, society, religion or by any broader historical societal theme. Such conditioning then becomes the basis for repression.

The Saturn skipped step can indicate a need for maturation, for taking responsibility for one's own life at a core level without succumbing to the delusory temptations of blame, excessive fear or self-control.

This placement can indicate an issue of genuine guilt, an authentic sense of having done something wrong (the nature of which will be indicated by the house/sign/aspects of the planet squaring the nodes and the nodal axis of the Moon). In contrast to the introjected guilt found in the Mercury/Virgo/6th house archetype, which is internalized from others blaming or criticizing, the Saturn archetype involves the self recognizing past mistakes and making direct reparation for those mistakes.

This placement emphasizes the importance of the Saturn Return.

Uranus

When Uranus (or a planet in the 11th house or Aquarius) squares the Moon's nodes the unresolved material indicates a need for liberation from conditioning, and liberation from the past. This stems in part from past wounding and from exposure to excessive conditioning influences.

With this placement, the nodal axis of the Moon can be understood as a trauma signature (see chapter 3) indicating that the unresolved trauma is a critical part of the skipped step. An analysis of the house and sign, aspects to the skipped step planet, and aspects to the nodal axis of the Moon will help identify the nature of this unresolved trauma.

This placement also symbolizes a crisis in individuation. The person has started to detach themselves from prior conditioning but they have either not been able to maintain this process, or they remain blind to a critical aspect of how the conditioning imprisons them, which then results in a block to the true expression of their individuality.

This placement can indicate a specific fear or post-traumatic stress that blocks access to the true self. It can also mark the need to reintegrate some former illumination that has been lost or resisted. There is a powerful requirement to embrace the transformational nature of the self. Regression work or depth therapy can aid in recovering deeper unconscious material – both traumas and gifts.

This placement emphasizes the importance of the Uranus opposition.

Pluto

When Pluto (or a planet in the 8th house or Scorpio) squares the Moon's nodes the unresolved material relates to the deepest unconscious self – its motivations, compulsions, resistances and its urge for transformation. In some ways this is the ultimate skipped step. Pluto square the nodal axis can be likened to a fork in the road, a battle between the adaptive self and the higher self, between ego and soul.

This placement represents a fundamental encounter with deeper unconscious forces, either to evoke radical transformation, to become trapped in psychological attachments and compulsions or some combination of both. A critical divide in the deeper self needs exploration and resolution yet this placement indicates the potential (as all skipped steps do in some way) for tremendous resistance to the evolutionary goal.

This placement suggests that a struggle between power and powerlessness has been playing out over lifetimes. There exists a need to identify limitations in order to transform them as well as a need to form powerful relationships with other people, objects or teachings that are symbolic of the intended transformation in the self. In this way the self may learn by example via osmosis, absorbing the energy of otherness.

This skipped step may indicate a variety of power dynamics ranging from pronounced psychological disturbance to issues regarding the appropriate use of power and an enquiry into its source and origin. There may be issues of personal betrayal on every level – betrayal of self and others, and being betrayed by others. Or there may exist a need to confront limitations, both of self and others.

This skipped step demonstrates a critical juncture in the evolution of the soul involving a profound choice as to what to commit to in order to effect transformation. Furthermore it implies the necessary commitment has been intermittent or lacking in the past, emphasizing a need to honor the commitments made now in order to resolve this prior inconsistency.

Neptune

When Neptune (or a planet in the 12th house or Pisces) is square the Moon's nodes the unresolved material pertains to the subtle issues of one's sense of ultimate meaning, one's dreams and ideals. The skipped step can therefore revolve around the loss of meaning, profound disillusionment or despair that leads to loss of life force and will. In some cases the negative ramifications are so extreme as to lead to catatonic disassociation.

The Neptune skipped step may also represent an unresolved dream or ideal that the person has suppressed or been unable as yet to fulfill, that now demands exploration. Analysis of the *Evolutionary Axis* (especially the nodal axis of the Moon, the aspects that Neptune is making and the house ruled by Neptune) will illustrate the nature of these unfulfilled dreams and aspirations. Exploration of such themes can involve distinguishing whether or not such dreams need to be physically realized or can exist solely as fantasies fulfilled in the imagination.

The necessary discrimination required here is difficult to attain because this skipped step involves a struggle to clarify the difference between personal fantasy and objective reality. This placement can lead to spiritual crisis and transformation.

Just as easily this placement points to someone who has lost their spiritual way, who now wanders meaninglessly in cycles of despair, and perhaps is compensating for the loss with drug addiction or other similarly self-abnegating behaviors.

In rare cases this skipped step could indicate someone who has been exposed to a psychic attack of some kind, someone who has been possessed by unconscious or astral forces. But because of the possibility for distortion via fantasy and delusion reflected by this placement, this can be an especially problematic case to work with.

Fine Tuning the Details

Planets conjunct the Nodes of the Moon

Planets conjunct the nodes of the Moon reveal the ways in which the archetype represented by the planetary body has played a significant role within the prior-life development of the individual.

Pluto Conjunct the Nodes

When Pluto conjuncts the nodes of the Moon (with an orb of up to 15 degrees) a powerful karmic signature exists as the unconscious desires and focus of the deeper self are channeled directly through the prior-life personality experiences. This special circumstance within the *Evolutionary Axis* is central to an understanding of the natal chart, providing a useful representative of *all planetary functions* as they apply via conjunction to the lunar nodal axis.

Pluto conjunct the South Node of the Moon indicates a pronounced signature of *reliving the karmic past*. There exists the potential for some prior-life gifts or abilities to be channeled into the present life or for prior-life struggles, resistance or blockage to be recreated now. In extreme cases this signifies that the individual experienced either the fruition of a prior life capacity or a profound block or frustration. An example might be a person whose skill as a doctor is called for on a collective level. Individually they may wish to move on to a different form of self-expression but they are called by life to manifest their skill for others. Some people I have counseled with this placement feel a sense of restriction no matter what they do. This is then very difficult to handle though the causes can be explored through the chart, producing helpful insight for the individual to contextualize their experience.

However this more direct form of manifesting either as a gift or as a restriction brought forward from the karmic past is a rare occurrence. More often there is a combination of factors from prior lives playing out in the current life, a mixture of past abilities and knowledge alongside some critical blockage or restriction.

Whether the predominant form that manifests in this life is positive or negative, the essential quality remains: the repetition of past circumstances which in and of itself is likely to feel restrictive. *This is the most powerful signature of karmic repetition that can be found in the natal chart.*

Importance of the First Saturn Return

In those natal charts in which Pluto **does not** conjunct the South Node of the Moon, the first Saturn return (around age 28-30) represents the crucial point of rebirth from the karmic dictates of the past. Life experience up to one's late twenties tends to be driven by the volition of prior karma playing out through the circumstances of family, education and early incursions into the world. I am not making a case here for some predestined or prescribed reality, but rather pointing to the practical application of understanding reincarnation and the momentum of karma. So, on a personality level we do not consciously choose our family of origin, our formative school experiences or much of our early life context.

The Saturn return symbolizes the development of maturity. Young people often feel they mature at eighteen or twenty-one years of age. But experience shows that most people don't actually settle into a more fully-realized sense of their identity until their late twenties.

Pluto and the Second Saturn Return

In the case of Pluto conjunct the South Node of the Moon, the volitional power of the prior karma is such that the **second Saturn return** (around age 56-60) becomes the *key moment of rebirth* more so than the first.

However, there are mitigating factors to consider. Planets conjunct the North Node of the Moon indicate that previously-developed capacities can be harnessed to offset this trend. Whereas transits of Saturn, Uranus and Neptune, or powerful progressions to the North Node of the Moon that occur *prior to the second Saturn* return can reveal the potential to break free from the karmic grip of Pluto.

For example, one of my clients has Pluto conjunct the South Node in Virgo in 8th house. A 40-year-old virgin, he was a very stuck individual, vigorous in mind yet paralyzed materially. After two failed attempts at a PhD and eight years of trying he simply stopped doing anything. But when Uranus in Pisces made a conjunction to his North Node he became involved sexually with a woman. Shortly after that he had a brief period of depression after which he actually got a job. Although he feels just as stuck as before, the transit to his North Node did precipitate a kind of step up from him being totally alone and sitting in his apartment all day long doing absolutely nothing.

When I first began studying Evolutionary Astrology I had difficulty accepting this concept. It seems to imply restrictions on an individual's potential. When I started teaching, during my own Saturn return, I feared encountering a chart with this signature, unsure how I should counsel a younger person who was in this karmic situation and still many years away from their second Saturn return. When this eventually happened, I chose to share the teaching in an honest way, with the caveat that I had yet to see if it correlated to people's lived experience. And to my surprise I found that this was very useful information for the individual whose chart I was reading.

I have since read for many clients with Pluto conjunct the South Node of the Moon and this approach has resonated deeply with all of them to date. But as with all the methods and approaches delineated in this book, I encourage you to *test your accuracy* against the experiential reality of those whose natal charts are being explored. Some questions you can ask clients in this situation include:

- Do you feel as if some powerful past influence is now present in your life?
- Do you feel you bring gifts or abilities with you that you're compelled to share, or do you feel blocked in expressing these gifts?
- Do you feel restricted in some critical way, the causes of which seem to resist understanding?

In my practice, these questions have proven to be both a respectful invitation (my preferred approach) and a powerful gateway into deep aspects of the individual's relationship to their own experience.

Other Planets Conjunct the South Node

With any planet conjunct the South Node of the Moon, issues pertaining to that planetary function have been important in the past experience of the individual. A planet conjunct the South Node adds another layer of meaning to the archetypes at play, and can often contradict or create a paradox in meaning.

For instance, if Mars is conjunct the South Node, but the South Node is in the 4th house/Cancer, the 1st house/Aries archetype is added to the mix. This person will not only manifest 4th house/Cancer archetype, but also the 1st house/Aries archetype.

Furthermore any planet in this placement has the potential to manifest as an ability or awareness that has been developed in the past, just as well as it might represent a restriction of the kind symbolized by its nature. More often than not the planetary function will represent something that is partly realized but also partly unresolved and restrictive.

The planet conjunct the South Node will always represent something directly experienced in the past being brought forward into the life of the individual in the present. As this experience comes in from the past, the early childhood will often be a primary mode of expression of the issues that are symbolized by this planet.

Pluto Conjunct the North Node

Pluto conjunct the North Node of the Moon indicates that in a recent prior life the individual began to commit to the evolutionary intention symbolized by the North Node of the Moon. The intention is then to continue to develop through the evolutionary gateway of the North Node. This is the **only time** in analyzing the *Evolutionary Axis* that the polarity point of Pluto is ignored. This is because the North Node of the Moon has become the polarity point of Pluto as its development has propelled the individual forward in their evolution and the crux of the chart is to continue this journey.

This does not mean that with planets squaring the nodal axis, skipped steps, or planets conjunct the South Node of the Moon that other parts of the chart do not reflect the need to re-enter the past in order to heal, but it does point toward the resolution of the chart lying in on-going development of all that is symbolized by the North Node of the Moon and its ruler.

Other Planets Conjunct the North Node

When any planet conjuncts the North Node of the Moon it represents a quality that has been developed in recent prior lives which is useful in furthering the evolutionary intention. However we still acknowledge the polarity point of Pluto. This can be understood through the following example.

A student of mine has Saturn in Aries conjunct the North Node in the 10th house. She has a natural maturity and capacity for responsibility, and the courage to express herself in the world. She was able to set up a vibrant healing and body work practice even though her family was critical and judgmental and her husband was dismissive of her efforts. Today her work has helped hundreds of people. The family dysfunction hurt her deeply and eventually her marriage ended. And yet she was still able to manifest this tremendous expression of her physical and psychic gifts.

Saturn conjunct the North Node in her chart represents a decision in her will, taken in a recent prior life and remade in this life, with the resulting courage (Aries) to take responsibility for the difficult relationships that had gone on in her family. This led to the capacity to express her potential in the world even as her personal relationships were unrewarding or even painful. Nothing could stop her from expressing this gift.

The Rulers of the Nodes Conjunct the Nodes

When one of the node's rulers is also conjunct one of the nodes, we see the need to relive prior-life experience in the current life.

Ruler of the North Node Conjunct the South Node

If the ruler of the North Node of the Moon is conjunct the South Node of the Moon we see that the very quality that facilitates the evolutionary intentions (ruler of the North Node) is being brought in through the karmic past (conjunct the South Node) and as such indicates the capacity to bring in past gifts, or blocks to growth. The essence of this signature, whether helpful or restrictive, is the necessity to repeat the past because the prior karmic energy around the issues symbolized by the planet conjunct the South Node is so strong.

Ruler of the South Node Conjunct the North Node

With the ruler of the South Node of the Moon conjunct the North Node the necessity to repeat prior karma occurs early in life (South Node ruler) in order to kick-start the evolutionary intentions for the future development (conjunct the North Node of the Moon). This is a signature that expresses a need to relive explicit events or themes symbolized by the planet ruling the South Node of the Moon so that in reliving them the individual is propelled into the expression of the North Node intention. It is as if a karmic theatre replays a certain theme that the individual had already (in prior lives) begun to learn from but in being replayed the need to move forward is clarified once again.

Respect the Client's Experience

I encourage all who find the techniques described in this book interesting or potentially useful to adopt an invitational approach to reading charts as it establishes a primary respect for the client's life experience. It's easy for us to get caught up in trying to prove astrology works, or to prove our professional competence. However, our most profound work occurs when we can set those motivations aside and instead start with the client's experience, building our understanding of the chart from there.

Some prominent astrologers prefer to dazzle the client by explaining everything they see in the chart before the client even says a word. I don't see the use in this approach. My first question when reading a chart or even conducting an individual tutorial is, "How might I help today?" Or even, "How might we best meet your needs together?" This collaborative approach is one that I believe best acknowledges the person as the most authoritative source of information. The chart then, being a secondary tool, a map to the potentials that this individual might access, must itself be translated according to *their specific needs and concerns.*

This is why there is not one right answer across the board as to the meaning of a planet in a certain house and sign, only a series of possibilities.

Case Study: Kay

I present the following case study to share a real-life analysis of the Pluto placement and the nodes of the Moon as a way to establish a foundation for understanding an individual's prior experience and the evolutionary intentions that stem from their karmic past.

I am grateful to all the clients with whom I have worked and all of those people who have given me permission to refer to their charts and their personal journeys in my writing and teaching work. I have been fortunate in experiencing many thousands of hours of work with clients and students and so have access to a plethora of case study material. However, for the purposes of this book I have opted to include only a small number of case studies explored in relative depth which can then serve as a touchstone to refer back to.

In this way it's my intention that it be easier for the reader to focus on the method and its implications more fully. One disadvantage of this approach is in the lack of empirical data, however this is remedied in the classes and workshops I teach. Additional charts may become the focus of later writing.

I have named this example chart Kay as an echo of the symbol for Chiron (the wounded healer) and to allude to the hero of Kafka's *The Trial* for reasons that should become apparent as the case study unfolds.

Kay's Birth Information (see chart, fig. 4)
March 19, 1964, 4:55 am GMT. Whiston, England (2W50, 53N25)

With Pluto in the 7th house, Kay has desired to initiate a diversity of relationships in order to learn about herself through comparison. There has been an on-going attachment to the meaning that other people have to her and a potential compulsiveness in creating patterns of relating.

With Pluto in the 7th house the desire has been to learn balance in relationships. To the extent that this need for balance has not yet been achieved, Kay may have manifested cycles of excessive dependency upon others. Or she may have experienced social exhaustion alternating with periods of loneliness or social exclusion as a counterpoint to the value she placed on others or their demands upon her time and resources.

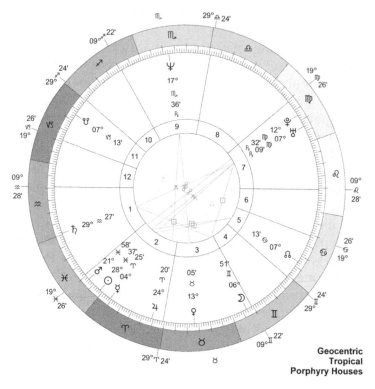

Figure 4. *Kay's Natal Chart*. March 19, 1964, 4:55 am GMT.
Whiston, England (2W50, 53N25)

Additionally, with Pluto in the 7th house there has been an on-
going need to learn how to really understand other people's experience in order to mitigate a tendency for the projection of meaning
onto others. Her projections could take the form of:

- Unrealistic expectations of others
- Others distorting her perception of their feelings
- Patterns of manipulation as she herself, or others with
  whom she is involved, overtly (or covertly) attempt to control the other person

With Pluto in the 7th house, Kay's relationships have become
the battleground for the struggle with the self, and the patterns of

relating that she manifests are indicative of the nature of the feelings she has about herself.

One danger for a 7th house Pluto person is that other people become overwhelming to the personal experience of self. This is the case whether the experience is an actual reality or a projected one. The individual can become lost in the various points of view that other people hold about them. If this individual has powerful unresolved feelings about themselves, this process can become easily disengaged from the true experience others have of the situation. Important questions for this kind of individual are:

- How do other people really experience me?
- What is real and what is not real about what I think they're experiencing?
- What do they really think of me?
- Do they really care about me?

There is enormous room here for distortion of meaning in relationships. Kay's patterns of behavior are based on what she thinks other people think of her, usually without validating her assumptions with the other person. Due to the power of these projected assumptions and the subsequent reactions from partners to the 7th house Pluto person's projections, there is considerable potential for delusion and disappointment when the illusory perceptions are shattered. This pattern is the basis for all sorts of problematic endings to relationships in prior lives and also in this life.

Abrupt and painful endings to relationships are commonplace in this placement, as relationships are entered with unacknowledged, unmet needs and expectations, which then either remain met or are proven delusory, leading to the painful break. This creates the need for the soul to encounter people in the current life with whom the individual has powerful unresolved feelings left over from the past.

For Kay, an unconscious imbalance in current-life relationships exists right from their inception as compelling patterns (Pluto) are already in place.

As there are powerful dependency needs underlying the 7th house Pluto person's experience, there may have been past situations in which Kay has manifested either a dominant (if the partner is dependent) or submissive (if the individual is dependent) role predominantly within relationships. Such roles become a foundation for manipulating other people, or can indicate a proneness to being manipulated by others.

Pluto in Virgo

Notice that in the house placement of Pluto alone we can gain insight into a range of potentials representing the depth concerns and issues of the individual. Now we can start to blend the archetype of the house placement with the sign of Pluto, which in Kay's case, is Virgo.

With Pluto in the 7th house/Libra, Kay is looking to meet other people on an equal basis. Virgo is a transitional archetype in which the pyramid structure of reality – with the self in ascendancy in Leo – is reversed so that the self might be humbled to undertake a process of self-analysis and self-improvement. This being so, the desire to meet others (Libra) occurs without the excessive egocentricity of Leo. With Pluto in Virgo, Kay has been learning to analyze herself with an eye on the nature of her personal motivations and egocentric aspirations or delusions. Pluto in Virgo exhibits the potential for crisis relative to the extent that one's personal reality and creative aspirations (Leo) are overly identified with.

The Pluto in Virgo generation are born to experience a crisis of the personal will and the manner in which their sense of the self (Leo) is internalized and adapted to meaningful work within larger societal structures. This crisis has a mental aspect (Virgo is ruled by Mercury) and results in an inner dialogue regarding the nature of personal experience.

With Mercury ruling two signs we see in the first sign, Gemini, its outgoing or yang nature as the self seeks out information about the world. In Virgo, the second sign ruled by Mercury, the mental function is in its introverted or yin quality representing an internalization of the mental life.

The positive/yang or negative/yin quality of the signs fluctuates back and forth in order as we move through the Zodiac: Aries yang/Taurus yin, Gemini yang/Cancer yin, Leo yang/Virgo yin and so on.

With the Libra archetype, Venus is in its yang or outgoing form, initiating relationship (as opposed to its internal form in Taurus in which the relationship with one's self predominates). The internal or yin aspect of Mercury in Virgo represents an inner dialogue within the self in order both to explore the identity crisis and to form a foundation for a realistic sense of one's relative value within the collective.

Kay has Pluto in the 7th house so she has the desire to meet others on an equal footing. But that Pluto is in Virgo suggests a potential crisis of lack or disparity between self and other. The crisis inherent is that the individual has not yet attained this insight or parity, the result being that Kay was born experiencing an identity-crisis themed around learning to relate to others on an equal basis. As this crisis originates from the *humbling of the self* within the Virgo archetype, it is likely that in her tendency to struggle for equality in relationships, Kay has manifested an inferiority complex or chronic undervaluing of herself in her dealings with others. This undervaluing becomes the basis for distortion within the context of projected meaning, whereby Kay might tend towards hearing what others say about her in an overly negative light, or seeing critical behavior directed at her from others.

In this way the projected needs and expectations of the 7th house Pluto person are co-opted by a negative or self-critical stance in a way that forms evidence against the self in the internal dialogue.

Enter Uranus

The natural capacity for self-criticism and the psychology of self-defeatism is generally implicit within the Pluto in Virgo archetype. However another planet complicates this part of our analysis: Uranus, which is in a close conjunction with Pluto in Virgo in the 7th house. In the next chapter I explain the relationship of stressful aspects from Uranus, Aquarius and planets in the 11th house in depth, but here we note simply that Uranus conjunct Pluto indicates a trauma signature. And as such, lends weight to the growing body of evidence that Kay has tended towards self-critical or self-defeating patterns of relating in past lives which will likely continue in her current life if these patterns remain unconscious.

The alignment of Uranus with Pluto gives credence to the more difficult aspects of the Pluto in Virgo crisis in Kay's journey.[6]

Synthesizing Pluto, Uranus, Virgo and the 7th House

Some of the more difficult aspects of the Pluto in Virgo crisis, which here is heightened by Kay's Uranus-Pluto conjunction, are experienced through a self-dialogue in which the individual seeks a more honest understanding of themselves but instead becomes lost in defeatism on encountering any negative self-assessment.

Furthermore this crisis can involve persecutory messages from others which confirm the feeling of inferiority. The individual with Pluto in Virgo intends to take on more honest feedback from others in order to improve and grow; however when their attempt to improve flounders in self-criticism and despair the feedback can assume a persecutory intensity. It can seem as though others have discovered one's shameful secret, that one is fundamentally empty, a fraud.

With Pluto in Virgo in the 7th house Kay has the pronounced tendency to elevate others' points of view above and beyond her own. The traumatic aspects of the crisis manifest in her having introjected harsh criticisms and persecutory messages. These messages infiltrate her self-dialogue and contaminate it, running over and over again like a tape loop. This exacerbates her existing tendency to feel bad about herself, laying the foundations for a masochistic internal psychology.

The Virgo archetype in crisis has introjected toxic messages regarding the meaning and value of the self. Virgo correlates to an injected guilt received via external agencies and third parties in general, particularly via cultural or religious teachings that emphasize the sinful or imperfect nature of the self. The Pluto in Virgo individual is acutely sensitive to these messages due to their desire to self-improve and accept outside advice and instruction to that end. So their natural evolutionary intentions leave them prone to this negative pitfall.

As we've said, the feeling of guilt that arise here stem from extraneous messages that become internalized. This kind of introjected guilt (guilt through osmosis from an outside source that overpowers positive self dialogue) can be contrasted with the guilt of the Capricorn archetype in which genuine guilt or remorse for past behavior becomes a stepping stone in the process of maturation.

In Capricorn one takes responsibility for the mistakes one has made and the wrongs or injustices one has perpetrated as the basis for genuine maturation. When fear or shame dominates an individual with a harsh Saturn placement, they may repress or deny authentic guilt. But in principle, the Saturn archetype holds the promise that by owning our misdeeds we grow in maturity and wisdom. By comparison, the problem with the introjected guilt inherent in the Virgo crisis is that there is often no clear wrongdoing, no act from which to base reparation. The terrible irony is that the innocent person internalizes guilt which they struggle to expiate and the guilt is all the more tricky to process for having no clearly defined origin. As such it can permeate the consciousness leading to an unconscious desire to be punished or mistreated in order to make atonement.

In extremis novel *The Trial*, the anti-hero Joseph K. is arrested for a crime which is never specified. And no matter how far he delves into the labyrinthine halls of power he is never able to discover of what he stands accused.

In fact this kind of injected guilt is caused by the residue of narcissism leftover from the Leo stage of development that the Pluto in Virgo individual struggles to balance. In its own way a masochistic or self-defeating psychology is as egocentric as a self-aggrandizing psychology, merely inverted. To internalize guilt we must have a self that is unequal, one that is lacking or *less than* – a subtler variation on narcissistic self-importance. Both are delusions which essentially refute the archetypally Libran concept of equality.

The problem with the unequal self in this context is that to the extent that Kay has developed an internal foundation of guilt that has no specific cause (and therefore no easy way to assuage it) then she will manifest all sorts of "proof" to herself that she is deserving of punishment. Here we see the potential for Kay to have manifested a primarily masochistic way of interrelating which then becomes an attractor field to a harmful type of damaged individual: the sadistic type.

Both the masochistic personality type and the sadistic type share a feeling of victimization and disempowerment (a fundamental inequality with others). But alongside the sense of victimization in the sadistic type runs an anger about their situation that impels them to hurt other people as an expression of their own pain. When discussing this sadomasochistic pathology in relationships we are not discussing the sexual practices of those interested in bondage or BDSM, nor necessarily the sociopathic criminal element in modern life, but rather a complex of psychological and emotional patterns that can influence people on a core relational level.

Coming back to Kay's Pluto-Uranus conjunction in Virgo in the 7th house, we see that Kay has the potential to have manifested an on-going pattern in relationships that could relate to a sadomasochistic pathology, with its foundation in a distorted negative self-image, fuelled by internalized persecutory messages from others. This pattern can leave Kay prone to attracting others into her life who confirm her own negative self feelings. These people, because of their own loss of personal power and anger, may seek to manipulate and abuse her. Kay might then justify their behavior to the extent that she has internalized a pervasive sense of guilt. This guilt can manifest as an unconscious need for punishment as atonement.

Kay's South Node

In our analysis of Kay's Pluto placement thus far, I hope to have illustrated just how much information can be gained simply by focusing first on Pluto. Now as we move our attention to the South Node of the Moon, our emphasis shifts to the prior-life ego identities that have endeavored to express the Plutonic purpose. We can also relate what we find to the early life experience and the extent to which Kay's prior-life identities are now conditioning the formation of the ego in this life.

The South Node of the Moon in Kay's chart is in **Capricorn** and as such relates to her prior-life experiences of judgment and responsibility. As we explore the themes of Kay's prior lives through the South Node of the Moon we need to relate them back to the Pluto placement since Pluto represents the purpose or deep underlying intentions (unconscious) that formed the basis for those specific conscious issues and memories.

So as Kay struggled with issues of judgment (Capricorn) in prior lives we can relate that back to her own underlying insecurity and crisis in relationships with others symbolized by her Pluto placement, and assume that at times Kay has been very vulnerable to judgments from others.

Kay has a stated fear about expressing her individuality and we can put that into context now, with the idea that her fear might stem from difficult conditioning influences imposed on her from structures outside herself (South Node of the Moon in Capricorn).

It is likely that these kinds of experiences have colored Kay's early childhood experiences in this life. To the extent that Kay has already developed a negative self-psychology and feelings of inferiority or criticism in relationships (Pluto in Virgo in the 7th house), experiences of cold or judgmental families of origin will cement these feelings. The judgments or lack of warmth/love (Capricorn as it relates to the Moon, through the Moon's South Node) will likely be evaluated by Kay as evidence of proof of her underlying feeling of lack.

Kay's South Node of the Moon is in the **11th house**. Trauma signatures relate to Uranus, Aquarius and the 11th house, when under stress by aspect, and here Mercury is square to Kay's nodal axis. Because the south node is in the 11th house squared by Mercury, we see an additional trauma signature that echoes the message of the Pluto-Uranus conjunction. Therefore we can describe Kay's entire *Evolutionary Axis* as a trauma signature, one that, in relationship to the South Node of the Moon, has a Capricorn quality.

Trauma signatures expressed through the Capricorn archetype can refer to intensely dysfunctional family systems, or societies with totalitarian regimes and/or severe hierarchical structures with little or no compassion for those at the bottom of the scale. Also indicated are merciless or persecutory judgments, or collective events such as war, famine or forced migration.

Kay's Pluto placement in Virgo reveals an evolutionary intention to be at the bottom of the scale and we see Kay's vulnerability as the potential family "black sheep" or, in another context, the group scapegoat within punishing social structures. The potential exists for Kay to have experienced complex cycles of persecution and mistreatment both on an intimate level (within the family) and as part of vulnerable communities, either through warfare or through being marginalized within the given culture. Such experiences would have only served to compound her fear of breaking free from the consensus mentality (Saturn/Capricorn) that is inherent in the early stages of individuation.

With the South Node of the Moon in the 11th house, Kay has been seeking to break free of past bondage and to re-orientate her experience of reality by detaching from those past circumstances and learning to see herself in a more objective light. This intention, gleaned through the South Node in the 11th house, ties in with her underlying Pluto in Virgo intention to examine the motivations of the personal self in order to discover a more realistic and honest understanding of where she was (and is) coming from. With the South Node in Capricorn she has desired to take responsibility for what has occurred in the past and to find a new level of maturity both in her relationships (Pluto in the 7th house) and in her understanding of herself and how she might contribute to society as a whole (Pluto in Virgo).

The South Node Ruler

The ruler of the South Node of the Moon represents further information as to how the individual fared in their effort to express the Pluto purpose via their prior-life identities. The ruler of the South Node in Kay's chart is **Saturn in Aquarius in the 1st house**. This emphasizes the Aquarius archetype for a third time. Saturn is in opposition to Uranus in Virgo in the 7th house, even further accentuating the trauma signature. This makes the archetype of Aquarius dominant within the *Evolutionary Axis* and reveals the importance of her individuation journey, her struggle with feeling different or in experiencing herself on the edge of the mainstream, and her need to detach from the circumstances of the past and to understand herself anew.

Saturn is at 29 degrees of Aquarius, emphasizing this transformative urge even further. Any planet in the **last degree of a sign** embodies an intensified meaning of the archetype in question. This is a signature of culmination, the epitome of all that the planet and the sign symbolize. Saturn represents the structure of consciousness and the embodiment of structures within collective experience. In Aquarius it signifies a consciousness built around detachment. It also expresses a fundamental conflict in that Uranus seeks to liberate from the conditioning influences represented by Saturn. This placement indicates a culmination of Kay's ability to take on any more judgment or conditioning. It represents the need for a radical break with the past.

Kay's Skipped Step

The square from **Mercury in Aries in the 2nd house** is a *skipped step* which adds further complexity to our understanding of Kay's karmic past. In this case, Kay's North Node of the Moon (in Cancer in the 5th house) becomes a *de facto* South Node since it represents here a partly-developed evolutionary intention that was disrupted. Kay intended to develop an emotionally secure personal reality (North Node of the Moon in Cancer) that allowed her to creatively self-actualize (North Node of the Moon in the 5th house). Her attempt to realize this personal security and creative development were restricted in the past, as symbolized by the Mercury *skipped step*.

A square to the nodal axis of the Moon represents unfinished business on an evolutionary level and the reintegration point is signified by the node of the Moon which last transited it. In this case the South Node of the Moon is the reintegration point. This indicates that Kay needs to go back into the past experiences that repressed or traumatized her in order to find her voice and to understand the nature of what has occurred (Mercury).

Kay's Mercury *skipped step* also indicates a loss in her capacity to understand her own experience, and a silencing that occurred through past judgments and traumatic circumstance which left her isolated or bereft in some critical way. With Mercury being in Aries, we see that this blockage occurred on an instinctual level and that Kay may have difficulty in speaking or allowing her body to express its needs (Mercury in the 2nd house). Because it is the ruler of Virgo, Mercury has a heightened importance due to her Pluto in Virgo placement. So we can also see the potential for disruption in the internal dialogue, or for looping cycles of repetitive thought-forms from the past.

Suicidal Tendencies

As the opposition from Saturn to Uranus indicates past physical trauma in the nodal axis (Saturn as ruler of the South Node) and now the *skipped step* is in the 2nd house (which we can relate to biological survival issues) we can see that unnatural prior-life deaths or physical damage occurred, possibly to the throat (strangulation, hanging or being collared or chained). It is possible that the damage was caused by speaking out or not speaking out (damage from others, Pluto in the 7th house). This, when related to the most intense cycles of negative self-analysis of the Pluto in Virgo, could signify the potential for self-harm, prior-life suicide, suicidal ideation or passive suicide (giving up the will to live) as the distorted but "logical" answer to extreme self-loathing or in response to the past traumas.

Suicidal ideation occurs when an individual repetitively returns to thoughts of suicide. Passive suicide can be defined as not taking appropriate measure to preserve or prolong one's life because internally one has given up caring. Such a lack of safety concerns on the biological level would then represent a fundamental block to the intention to develop a safe and secure personal reality as the foundation for the creative actualization of the self (North Node of the Moon in Cancer in the 5th house).

This analysis of the *skipped step* serves to illustrate its impediment to the intended evolutionary goals of the North Node of the Moon. In fact such experiences may even have threatened the fundamental cohesion of the ego identity (North Node of the Moon in Cancer) through verbal and physical abuse (Mercury in Aries in the 2nd house square to the nodes) that related back to recurrent themes of judgments and traumatic loss (South Node of the Moon in Capricorn in the 11th house).

Parental Figures

Since we're considering the North Node as operating in Kay's chart like a South Node (because of the *skipped step*), and we have the archetypes of Capricorn and Cancer at play, the potential exists for specific karmic stories or enmeshment with the souls manifesting as Kay's parents in this life. In some fashion both are likely to have taken part in the experiences that shaped Kay's past. So as the Pluto intention is the development of relationships in order to learn about the self, we can deduce that Kay's parents are two critical figures with whom she may have experienced projected expectations, delusions or difficult prior-life endings. Further to this, her parents in prior lives (not necessarily known to her in the current life) will have played important roles in effecting the lack of safety, judgment and persecutory violence that are indicated through the nodal axis of the Moon and the *skipped step* to that axis.

The experience of Kay's early home-life then relates back to the Pluto purpose to achieve an understanding of relationship dynamics. The manner in which Kay experienced her parents in early childhood becomes representative of her desire to achieve parity with others on a soul level. Past problems of inequality in relationships and her internalized sense of lack or inferiority may very well play out as problems with the current life parents, feelings of not being good enough, of being unloved.

With the *skipped step* being Mercury, the ruler of Gemini, we can see that siblings could also be an issue. Not having siblings may compound Kay's sense of isolation. If she has a sibling or siblings, they too may have a specific karmic connection to Kay's past. It is possible, through her Pluto in Virgo need for humbling self experience in order to achieve a more authentic stance, and with the Mercury *skipped step* resolving via the South Node in Capricorn, that Kay might feel judged by her siblings, experiencing herself as inferior or struggling to experience parity with them.

Kay's Story

I have selected this example from my client files so that I may share with you the insights gained from the regression work that we undertook together as part of her therapy. This work illumines deeply explored issues that will best illustrate the potential for this form of astrological analysis. The current life issues that Kay faces could occupy a case study in and of itself but in line with the purpose of exploring the reincarnational dynamics alluded to in the *Evolutionary Axis*, I will, at this point, explore only those aspects of our work together that relate to prior-life experiences, experience inside the womb and states of awareness originating between lives on earth.

Kay initially approached me for therapy. Kay had been seeing a therapist (for whom I had done an astrology reading) for a finite number of sessions who, at the end of their therapy, recommended that she continue her work with me. From the moment Kay first sat down opposite me in my client room I intuitively saw a pantry, or a system of shelves, with bags of food and jars with contents open and strewn across the floor behind her. As she spoke it seemed as if she was speaking about the mess behind her. In some ways this image reflected our early concern of whether to work together. It was going to be a big job just to clear up what had been spilled or was out of its container, even before trying to restore order or find meaning in those containers. This image was relaying to me her state of mind and the nature of her unconscious.

It was only after six sessions that I saw her natal chart, the understanding of which informed my work with her from that point forward. The image of a messy pantry seemed to me related to the nodal axis and its intended expression of nurture and sustenance, counterpointed by its actual state of traumatic discord and lack of boundary.

The level of chart analysis we've pursued here was at my disposal long before Kay was able to describe some of what had occurred in her life. However this unconscious knowledge expressed itself in a radical way after we had established a basis of therapeutic trust.

While conducting a simple grounding body-scan exercise in which I led Kay through feeling the top of her head to the tips of her toes, Kay had an image of being chained and in a dark cellar. Being in therapist mode, I understood this at first as a symbol of Kay's heart (that she found the image as the body scan reached the heart) and the way a part of her loving nature was chained by her experience of rejection and held in the unconscious (the basement). However this explanation proved to account for only one level of what was occurring.

The following day Kay phoned me in a panic. She had decided not to go to work that morning and could not get the image of herself chained to a cellar wall out of her mind. I happened to have space for her to come in right away and within moments of our meeting Kay was recounting a memory of being a girl who was chained to a cellar wall. I encouraged her to explore this experience, using techniques from a hypnotherapy training course from which I had just graduated. Although I was using prior-life regression techniques to keep Kay moving through her story it was only after a certain amount of time that I myself realized she was in an experience of prior-life recall. It became apparent that the events she was describing could not have happened in her current life. Kay had no previous experience of past-life regression and both of us were surprised by this powerful incursion of past material.

Kay had no interest or belief in prior lives. She had been a Christian in her early life and though she did have an interest in

Reiki healing she had never seriously considered the question of prior lives. Watching her powerfully relive one, accompanied by somatic experiences of writhing in her seat as if in physical pain, was a critical experience for me in understanding the psychic importance of this process. Without even consciously trying, this deep level of memory demanded expression.

In understanding that Kay's 2nd house Mercury in Aries skipped step resolves via the South Node of the Moon in the 11th house (understanding of traumatic memories) we may predicate that Kay needed to relive what happened in order to speak of it (Mercury) and somatize its expression (Aries in the 2nd house) in order to heal. This process was of critical importance for her in the present to gain sufficient detachment and awareness (South Node integration point in the 11th house) so that she could begin to take responsibility for events and consequently mature (South Node integration point in Capricorn).

The narrative content of Kay's traumatic memory involved being kept prisoner in a cellar, chained to a wall and collared by a man who turned out to be her father. He would routinely bring her food and violently rape her (linking the association between nurture and abuse, alongside explicit issues with food).

Eventually allowed back upstairs to live in the main house with her submissive mother, in time she met a man and married. The man was kind and they enjoyed some quality of life together, albeit financially dependent upon and controlled by her father, who one day returned from a hunting trip declaring that her husband had been killed in a freak accident. She was then forced to return to life with her family, brooding on the likely murder of her husband by her father. She never recovered from these experiences or was able or allowed to have her own life.

That such events happen within families even today is something that the recent story of Joseph Fritzl demonstrates. In Fritzl's case, a shocked Austrian nation watched in horror as the details were revealed. Fritzl led a double life fathering children with his imprisoned daughter in the basement of the family home while maintaining the appearance of a "normal family" with his wife upstairs. Whether Kay's story is a literal prior-life memory or a non-literal expression of unconscious evolutionary themes, the chart demonstrates the validity of her experience. I witnessed the congruence of my client as she suffered through the telling of a story that was simply compelling – it demanded to be told.

Kay's story represents the symbolism of dependency, emphasizing the karmic role of the parents as primary factors in the cyclic extremes of relating (one dominant, the other submissive), persecution and abuse. In Kay's recall, as the father raped her he would call her names, saying "what a whore she was," and how she made him do what he did to her.

In doing this, the father from Kay's story set up a hallucinatory effect within the young girl's reality whereby the negative messages (Pluto Virgo) from others (Pluto 7th house) were internalized as part of an intense expression of desire and physical abuse (*skipped step* Mercury in Aries). The abuse originated from the father (South Node in Capricorn) in a traumatic cycle (Uranus signatures) which combined the physical and mental aspects of abuse within the emotional boundary of incest. In this combination of physical threat and emotional transgression the persecutory messages were encoded deep within the developing consciousness of the youth.

The depth of this experience eclipsed the conceptual shock that Kay encountered in her expression of such prior-life recall. There are those who, regardless of their views on reincarnation, simply reject the idea that the natal chart can have any capacity to describe prior-life experience. I hope that the examples throughout this book can offer an alternative to that seemingly limiting view. Kay is an excellent example. The *Evolutionary Axis* in her chart shows the importance of accessing prior-life traumatic memory in the first place, and also identifies the themes of those traumas.

Kay's Second Regression

We approached Kay's next regression more consciously after much discussion about the meaning of such experiences. We followed the negative introjects that Kay often returned to in her mind in which she felt it was her fault that she was alone. I asked her to go back to a time when she learned or first experienced them. Kay regressed to a very brief lifetime whereby, after a safe early childhood, her parents were killed while away traveling and she was sent to an orphanage, which was a cold and unpleasant place. Already struggling with the guilt that young children often carry when something tragic happens to their parents, she was falsely accused of something by someone at the orphanage and kept confined to her room (the Mercury *skipped step* referring to lies or false accusations, Gemini, internalized as part of underlying guilt, Virgo). This experience and the loss of her parents were instrumental in a decision she made in that lifetime to starve herself. She became emaciated and was taken to the sickbay where she later died from her self-imposed condition.

We saw in the *Evolutionary Axis* of Kay's chart the tendency to internalize blame, her dependence on others, the disruption in her personal security in the square from Mercury in Aries in the 2nd house. We saw that this *skipped step*, (through the Mercury rulership of Virgo relating to the Pluto critique of the self) can become destructive, leading to the capacity for self-harm or passive suicide. The events that transpired in that life were in no way her fault, but her own internalized guilt found expression in ending her life through overcoming her own survival needs (*skipped step* in the 2nd house) as an expression of traumatic loss triggered by an experience of blame.

The Case of Norbert

Stanislav Grof has identified these kinds of interwoven stories as COEX's: systems of condensed experience that ally biography, inter-uterine experiences of the birth process, and prior-life experiences into traumatic complexes of information.[7] In his book *When The Impossible Happens*, Grof offers the example of Norbert who experienced a long-term shoulder pain that was unresponsive to all but the most severe painkilling medication (and then only for the immediate period after injection), and also a fear of being choked.[8] During a session with Grof, Norbert drew his attention into the pain and recalled a childhood experience from around age seven. After building a tunnel in the sand he had entered the tunnel, which then collapsed. He only escaped suffocation thanks to being rescued by a nearby adult.

His attention then went further back into a protracted birth process during which his shoulder had become caught on his mother's pubic bone causing him excruciating pain and anxiety as he struggled to break free. Next his awareness took him to a scene from Cromwell's England in which he was a soldier on horseback whose shoulder was pierced by an enemy lance and in falling from his horse he was trampled underneath it, dying painfully as he choked to death on his own blood and crushed bones. In liberating this complex of interwoven memories, Norbert then experienced freedom from his long-standing pain for the first time in his life.

Systems of Condensed Experience

With that in mind, let's take a look now of Kay's COEX's or systems of condensed experience.

Kay's first suicide attempt occurred in her teenage years. The death of her beloved grandmother exacerbated her experience of her home life as an emotional desert.

An experience to which she would return several times in sessions was a memory as a fetus in the womb during which she could hear/feel her parents arguing and internalized their stress relating to their not wanting her. Alongside this emotional isolation she would find the umbilical cord wrapped around her neck like a noose.

The aforementioned prior life during which she was orphaned linked to another system of condensed experience, again through the feeling of not being wanted in the womb, which Kay could not experience as a nurturing environment.

This then linked to consistent overeating in childhood and teenage years to fill the hole inside left by the emotional and physical absence of her current parents. What was an act of starvation in a prior life became a pattern of extreme comfort-eating in the present life as an attempt to fill an inner sense of being starved of love and affection.

We can see then that issues linked to the *Evolutionary Axis* are expressed through multiple layers of experience: present life biography, the experience of life in the womb and transpersonal experiences of prior lives, or of states in between lives. This idea represents a profound topic for further exploration.

Kay's Land of Celebration

At the next stage in our work we found an ally in Kay's higher self, which it became possible for her to contact during our sessions. Via the guidance of this teacher/guide figure, Kay could move directly from the states of despair experienced within the womb into the state that existed prior to conception.

When Kay found herself in the womb she would begin to drift for long periods of time in a highly dissociative state in which she was unable to relate to or express feelings that had been real to her only moments before. It was if a switch inside clicked, or a fuse shorted, so that she would not have to endure her most anxious and self-hating feelings. Yet the energy of these emotions would permeate the room like ink from a squid spilling into a pool of water, an effect so rapid and overwhelming as to be quite shocking. If this energy caught me off guard I would find difficulty in staying conscious under the thick tide of oily emotional residue filling the room. This state was very toxic and at points seemed to threaten to drown Kay, or leave her lost in a weird limbo that I found equally difficult to experience.

The fundamental dilemma I faced was that I did not want to move away from this space just because I found it personally unpleasant. It was clear that change could occur when it was right for Kay. Conversely I had concerns about Kay's ability to survive extended periods in this zone without emotional aftershocks occurring for her outside of the therapeutic space.

So as Kay began to express her distress at being conceived I asked her to contact her higher self and to ask for this aspect of her consciousness to offer insight into where she had been before she was conceived in order that we might understand her distress. To my surprise the entire energy field in the room instantly lightened as Kay described being surrounded by a group of beings, some of whom she knew well, some of whom were more distant, like teachers, but all of whom radiated care and concern for her well-being. She recognized these beings as a kind of soul group and called the place in which they congregated the "Land of Celebration." For the first time in our work together, Kay radiated joy, which I understood as the soul's happiness as it recognizes home.

The "Land of Celebration" was such a beatific place to Kay, and so wonderfully evoked in the energy in the room that I encouraged Kay to stay with the experience as she breathed this quality into her being on many levels. In this approach I followed Roberto Assagioli, who insists that during exploration of the unconscious complexes we must develop strength and light within the self so as to not unbalance the psyche through premature voyaging into the deep.

Yet even after internalizing the celebratory energy of the "Land of Celebration," when Kay eventually moved back into the womb state she immediately went into a state of distress, this time one from which she was not so disassociated. She could see that her friends and guides loved her and supported her but as soon as she was removed from their comforting embrace she felt bereft and ill-equipped to meet the challenges she had prefigured with them.

Kay's attachment to dependency on others symbolized by her 7th house Pluto had returned. The Pluto in Virgo capacity to internalize and make a crisis about the lack of power returned the moment she was conceived so that even when she had just traveled from the supportive intermediate zone she felt abandoned to a life-mission that was doomed to fail.

This entire phenomenon is a clear illustration of the deep compulsions of the Pluto placement and its relationship to powerful karmic patterns of attachment that are capable of superseding other, more positive levels of experience. However, by remembering the "Land of Celebration" for the first time in her current life, Kay introduced a vision of hope and an exotic but powerful expression of the desire of her North Node of the Moon in Cancer in the 5th house – a safe and secure reality in which her creative actualization is dominant rather than marginalized.

More Work with Kay's Parents

Through Kay's lunar nodes, we observed the potential for specific karmic events involving her parents in this life. After experiencing a past-life death in her first regression, Kay had (with the support of her higher self) recognized her father in this life as being the kindly but ineffectual husband who had been murdered by her abusive father from the past life.

Kay subsequently underwent a series of regressions involving her current-life mother. The most powerful of these figured Kay as a young woman, a maid for the older but more attractive lady of the house (her current life mother) with whom she had an affair. As they got to know each other over time, the younger woman (Kay) felt she could really open up with to the older woman. And in their sexual relationship she felt loved and appreciated like never before. Her ongoing issues of abuse by men melted away under the soft touch and real sense of being wanted by another.

Later the lady of the house became ashamed by her congress with a servant and she banished Kay to duties in another of her households, not seeing her again for many years. Kay felt emotionally abandoned. All subsequent relationships failed to recreate the sense of openness and real love that she had felt with this woman. Kay became uncertain whether this woman ever had any real feelings for her.

When she became ill and was on her death bed, the lady of the house summoned for her serving maid to return to her side to care for her. Kay was delighted, as if the many years of loneliness and insecurity as to the value of their union had melted away. In caring for her in her last moments, Kay learned of the lady's difficulty in reconciling her feelings due to the social stigma they represented. While the older woman never truly overcame her shame for what she had done, the indications of her struggle allowed Kay to feel that she was wanted.

As the lady approached death, she entered a state of shock and terror. Kay was so attuned to her suffering that she wanted to give her something but did not know what to give, so with a powerful inner intention she gave (sacrificed) her heart to this woman to ease her transition into death. This seemed to soothe the lady in her passing but after she was gone Kay felt a terrible emptiness and a hole inside that she was never able to fill.

This experience had a parallel in Kay's current life. An emptiness and guilt had overpowered Kay when her mother died, haunting her for many years, relating to Kay having signed a medical notice allowing her mother's organs to be donated for others in need. She did this although she felt it was against her mother's intentions. Kay's mother had not specifically stated she did not wish her organs to be used but Kay felt strongly that she would not have wanted this. Kay was subsequently burdened with guilt for a long time in a strange echo of her ambiguity at having "given up her heart" to the lady in the prior life.

Under the guidance of Kay's higher self we were able to facilitate the return of Kay's heart while still indicating to the soul of her mother (and the Lady she loved in the past) that her love was real and did not require such sacrifice in order to be recognized as such. This event was very powerful for Kay and led to the release of much of her internalized guilt about her mother. As we conducted this ritual of love we both felt that the soul of Kay's mother was present on some level and understood our purpose.

In this story we see the sacrifice of the self as servant (Pluto in Virgo) for the love of the other (Pluto in the 7th house). We see that a powerful identification with the meaning of relationships (Pluto in the 7th house) plays out with specific family members in the current life. These relationships involve issues of status and the repression of feelings due to such status (South Node of the Moon in Capricorn). And the experience also includes disassociation and the splitting of the self (South Node of the Moon in the 11th house). We see that such splitting of the self takes on literal form within the structure of consciousness (the South Node ruler Saturn in Aquarius in the 1st house) with the literal/psychic offering of the body/ heart through an act of will. We see that the result leads us back to an experience of inner emptiness and lack (Pluto in Virgo) as the giving away of the heart becomes the perfect metaphor for the intention of the Pluto in Virgo to transcend the egocentricity of the preceding archetype, Leo.

This case study illustrates the complex ways in which the themes we can identify using this method might play out in a person's consciousness and life. It also shows us that the archetypal themes of prior-life events and their karmic implications can be accessed purely from in-depth analysis of the natal chart. Certainly this work had a profound impact on Kay, who is happy that it can serve as an illustrative example and potentially be of use to others. As we continued Kay's therapy she became experienced and articulate in employing the hypnotherapeutic approach we used. Kay was accepted into a prestigious hypnotherapy program and is herself now a fully-qualified hypnotherapist.

Chapter 3

Uranus: Identifying and Healing Trauma

Trauma: An Overview

In the landmark book *Trauma and Recovery*, Judith Lewis Herman makes a connection between three social movements and specific trauma signatures that proliferated during those times:

> Three times over the past century, a particular form of psychological trauma has surfaced into public consciousness. Each time, the investigation of that trauma has flourished in affiliation with a political movement. The first to emerge was hysteria, the archetypal psychological disorder of women. Its study grew out of the republican, anticlerical political movement of the late nineteenth century in France. The second was shell shock or combat neurosis. Its study began in England and the United States after the First World War and reached a peak after the Vietnam War. Its political context was the collapse of a cult of war and the growth of an anti-war movement. The last and most recent trauma to come into public awareness is sexual and domestic violence. Its political context is the feminist movement in Western Europe and North America. Our contemporary understanding of psychological trauma is built upon a synthesis of these three separate lines of investigation.[1]

We will explore these three social movements, as well as introduce a new fourth movement, in order to more clearly understand the nature of traumatic experience in our current time. The fourth movement concerns the more recent collective awareness of the evolutionary perspective of the soul as explored through conscious memories of inter-uterine, bardo (in between lifetimes) and prior life states. This long-term memory (which includes the womb, and prior lives) holds imprints of traumatic experience. I will show how they can be identified in the birth chart and how healing work can be initiated.

The First Movement: Hysteria

When Freud, Breuer and Jung (following Charcot and Mesmer in France) began their early psychoanalytical work in the late nineteenth century, they were working within a societal context that was heavily conditioned by a patriarchal bias that excluded women's rights politically and in marriage. While hysteria was the great psychological issue of the nineteenth century, the use of the term is first found in the Hippocratic text *On the Diseases of Women,* in which the uterus is seen as "the cause of 600 evils and countless sufferings." This ancient viewpoint overtly echoes the proclaimed Biblical punishment that the daughters of Eve must suffer pain in child-birth, sickness and death.

Working from a 1969 paper in which Dr. Esther Fischer-Homberger writes, "Where hysteria is diagnosed, misogyny is not far away," James Hillman noted an association was being made between the diagnosed hysteric and the witch as early as the nineteenth century: "In nineteenth century French psychiatry, an old test for the witch – sticking her with pins and needles – was used in clinical demonstrations of hysteria."[2] The stage had been set even then to link the concept of hysteria with the female experience.

In the late nineteenth century, at the peak of Empire and post-enlightenment rationalism, the individual experience as we know it today was largely repressed by the compelling drives of rationalism, science and the Industrial Revolution. The young women who filled Charcot's demonstrations in Paris (and later became Breuer's, Freud's and Jung's first patients) represent the concept of a "return of the repressed": that which we sweep away comes back through more subtle routes such as symptoms, or dreams.

The historian Mark Micale sees hysteria as "a dramatic metaphor for everything men found mysterious or unmanageable in the opposite sex."[3] Indeed this diagnosis was an excuse for some men to rid themselves of "demanding" or "nervous" wives or daughters by sending them to sanatoriums and safe houses, "out of harm's way."

These "mysterious" or "unmanageable" aspects of the feminine psyche were more often than not simply the woman's suppressed potentials manifesting as symptoms. These powerful unmet desires were so strong in the famous case of Breuer's patient Anna O. (real name Bertha Pappenheim), that the case study reads more like a man falling in love than therapy. And indeed he broke off the work with her for the sake of his marriage in the end. In passing the case on to his colleague Sigmund Freud, the foundations for the Psychoanalytical movement were laid.

Pappenheim's "symptoms" were in many ways the simple expression of a bright young woman trying to manage under repressed circumstances. Pappenheim, who coined the term "talking cure", later became a social pioneer, founding the League of Jewish Women.

Breuer, though having paved the way for others, was uncomfortable with the feelings brought up by working in close proximity with Pappenheim and stopped working with patients. This is a solid example of a counter-transference response to the transference of a patient. Pappenheim's feelings, and her erotic passions, buried in grief at the loss of her father, were transferred on to the older Breuer, evoking from him his own passionate response which, within the narrow confines of the social mores of the period, he was too uncomfortable with.

The Second Movement: Combat Trauma

The suppression of the feminine is one of the most important distortions in our current culture. Equally tragic is the dominance of global conflict. Tens of millions of young men died in the great wars of the last century, whole generations falling like corn under the scythe of the industrialized war experience. In some ways the mass slaughter in Europe, North Africa, the Pacific Island and Asia was the inverted initiation rites of the Industrial Age as millions of teenagers felt compelled to fight and then watched their friends die or died themselves.

In famous battles such as the Gallipoli Campaign, to fight was in fact simply to choose to die en masse with one's brothers in arms. Churchill, the admiral of the Navy at the time, felt so aggrieved at the pointless deaths at that particular battle that he stripped himself of his rank and went to fight in the trenches alongside the common soldiers. Shell shock – the experience of a person literally shaking in fear that the huge explosions routinely heard might blow them apart – was initially viewed as an offence. Scores of young men/ boys experiencing shell shock were rounded up and shot as cowards. That some freethinking doctors and psychologists eventually began to recognize this experience as a disorder of the mind rather than a lack of moral caliber forms the basis of the second wave of understanding regarding trauma.

The world was reeling from the pain of loss and the brutal violence of the two World Wars. The loss of life was staggering. As the cold war gave way to Vietnam, a new dynamic emerged. More men end up self-harming or taking their own life in that war than died in active service. Why is this?

In the Second World War, trauma studies show that most soldiers suffered traumatic stress longer when separated from their unit. Many would return to the fighting with serious injuries simply to be with their group. When the war was over, those on the victorious side were able to return to their communities as heroes and liberators. But in Vietnam the problematic political context of the war ensured that no sense of community could be maintained in civilian life once one's tour of duty was complete. There was no safe community to return to that could understand or hold the experiences that had occurred.

Without political rationale and support from folks back home, the atrocities endured during the Vietnam War led to soldiers experiencing a form of traumatic stress that no medications were strong enough to address. Studies of post-traumatic stress disorder began to proliferate after this conflict and continue today.

The Third Movement: Domestic Violence

We turn now from the collective experience of the tragedies of war to the more personal trauma of domestic violence and sexual abuse. That there is a link between domestic violence and war is undeniable: the incidence of rape and systemized sexual abuse is prolific within the context of large-scale violence. What's more, we find in this subject a common thread between the three movements discussed, as the victims of sexual violence are nearly always women.

One of countless examples of the co-mingling of these two types of trauma during war time is the existence of "joy divisions" of Jewish women forced to service Nazi officers in concentration camps. The high incidence of rape as revenge with the Russians in Berlin, and throughout the Balkan conflicts, also reveals the use of rape to distort the blood lines within an ethnic conflict. To destroy the purity of the enemy blood through the multi-ethnic children of rape escalates the conflict into another, more intimate, territory.

Countless examples such as this demonstrate the manifold violence to the feminine that occurs within the patri-focal (from the lineage of the father) civilization dominant in the world today. During times of conflict and war, this violence is directed outwardly towards the "other." But the cycle continues unbroken at home through domestic and sexual violence.

When one meets or works with victims of domestic abuse one enters a world shrouded in secrecy. It is hard for many to understand the impact of routine abuse on an individual. Victims attempt in vain to express personal power, and instead find themselves bound to their poisoned nest. The drive inside the abused person to do something positive to change their situation eventually atrophies and dies. A Home Office Study in the UK found that a woman will be assaulted on average 35 times before reporting it to the police.[4] A high level of self blame among victims of domestic violence and a pattern of chronic victimization work in tandem to keep people trapped in the situation despite their suffering.[5]

Routine violence towards women is an expression of our distorted relationship to the feminine within the industrialized world. We can expand our view outward and see the inherent relationship to the violence we do to harm the earth and control nature. This violence towards the feminine represents a collective traumatic imprint and a shadow across all of humanity. Our growing awareness of this insight has begun to create a context for healing a problem of which the scale within Western cultures is truly shocking:

The most sophisticated… survey was conducted in the early 1980's by Diana Russell, a sociologist and human rights activist. Over 900 women, chosen by random sampling techniques, were interviewed in depth about their experience of domestic violence and sexual exploitation. The results were horrifying. One woman in four had been raped. One woman in three had been sexually abused in childhood.[6]

The Fourth Movement: Evolutionary Trauma

I'd like to turn your attention now to a fourth movement which concerns the growing cultural attention to the effects of the unresolved traumas from birth and from past lives. It is here that we find a connecting thread between the insights of Evolutionary Astrology and many healing disciplines including Transpersonal Psychotherapy. By taking a closer look at this increasingly powerful subject, we will add a crucial layer to our understanding of traumatic experience.

In the academic astrological journal *Archai*, Richard Tarnas points out that both Carl Jung (1875) and Stanislav Grof (1931) have a natal T-square (with the planets Saturn-Uranus-Pluto) in their natal chart, which makes reference to the 2010 Pluto T-square to the Saturn-Uranus opposition.[7] This suggests that during these immediate years that follow, we might begin to more fully appreciate the contributions of these two key figures, who have both done so much to contextualize the underlying field of experience beyond the merely personal. The celebration of the publication of Jung's *Red Book* seems testament to this.

Jung and Grof stand at the helm of the most prominent wave of thinking regarding expanding perceptions of our experience. This transpersonal perspective, a realm of experience that is literally beyond the personal, is described by Jung's *complexes* of experience that ally to the collective unconscious. Grof has expanded on this idea with the term COEX's or systems of condensed experience, as explored earlier. Grof's COEX's refer to levels of experience that move beyond the personal or even collective cultural level into the collective unconscious, the world of the archetypes, prior lives and the spiritual realms.

Through Jung's and Grof's work, we can understand the individual as having a link from the birth experience (and what preceded it) to the collective archetypal experience of humanity. This insight fuels my current approach to healing the soul by first understanding the identity in this new and radically expanded context. This includes the traumas of birth, but for our purposes, we will focus on past-life trauma, as it is revealed through the birth chart.

Uranus: Trauma Held in Long-Term Memory

Past-life trauma includes those prior-life memories held within the long-term memory which is signified by Uranus/Aquarius/11th house.

The Uranus archetype corresponds to the individuated (un)consciousness of the individual. This deep state of the unconscious symbolized by the Uranus archetype can be brought towards conscious awareness through the attention and focus of the individual, as part of the process of individuation. Through contemplation, regression work, dreams and intuition, this state of awareness can arise as the experience of states of being that transcend the merely egocentric focus within the here and now. This new level of experience has the potential to expand the concept of the here and now into the new experience of an Always: an always having been, an always will be. In this context, flashes of insight can lead to revelations such as the idea that there are memories existing from other lives that can be accessed and that healing is a multi-dimensional experience that includes all that has gone before in the life of the soul.

The ultimate context of life is the All-ness from which the life of the soul or core self emerges. The archetype of Uranus corresponds to that part of the core self that holds memory, the subtle mental nature, and this subtle mind or memory can hold traces of trauma which can cause constriction, the formation of patterns within the subtle mind that can then manifest as difficult mental and emotional states, even physical circumstances within a person's life.

Just as this subtle mind can manifest trauma so it can function as the basis for the realization of the field of reality in which we live. The subtle mind can be likened to a magnetic presence of a certain type or quality, existing within an overall vast, perhaps infinite magnetic field. Trauma is an imprint on this magnetism, a distortion of its field. The individual magnet, this individual consciousness, can recognize the nature of the overall field and gain support from that.

In this way we are life experiencing itself through us, life enjoying life. This ultimate context, the overall field of reality, provides a backdrop of meaning that can help us contextualize our personal life experience, including our most traumatic memories and experiences. Because it is from this perspective that we realize that we are not just an isolated subject, ravaged by our experiences or past, but that we are a point of awareness held within a vast field. We are not alone, and although that idea may be quite hard to connect with under duress, we are all held by this larger field.

This insight forms the basis of the recovery from trauma through a holding environment, initially therapeutically, then by extension through being able to experience the world as safe again. This is understood within current psychological thinking as it corresponds to overt trauma in the current life: the person needs to be removed from the traumatizing environment and through safe relationship recovery can begin. The paradox from this perspective is that serious traumas may lay unresolved on the subtle level from other lives and they may require similar healing.

So, while other lives or past lives become the potential source of great learning, they can also contain very difficult or traumatic experiences which may still be impacting on our consciousness within the current life. Understanding these past traumas can produce a liberating impact on the present life of the individual. It is this liberation that is our goal as we analyze prior-life trauma through the symbol of Uranus, Aquarius and the 11th house.

Why is Uranus linked to Trauma?

In his 1993 work *Prometheus the Awakener*, Richard Tarnas likened the archetypal complex symbolized by the planet Uranus to that of Prometheus in Greek mythology, the titan who stole fire from the Gods.[8] As the story goes, gazing down on Earth one day, Zeus notices men cooking over open fires and realizes that Prometheus has stolen this tool from the Gods. He has Prometheus chained to a mountainside whereby a huge eagle visits each morning to eat his liver, which heals overnight so that the eagle can eat it again the next morning. Prometheus has stolen a monumental gift for humanity; his punishment is equally monumental.

It seems that even mythically the principle of individuation, the fire of illumination, is linked potentially to pain and suffering. The Greeks were very concerned with the concept of hubris, pride before the gods. Their pantheon was a particularly capricious one and the gods and goddesses therein are much of the time anthropomorphic projections of human qualities and distortions taken to an epic scale. In Greek mythology, if a human hero were to challenge the power of the gods, terrible things could and did happen. In the most definitive tales, a hero with a fatal flaw plays out their grandiosity and at some point falls, or is punished by the gods.

The myth of Prometheus alerts us to the possibility that to individuate, to elevate the human life to its apex of individuality, is a potentially dangerous path. Some of these dangers exist in the psychic realms when coming to terms with the unconscious. Uranus represents that level of the unconscious that does not forget – the part illumined in dreams, in regression work or in intuitive flashes of insight. How the psyche begins to integrate those insights is a matter for serious consideration, and indeed debate.

In following one's daimon (what the Greeks named one's indwelling genius, one's spark of individuality) one is following a path along which creativity and madness lie side by side. In his great mid-life transition, his Uranus opposition, Carl Jung had a break*down* that led to the greatest break*through* in his creative work. But by his own admission he was a madman for a period of time during the transition.

Uranus As Liberator

When exploring the Uranus archetype we also need to consider Uranus as liberator. The best question we might ask here is: Liberator from what? We find the answer in exploring Saturn, who, in Greek mythology was the father of Zeus. When we begin to think for ourselves, the potential for lawbreaking arises, hence some of the great control mechanisms employed by church and state over the centuries to control the masses. Yet let us not be naïve. Throughout great swathes of human history the great majority of people have not been able to differentiate truth from falsehood. A great many people followed creeds or had personal motivations which were untested, thoughtless or destructive. This became the justification – not wholly unreasonably – for the control procedures of the state.

Human history reads like the compulsively repetitive wheel of life described by the Tibetans, in which samsara rotates endlessly from godly narcissism to hell realms without meaning, without self knowledge. How to break free of this maya, this cycle of samsara, was the great question of Asian thought in the Axial Age, the period of the Buddha, the Upanishads, Zoroaster and Lao Tzu. The question arose: What was genuine liberation and what was just un-tempered psychic chaos? This is a critical question, an essential act of interpretation. It points directly to the archetypal conflict between Uranus and Saturn: Uranus is always seeking liberation from the structures and confining limitations of Saturn. In that sense there is an inherent tension between the two.

In terms of Trauma we can see that throughout history there have been countless violent and problematic regimes, vast environmental and political disasters, huge wars, famine, man's inhumanity to man. We are not separate from the violence of the historical whether we view history through the lens of the collective unconscious – the storehouse of all prior experience – or through the concept of the soul reincarnating over time, or even if we view the present as containing all the experiences of the past that have led to this point. The past still lives in us.

As we individuate, i.e. as we begin to embrace our full potential (Uranus), we begin to rebel and reject outmoded institutions or forms of behavior (Saturn) which can in turn become rejecting or punishing of this new direction we're moving in. This resistance can manifest as being teased or scolded for our new interest, just it can manifest in more extreme ways as severe restriction or condemnation. As Uranus compels one towards the new, Saturn directs one to maintain the old. In this way the struggle between the individuating spirit (Uranus) and the consensus (Saturn) can be a major source of prior-life (and current life) trauma and wounding.

Putting Trauma Into Context

From the new perspective of a truly evolutionary astrology allied with Transpersonal Therapy we can see that trauma is merely the re-flowering of a karmic pattern, memory or unresolved issue within the subtle mind, the deeper unconscious. This pattern is a knot that we carry within the thread of our consciousness as it existed in previous forms, prior to birth, and as it can exist again after death.

Sometimes we become caught in our experience of trauma, feeling like a victim of our circumstance, or expending valuable internal resources to repress painful memories. When this happens it helps to remember one core insight of the non-dual mystics and sages of humanity: that all that is exists in a state of constant unfolding within the luminous presence, the field of divinity. As the Buddhist scripture the *Heart Sutra* magically suggests, samsara *is* nirvana, the difference is merely a transition of perspective. In other words, the very world of troubles *is* also the enlightened world. The kingdom of heaven is now, spread out before us, we just cannot see it. The few brief times its light shines through the cracks in our world become the unforgettable, inspirational moments of our lives.

Within the experience of non-dual reality there is no separate self to be wounded, no place for an ego which can carry the hurt. One is instead not-two (the literal meaning of non-dual), nothing that is can be separate from awareness. In this state one is life *and* death, and what is not alive and cannot die. In that place there is no suffering self, no trauma.

While the dream or illusion (maya) of separateness exists, there will be the need to see through to what is real, there will be the need for grace. This is what a psychology of soul is open to: the grace of the divine; the grace of the realized beings who have walked the path before us, and on our behalf. For all the wonderful insights and gifts of psychotherapy in the last century there is no more powerful message of healing than those transmitted by great spiritual teachers as epitomized by the Buddha and the Christ.

Adyashanti, a modern teacher of Zen Buddhism poetically describes the nature of our true identity in the following spiritual message:

Have you not been told how grand you are, how uncontained, how limitless? I for one maintain that you are as unseen and eternal as the space that spans beyond the myriad universes. I praise the immortal self—not one self among many, but the self within all selves. For everywhere I go, and in each and everyone I meet, I greet my secret and unseen self. For I know each man and each woman as I know myself, none greater or lesser in essence or worth.

I have no desire or pull toward the gods, nor sacred relics, nor holy books. For I have waded through the various dogmas and found them lacking the essential vision, the unitary glance that reveals God's hand within every gesture. Why should we go looking for more than we are, when we are what we are looking for? Beware of a misguided longing, for it leads in the end to brutality. How much blood has already been spilled in God's name and how much more to come?

I bid you, dear companion: Throw off the yoke of belief, for to arrive at the nobility of truth you must be cleansed of all borrowed knowledge till you are as innocent as the day before you were born. You must forge from within your longing a fiery sword of discrimination, unsheathed from the past—starting now on this hill we stand upon, determined to never again take anything second hand, but instead prove true or false each statement yourself.[9]

Uranus as a Higher Octave of Mercury

The key to the identification of trauma in Evolutionary Astrology is found in the significance of Uranus, Aquarius and the 11th house. As the higher octave of Mercury the Uranus function is allied to the mind and memory. But while Mercury corresponds to the left brain and conscious thought, Uranus corresponds to the unconscious mind – the things of which we are not consciously aware but which may emerge into consciousness either at a critical juncture in life, or via specialized states of consciousness (i.e. dreams, meditation or hypnotherapy).

The Mercury function symbolized by Gemini is that which gathers information, opinions and ideas from the environment around us (e.g. the mimicry with which the young child learns words). In Mercury's expression through Virgo, this information then expands as the mind discriminates the appropriateness or reliability of the information gathered through the Gemini intake process.

Through Jupiter, Sagittarius and the 9th house, the information that we gather en masse (Gemini) and run through the process of discrimination (Virgo) then becomes part of our intuited and re-lied-upon belief system – the overall context within which we begin to interpret all this information and give it meaning.

Within this system, it follows that the archetype of Uranus and Aquarius/11th house corresponds with long-term memory, a strata of experience held within the unconscious. This may be contrasted with the conscious or short-term memory represented by Mercury. With Mercury we read, study and store information in a linear format, like we might while studying for an examination. With Uranus we experience the non-linear field of knowledge in which ideas simply appear to us, or in which certain altered states reveal new dimensions to our understanding. Uranus can be understood transpersonally as well. Uranus has to do with collective break-throughs – ideas that manifest in the world contemporaneously in the collective, often in different parts of the world simultaneously, at just the time that humanity is ready for them.

A good example of this follows from a therapy session I provided to a female client with Uranus in Scorpio in the 9th house widely conjunct the Midheaven and square to Venus in Leo. This woman had conscious memories of parts of the material she encountered in regression. For example, she remembered consciously that her brother had attacked her father one day when she was a young girl. When regressed however, she remembered hitherto forgotten details – the color of her childhood room, the patterned curtains, etc. She also vividly remembered feeling a lack of safety engendered by her brother's attack and at seeing her father so vulnerable. This combination of feeling and vivid detail had been absent in her conscious recall of the event. The vivid re-enactment, the feeling of actually being there again is the direct intrusion of the Uranian level of experience into her memory. The long-term memory, that aspect of the individual unconscious that does not seem to forget anything, is symbolized by the Aquarian archetype within Evolutionary Astrology. In this case, the Uranus signature is important due to its challenging square aspect to Venus.

In this woman's chart, Uranus is square to Venus in Leo (fear of betrayal, misuse of power). Venus in Leo is conjunct Saturn and Mercury (father and brother) in the 7th house. Her fears suppressed her sense of personal power and creativity (Leo) to the extent that she left her job (Uranus-M.C.) because she was too frightened of her boss. We used to joke that when she got over her overwhelming fear of coming to therapy (the re-encounter through the therapist of the fear of her stepfather and the chronic lack of safety she felt in the home) she would have gotten over the need to come to the therapy at all.

The Evolutionary Axis

In Evolutionary Astrology, the analysis always begins with Pluto as representative of the point of the deepest unconscious security with which we enter this life – the point on which we were focused prior to this life and are likely to gravitate back towards. Pluto represents our greatest interest, our greatest strength, and potentially our greatest blind spot.

From this understanding of Pluto we can then proceed to analysis of the South Node of the Moon to find out more about that past. As we have seen, the Moon in Evolutionary Astrology correlates to the nature of the conditioned self, the subjective lens that allows the concerns of the soul (Pluto) in this life to be focused on a meaningful sense of continuity moment by moment. The South Node of the Moon therefore refers to the nature of the conditioned self (ego) as it existed within former incarnations. The ruler of the South Node represents a further source of information as to the nature of these past egos and most specifically, how these past life egos facilitated their own needs and the point of security as represented by the current Pluto placement.

Uranus corresponds to memories or stored capacities within the larger field. It does not therefore always refer to trauma. It can also refer to the awakening or liberating potential of this larger field.

What distinguishes this difference in the natal chart is the nature of the aspects involving Uranus, Aquarius or the 11th house. If the aspects are stressful (conjunction, square, sesqui-quadrate, quincunx or opposition) then a trauma signature is indicated. The larger field of insight symbolized by Uranus is memorably illustrated by Stanislav Grof in a personal LSD session he undertook at the Maryland Psychiatric Research Centre:

> I suddenly had a vision of a dark rock of irregular shape that looked like a giant meteorite and seemed extremely ancient. The sky opened up, and a lightning bolt of immensity hit its surface and started to burn into it some mysterious, arcane symbols. Once these strange hieroglyphs were carved into the surface of the rock, they continued to burn and emit blinding incandescent light. Although I was unable to decipher the hieroglyphs and read them, I sensed that they were sacred, and I could somehow understand the message they were saying. They revealed to me that I had a long series of lives preceding this one and that, according to the law of karma, I was responsible for my actions in these lives, although I could not remember them.[10]

This is a classic intrusion of the Uranus level of reality into the personal consciousness – the lightning bolt literally writing in the stone the reality of the reincarnational past. The importance of Uranus is such that I hold it as a strange and powerful interloper alongside the main analysis of the *Evolutionary Axis*.

While the dimension of experience referred to by the Aquarian archetype is not inherently traumatic, stressful aspects from Uranus or planets in Aquarius/11th house indicate long-term memories, prior life memories of being overwhelmed or that have had such impact as to have problematically affected the development of the individual. As this aspect of traumatic memory can have such a powerful unconscious hold on people it is of critical importance to analyze and resolve it.

Unresolved memories of trauma in the long-term memory constellate whole series of prior-life and current-life issues. These systems of condensed experience include emotional material, repetitive patterns of thinking or introjected meaning, powerful feelings of being crushed by larger forces and symptoms of physical illness. Groups of lifetimes or long chapters of the current life story can be dominated by certain themes that originated in one central traumatic event or in a series of events in which the individual consciousness was overwhelmed. These events are stored in the subtle field of memory represented by Uranus.

Uranus as the Critical Astrological Signification of Trauma

While any stressful aspect between planets may indicate areas of difficulty within a person's life, a critical trauma signature is found when the Aquarian archetype is involved. A trauma signature in the natal chart occurs with any one of the following significations:

1) When a planet in the 11th house forms a stressful aspect to another planet

2) When a planet in Aquarius forms a stressful aspect to another planet

3) When a planet forms a stressful aspect to Uranus

Note: stressful aspects in this context include the conjunction (0 degrees), semi-square (45 degrees), square (90 degrees), sesqui-quadrate (135 degrees), quincunx (150 degrees) and opposition (180 degrees).

The nature of the planets involved in stressful aspect to Uranus, a planet in Aquarius or the 11th house will provide further information about the nature of the trauma. For example:

• When **Saturn** is involved this can indicate the physical nature of a trauma. It may involve a physical wound, depletion (malnutrition, starvation) or prior-life death.

• When **Pluto** is involved this can indicate the fact that the trauma has a primarily emotional or psychological nature, for example a betrayal, or severe psychological compulsion or disorder.

- When **Neptune** is involved this can indicate that the trauma has a psychic nature, for example experiences of severe disillusionment or meaninglessness that in extremis can produce catatonia, a state in which the individual has given up even though the biological form survives.

The trauma signified by the stressful aspect to Uranus itself indicates a mental trauma, where the more subtle aspect of the mind remembers what has occurred in the past. The memory is held in the individual unconscious on a psychic level and in the cellular memory on a physical-etheric level.

When **Uranus is in stressful aspect to a planet,** the nature of that mental trauma is revealed. For example, if Uranus is in stressful aspect to the Moon, there has been trauma associated with the conditioned self or the sense of personal security in the past. The parental experience, specifically the experience of mothering or of security through the primary caregiver in the present life (Uranus with Moon) may contain echoes of the prior-life traumatic memories. So hypothetically, while the current life mother may be erratic or distant at times (Uranus-Moon) she can trigger prior-life memories of traumatic separation or insecurity in the child. In this way the early childhood experiences carry the traces of prior-life experience, or karma.

What distinguishes trauma from mere stress within the chart (and the distinction may often be blurred in individual lives) is the severity of the impact of the event and also the tendency for the trauma signature to reveal painful themes that have been ongoing for an individual throughout multiple lifetimes. As a result, the issue of the identification of the nature of this trauma and its potential for resolution is of critical importance in the individual's life. This importance is further emphasized when Uranus, or a planet in the 11th house/Aquarius also forms a significant aspect to the *Evolutionary Axis* (Pluto, the nodes of the Moon and their rulers).

Kay's Uranus Trauma Signature

Let's take another look at Kay's chart, our case study from Chapter Two. Kay has **Pluto conjunct Uranus** indicating that the mental trauma has a psychological aspect and a tendency towards compulsive behavior and feelings of betrayal. Kay's South Node of the Moon is in the **11th house** with a **square from Mercury** in the 2nd house, indicating that the South Node of the Moon is a mental trauma signature revealing the dominant nature of traumatic memories within many recent prior lives.

With Pluto and the Moon's nodes involved, this trauma signature engages the entire *Evolutionary Axis*. This kind of signature indicates that a plethora of unresolved traumatic memories are stored in the unconscious of the individual. With multiple trauma signatures occurring in this chart it is very likely that traumatic experience has dominated long cycles of prior-life experience and also a good portion of the current life.

With the *skipped step* or square to the nodal axis resolving via the South Node of the Moon **in the 11th house**, we see that Kay has a critical need to understand and to then express that understanding (Mercury as the unresolved issue) of her prior-life memories in order to heal.

With the ruler of Kay's South Node, Saturn, in Aquarius and opposite Uranus we see that her prior-life traumas have had physical components and impact, most likely resulting in prior-life deaths.

The Potential for Many Trauma Signatures

Since any stressful aspect from Uranus or a planet in Aquarius or the 11th house reveals a trauma signature, then many people's natal charts will show the potential for trauma. This is really not all that surprising. All people are living their lives under the influence of prior-life experiences and for the great majority, such events may contain unresolved traumatic experiences or memories. Such traumatic memories frequently carry over unchanged into the present life unless sustained and meaningful effort is exerted in transforming the pattern underlying the trauma.

The Interconnection of Trauma, Healing and Liberation

Because Uranus is a higher octave of Mercury corresponding to the long-term memory, this higher mind function contains many memories and strata of awareness other than traumatic ones. In fact, we might consider the traumatic memories to stand out as difficult moments that have proven hard to forget. But even in their painful experience they may hold moral or educational seeds, such as the potential for remorse following a selfish action. Just as there are painful prior memories there may be other essential qualities held within that aspect of the mind symbolized by Uranus. For example, the mind can hold potentialities and insights that can assist the individual in their life purpose.

Next we'll explore some of the meanings of Uranus in each of the sign and house placements.

Uranus through the Signs/Houses
Suggested Starting Points for Analysis of Trauma

Uranus in the 1st House, Aries or in aspect to Mars

With this placement trauma can result from a difficulty in accepting limitations. Such limitations may be physical or psychological and the trauma occurs in the individual's struggle to maintain personal freedom. In difficult cases there is a superhuman complex in which the individual fundamentally denies the limitation, and then pushes themselves to the point of exhaustion, illness or breakdown.

This placement may correspond to memories of having died at a young age in recent prior lives. The subconscious fear of this happening again drives the individual to further push themselves. To the extent that prior judgments or limitations were externally imposed on the individual there may be a fear of further entrapment, or if such limitations have been internalized, there is a fear of losing control. As the will becomes frozen by traumatic experience there is the potential for the individual to experience the subconscious fear that taking action will itself lead to destruction.

Uranus in the 2nd House, Taurus or in aspect to Venus

With this placement trauma occurs around the issue of the value system. Imposed change to a cherished value system or identified resource can cause upheaval and mental suffering. This trauma can arise either from without (via an external event or authority) or within (via a new insight). There may be memories of huge shifts in fortunes and material resources.

To the extent that fear and the desire for egocentric control saw the individual manipulate others for material or psychological gain in past lives, they may experience profound loss or reduced circumstance in direct proportion to the prior misuse of resources. This signature can link to personal and collective experiences of loss (war, mass displacement and famine for example), including loss of life. Memories of such losses may produce a tendency in the individual to become stuck in survival mode in which they have limited the extent to which they open their consciousness to new experiences or to other people because of prior-life fears of loss. In these cases, the incursion of events or the needs of others challenge the person, who has intentionally walled-off their consciousness to new experience. Opening to these new influences can become the basis for re-traumatization if mishandled as the stress of the new opens the condensed insecurity of the past, which then threatens to overwhelm the person.

Uranus in the 3rd House, Gemini or in aspect to Mercury

With this placement trauma is caused by external or internal confrontations to the way one intellectually understands one's reality. A strong identification with the thinking process and nature of one's beliefs can cause huge stress if those thoughts/beliefs are undermined. At its worst this can manifest as the individual feeling alienated from the world around them, as they experience themselves as being on a completely different wavelength from others.

Trauma can occur through a lack of reception for the ideas one does communicate, leaving the individual unheard or silenced. Isolation can occur through resisting participation in the world around them either because of actual rejection or through rigidity in the mental life formed as a defense against potential rejection.

Uranus in the 4th House, Cancer or in aspect to the Moon

With this placement trauma originates in the lack of nurture or emotional empathy in the early home life. This then leads to the displacement of emotions, whereby the unresolved childhood feelings arise during adulthood in problematic ways. These emotional ghosts or residues from the past can lead to a re-traumatizing effect, whereby the original pain experienced with the parents is recreated without resolution via intimate partners/friends.

There may be a problem with the mother in this life, an issue that often has prior-life roots. Many of these individuals have experienced lifetimes wherein the family or early life context has lacked safety. This had the effect of creating radical insecurity in the individual – the feeling that, emotionally speaking, there is nowhere one can feel at home. The individual is then forced to redirect their attention inside in order to discover a source of security from within. However, this internal redirection may or may not happen. This process in itself can be traumatic and can lead to ego fracturing, mental splitting and breakdown in some cases.

Uranus in the 5th House, Leo or in aspect to the Sun

With this placement trauma can result from the lack of acknowledgment of one's gifts or creative contribution to the world, and also corresponds to periods where one has experienced a fall from grace. Trauma could have occurred in the past because the self image was unrealistically high – a feeling of superhuman ability or that one exists without fault. Feedback in this life to the contrary can be destabilizing.

Prior-life unconscious memories of achievement or high status only fuel the frustration experienced around lack of acknowledgement. This also corresponds to an internally or externally directed need for total change (Uranus applying to the Sun, the centre of the life force). This situation is inherently insecure as most people base their sense of security on what is familiar, and this change in extremis can promote traumatic mental disassociation or breakdown.

Uranus in the 6th House, Virgo, or in aspect to Mercury

With this placement trauma can occur through experiences of persecution or critical feedback from the external environment. Such persecution can be either objective (e.g. the Inquisition) or subjective (fear of the Inquisition). The incursion of both objective persecution and then the subjective fear of such persecution can problematically intertwine throughout multiple lifetimes. This may result in a deep-rooted sense of inadequacy, a feeling of not being ready for life or good enough to make life work.

The individual may struggle to find the right work, or to re-form the work that they do. Trauma can occur when the work is compromised, denied or morally corrupt in some way. The feeling of never being ready, of never fully self-actualizing can become its own vicious cycle whereby the individual is re-traumatizing themselves over and over as they move from one crisis to another. Here crisis itself can become a mentality, a method, an addiction. A feeling of victimization as a result of the pattern and a resulting isolation only compounds the problem.

This placement can also indicate a situation in which the powers of discrimination were fractured or flawed in some way, leading to the potential for extreme cycles of behavior – total lack of discrimination in chaotic hedonism or near puritan levels of restriction, for example. Both extremes involve the attempt to respond to the inner emptiness and self-criticism.

Uranus in the 7ᵗʰ House, Libra, or in aspect to Venus

With this placement trauma can be experienced through sudden or unexpected changes within the given relationship structures of a person's life. Unexpected termination of partnerships, the sudden shift from partner to friend, friend to partner can all cause problems for the individual who has based their security on the previous form of the relationship.

Trauma here is experienced via expectations that the individual projects onto others and the projections made from others onto them. A high degree of irrational thought and action may exist within relationships. The scale of trauma runs from excessive dependency to fear of dependency (destroying any relationship that comes close to really mattering). As a result of sudden change and loss some of these individuals will develop a detachment from others that is traumatic to the extent that it is dissociative and can result in pronounced loneliness.

Uranus in the 8ᵗʰ House, Scorpio, or in aspect to Pluto

With this placement trauma often occurs through an experience of betrayal (real or imagined) whereby the person to whom one has been committed appears to (or actually does) undergo a nightmarish change of personality or direction, leaving the individual bereft.

There can be trauma with this placement relating to sadistic abuse and/or psychological torture of or by others. This may take the form of sexual abuse or the use of sex to manipulate or hold power over another. The impact of such experiences can leave people unable or unwilling to trust again. The individual may approach relationships as a process of psychological confrontation, or test of wills.

Understanding the history of these experiences can result in the individual amassing acute psychological understanding but also brings with it the potential for such knowledge to be used aggressively – with the aggression fuelled by the fear that has resulted from prior experiences of betrayal. This can result in a "get them before they get me" mentality.

Uranus in the 9th House, Sagittarius or in aspect to Jupiter

With this placement trauma occurs via personal belief systems which may run counter to the prevailing norms in the environment. This can lead to alienation from the culture or family unit into which one has been born. This alienation may pervade the consciousness, leading to an ongoing fear of misjudgment, of being taken the wrong way.

Traumatic experiences may result when belief systems that are extremely fixed and important to the individual are challenged in some way. Mental suffering occurs in direct proportion to the identification that was invested in the belief system in the first place. In extreme cases the alienation or loss of belief can promote a state of complete defeatism or despair, as if the world experienced inside has absolutely no relationship to the one "out there."

Fundamentalism and/or holy war against others who threaten dearly-held beliefs become possible responses.

Uranus in the 10th House, Capricorn or in aspect to Saturn

With this placement trauma can occur through one or both of the parents being dysfunctional or completely lacking in empathy. The lack of validation on a parental level can easily extend into society, whereby the person can struggle to feel accepted or validated. At its most extreme the mental trauma of feeling such a lack of acceptance or judgment from one's family or society can produce deep depression and despair.

Many prior-life memories of a judgmental family and/or culture of origin may compound the problem. This can produce a compressed psychology, a repressive emotional make-up and a psychology of futility as those in power never offer understanding or validation. As a result the individual can feel that there is no point to their life or to anything that they do. Trauma emerges from the sense of being judged and shamed. There may be prior-life memories of being scapegoated by family or tribe and carrying a burden of guilt in isolation.

Uranus in the 11th House, Aquarius

With this placement trauma occurs due to a realization that the individual is not living a life that reflects their true nature. The discovery of the inner lie or false self can be profoundly shocking. There may have been an experience of rejection or punishment when trying to live in a different fashion to the mainstream. Such shocks or fears of imagined (or actual) responses from the environment can promote a psychology of hiding which itself becomes the basis of feeling that the individual is living with an inner lie.

Trauma may be experienced though friendships or groups, in that they suddenly change their view of the individual and may even be highly critical or persecutory. This placement refers to the evolutionary intention to detach and in so doing to experience a radical break from all restrictive prior conditioning. As security is constituted primarily through familiarity, this need can create enormous mental stress and anxiety which can cripple the person and prevent them achieving the desired freedom from the past.

Uranus in the 12th House, Pisces or in aspect to Neptune

With this placement trauma can occur as the personality itself begins to dissolve or fall apart under external or internal pressure and stress. This can result in a need for escapism, either through substance use, excessive fantasy or delusion, all of which can lead to madness and/or disturbed behavior.

Trauma corresponds to memories of imprisonment and persecution which inculcate a psychology of hiding from others and from life itself. To the extent that the spiritual impulse remains unrealized there exists a capacity for powerful disillusionment, fear and loss of meaning. In extreme cases, states of catatonia, mental imbalance and psychosis all represent the epitome of withdrawal from life.

Others may endlessly sleep or retreat into fantasy life to escape the demands of the actual. Still others may never properly sleep, haunted instead by dreams which include present anxieties blurred into prior-life memories of struggle and meaninglessness. In rare cases the phenomena of psychic attack, possession by "entities" and feelings of having lost a part of the self may have occurred.

Case Study: Oak

Oak's Birth Information
March 6, 1971. 5:10 pm CET. Newport, Wales (3W00, 51N35)

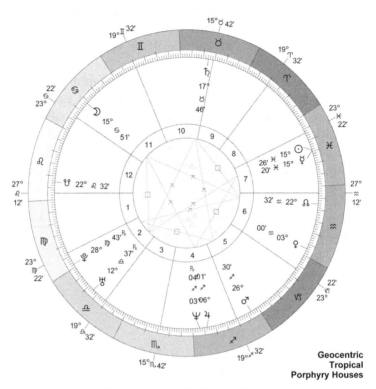

Figure 5. *Oak's Natal Chart.*

In prior-life regression work, clients typically access prior-life abilities or awareness in parallel with traumatic memories. Oak had done a whole series of regressions before undertaking further sessions with me and was already aware of some of the more crucial traumatic events from his prior lives. He underwent two regression sessions with me over the course of several months in which he had been struggling with a sense of meaning and purpose at work. He found his work as a transpersonal psychotherapist for university students satisfying, but the bureaucracy of the work was weighing heavily on him.

In one of our sessions, Oak recalled his feelings of the point-lessness of a particular meeting that went on all day, as the sun shone outside on the fields that he wanted to walk in. He felt imprisoned, gripped by a conviction that those in authority had no clue and would betray any real value that he found in his work with others. We can see from the chart that these feelings were core aspects of the *Evolutionary Axis*.

With Pluto in the 2nd house of his chart, Oak has needed to isolate his internal resources in order to maintain a strong self-reliance and inner resilience. The question arises, was this inner resilience needed because of core survival pressures? The problem when focusing exclusively on the personal needs and resources is that the individual can become stuck or repressed in some crucial way, seeing one part of the sky and mistaking it for the whole.

Oak may have tended towards social isolation and/or withdrawal in order to preserve the quality of his inner relationship and to protect the self (indicated by the Pluto placement but further emphasized in the placement of the South Node of the Moon in the 12th house).

With Pluto in Virgo, Oak has intended to humble or purify himself of excessive egocentricity, and to analyze his own motivations carefully in order to equalize himself with other people. The issue of right work is emphasized, as is the issue of whether his work is morally pure and/or useful to the collective. Also of concern is whether he can identify his internal resources (Pluto in the 2nd house) in order to achieve service for others (Pluto in Virgo). There may be, or may have been, a crisis (Virgo) with regard to being able to dig deep (Pluto) and find the necessary resources (2nd house) to survive and achieve his work or service in the world.

With South Node of the Moon in Leo there has been strong creative development in the past. In past lives Oak has developed gifts and capacities for self-expression that may also help others. This may indicate an awareness of certain egocentric attitudes that he is working to transform via Pluto in Virgo.

With the South Node of the Moon in the 12th house, Oak's prior-life egos have tended toward experiences of isolation or retreat in order to develop their capacities. There may have been strong religious or spiritual concerns as part of that prior development indicating a search for a transcendent belief system such as Christianity. Because his Pluto is in the 2nd house, we can deduce that this belief system may have become compromised or overly narrow.

Again referring the South Node of the Moon in the 12th house back to the 2nd house Pluto placement, we can see that prior-life survival issues (2nd house) correspond to the sacrifice (12th house) of the personal self because of the nature of religious or spiritual beliefs. There also exists the capacity for the self to have become overly identified with prior beliefs to the extent of experiencing delusions or having come to some kind of personal crisis.

With Saturn in the 10th house in Taurus square the nodal axis of the Moon we see a *skipped step* and as such, we read both nodes of the Moon as *de facto* South Nodes by dint of both of them referring specifically to qualities or experiences experienced in past lives. The North Node goal of developing methods and techniques of serving (Virgo) a larger humanitarian cause and personal individuated expression (North Node of the Moon in Aquarius) has seen interruption by heavy conditioning factors represented by Saturn in its own house squaring the nodes.

Oak's North Node is in Aquarius and is squared by Saturn. This is a mental trauma signature carried from past lives and one that is compounded by a physical component (Saturn), most probably including the loss of life. This echoes the Saturn quincunx to Uranus in the 2nd house, another trauma signature, and one clearly showing loss of life (2nd house, survival) through lack (Virgo) imposed by external authority (Saturn in the 10th house).

Saturn square to the nodes of the Moon, relating back to the issue of resources in the Pluto placement, represents the source of the conflict with authority, the feeling that bureaucracy and unhealthy structures are restricting Oak's capacity for meaningful work. This represents a series of lifetimes or experiences with prior lives (and this life) in which a conflict with authority or some judgment system has impeded Oak in his evolutionary intentions. The demands of society and of authority figures such as priests and elders, has in some way proved an obstacle to Oak's capacity to help himself and others.

The Saturn square may also indicate a specific shared karmic story with the soul who is his father in this life.

The Saturn *skipped step* integrates in Oak's chart via the North Node of the Moon (the node that last transited the Saturn placement). So Oak is meant to integrate his unresolved patterns of judgment and misplaced authority through the development of the North Node purpose of service, work and individuation.

Regression Work

This case study resembles our first one, in that the node of the Moon with which the *skipped step* integrates has an Aquarian signature (Kay's was to integrate the Mercury *skipped step* through the South Node in the 11th house). This is not unusual, as such a nodal signature indicates the need to gain a detached and conscious awareness (Aquarius, 11th house) of what had gone on before in order to heal. Such a signature indicates a proclivity for prior-life regression work and how potentially significant that work might be for the individual. Again, like Kay, Oak had a natural capacity in our sessions to enter deep trance while remaining clear, rational and detached.

We used Oak's feelings of resentment and betrayal as verbal cues to initiate his regression. Initially Oak saw himself surrounded by a misty darkness and I wondered if the trance required deepening in order to support his memory, but in fact Oak was experiencing the encroaching dawn above a slight mist on the Nile. He had entered into the consciousness of a young Egyptian priest. I am often reminded in regression work that staying with the unknown (the natural territory of Uranus) and trusting the process (rather than pushing forward) leads ever deeper into the reality even though I find it challenges my everyday consciousness to stay with the mystery.

In the past life Oak recalled, as a promising, bright and moral young man from a family with standing (Saturn in the 10th house), he was being groomed to become the next High Priest and to assume the mantle of high office once the aged current leader stepped down. The crisis (Pluto in Virgo) came from the failure of the Nile to flood that year, the consequence being infertile land and the starvation of many in the community (Pluto 2nd house). Unbeknownst to the masses, the Temple had stockpiles of several seasons worth of grain. Oak wanted to share the grain with the people so that they could eat. The High Priest denied that this was possible and when Oak would not budge on the issue Oak was sacrificed (Saturn square to the South Node of the Moon in Leo) by being sent on assignment with a struggling band of soldiers deep in the desert, knowing that with the mass struggle for resources he would never be seen again. Oak's moral outrage at the selfishness of the priestly caste (Pluto Virgo) cost him his life (Pluto 2nd house). If he had been prepared to lie to preserve the lifestyle of the privileged, he would have been rewarded with power, but he chose not to.

Oak's death in that life happened when he stopped to help a wounded man. After realizing that the man he was tending to wasn't going to make it, he looked up and saw that the other soldiers he was with had marched on. With the water and supply situation critical (Pluto Virgo 2nd house) he made the decision to stay with the wounded man and administer his last rites, knowing that this would be his last act since he had no way of surviving alone. He did this and then died.

As Oak saw his spirit rise up above the bodies in the sand I asked him (addressing this aspect of his higher self or soul in transition) if he recognized anyone from the Egyptian life that he knew in his life today. He saw that the man he'd given last rights to was his own father in this life. Saturn square to the nodal axis indicates the shared karmic story with his father, a man of humble origins who had worked hard all his life to give his brilliant and intellectual son the start in life he needed. Such an insight felt like a soulful boon.

In the next life Oak recalled, he was part of an Asian tribal community, as an apprentice to a tribal elder. He became his elder's successor as shaman and leader of the community – both roles which gave him a powerful sense of his potential for service and community. In this life Oak was able to spend time apprenticed to a powerful shaman who left to perform a collective rite for the tribe only to die on his return. Oak's sadness at his passing culminated in a crisis of confidence (Pluto Virgo in the 2nd house) as to whether he possessed the resources to serve the community in the way that his mentor had. However, when he went out on his first solo journey he found himself able to track animal prey while in trance (South Node of the Moon in Leo and the 12th house) and was successfully able to hunt and provide for his community. He then spent many years attending to his tribe's rites of passage, dying peacefully much later.

The recall of both of these lives (accessed over the course of a year) symbolized a movement in Oak's current life away from regressive work situations and/or institutions in which he felt angry and resentful at the bureaucracy and incompetence. Even though both lives expressed a very different relationship to authority – in one producing a terminal crisis, in the other crisis as a stepping stone to a long and fulfilling life – in death they were very similar. As both prior-life selves died, Oak felt a profound release and graceful lightening of his astral form above his dead body, rising and rising into an eventual bliss. The young priest in the desert had served his moral compass and died at peace as did the Asian shaman. The difference is that in the first life, representative of the failure to integrate personal vision and integrity within the collective structure, he had learned a mistrust of those who ought to morally lead the way.

Oak had undergone some previous regressions before working with me. At the end of one life he perceived the total emptiness of all the roles he had played (Saturn *skipped step* in the 10th house), none of which had expressed who he really was (Saturn square South Node in Leo, North Node in Aquarius). In the most traumatic of his previous regressions he had been a priest in the Inquisition cleansing the south of France from the Albigensian heresy. He was utterly sacrificial of his personality (South Node in Leo) to the fundamentalist cause (South Node 12th with Pluto 2nd, narrow or stuck). When he used his authority (Saturn *skipped step* in the 10th house) to personally kill the leader of a Cathar community he got the insight that he actually aspired to be like this man (North Node Aquarius), which he only realized as the man's peaceful face looked at him while his blood flowed over the blade of the sword that was killing him. The real inner power of this *parfait* or Cathar priest moved him more than the parody of forceful authority that he had become (Saturn square to nodes, quincunx Uranus). The resulting crisis (Pluto Virgo, Uranus quincunx Saturn) led to him leaving the church and entering the wilderness. After this particularly powerful regression, Oak somatized the blood as a red rash on his hands during a trip to southern Europe to visit a friend (Saturn as physical symptom).

Just as the Uranian archetype expresses traumatic memories, so it also holds the insights from those memories. When Oak died in the past life as a servant of the Inquisition, in the state after death he made a connection with the Cathar leader he had killed, who

was his true equal (North Node of the Moon in Aquarius, its ruler Uranus in Libra). From that place of connection he resolved to
never make the same mistake again. Thus the long-term memory
holds gifts and awareness just as it holds trauma. Sometimes they
are almost one and the same.

Gifts of the Uranus Placement

The Uranus placement in the chart (along with Aquarius and planets in the 11th house) represents one of the key potentials we have with which to offer insightful therapeutic assistance. We can use the natal chart to identify trauma knowing that the same symbols that identify trauma can offer the realization of potential and the expansion and integration of a new evolutionary awareness.

The Aquarian archetype symbolizes the greater potential within us, the inner butterfly struggling to awaken from the cocoon of our conditioned world. As there is but one life (or one taste as the Buddhists say) and we are all points of view within one overall field of consciousness, then Uranus is the electrical connection to the larger reality and potential of our lives.

On a universal level this knowing field can be seen as the symbol of the entire Zodiac, of all the potentials of consciousness. On the personal level the Uranian fire, through memory and flashes of insight, leads us into our own butterfly effect. In this sense Uranus is electrical potential within the higher mind of the individual that sets the frequency or tone for the type of life experiences and their understanding (rather like the selection of a radio frequency to a particular type of program). Traumas manifest to the extent that past experience blocked the range of frequencies allowed by the person. In the acknowledgment and release of trauma, individuals can find that the range of possibilities for their life opens up enormously.

Uranus vs. Saturn

In understanding the specific connection between trauma and liberation (the dual role of Uranus, Aquarius and the 11th house) we must also acknowledge the archetypal conflict between Uranus and Saturn. *Uranus is always seeking liberation from the structures and confining limitations of Saturn.*

As a person faces change that might lead to him finding himself at odds with a partner, group or social structure, he faces three basic options. One, he could accept his new identity and leave the partner/group/structure behind. Two, he could resist change, inhibiting his growth in order to stay within the limitations of the existing relationships (now understood with a greater degree of painful acuity). Or three, he could work out a way of growing together with the partner/group/structure.

The Natural Square from Taurus

The natural square between Aquarius and Taurus reveals that an aspect of all traumatic experience relates to the primal sense of one's survival being threatened. While this may not always be a literal threat to biological continuance it always involves a shock or threat to a level of meaning that makes the individual *feel* threatened at the core survival level.

For example, if the individual witnesses severely traumatic events, such as the sexual assault of a loved one, they can become fixated and trapped in the experience of traumatic loss just as much as if they themselves had been the victim. From the perspective of Evolutionary Astrology, we see that many traumas are echoes carried over from prior lives. In the current life a person may have had no traumatic experiences beyond the ordinary (death of a relative, first day of school etc.) but they may carry such memories as imprints from prior lives. To the extent that the survival response was threatened in the past, the imprint that needs to be released exists even without having evidence in this life.

Case Study: Drive

Drive's Birth Information
Oct 23, 1983. 3:30 am, Bristol, England (02W35, 51N27)

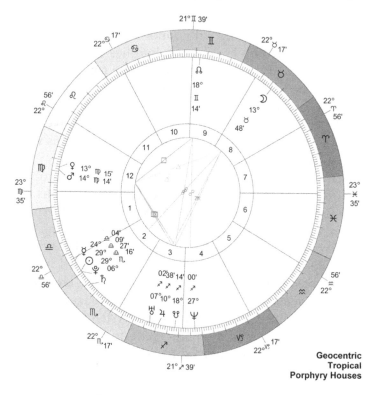

Figure 6. *Drive's Natal Chart.*

In this young man's chart a trauma signature exists with Uranus conjunct Jupiter in Sagittarius in the 3rd house square to his Venus-Mars conjunction in Virgo in the 12th house. This individual was experiencing a post-traumatic stress disorder when he came to see me for counseling. On driving to our appointment each time he would inevitably be delayed, having experienced visions en route of having hit a pedestrian or cyclist with his van. Sometimes he would detour back around the entire one-way system just to check if the police were there or to see if there was a body on the ground. In actuality, he had never hit anyone.

Drive had recently left the Army having served a tour of duty in Afghanistan where a traumatic driving experience seemed to point toward the source of his distress. He had been driving a jeep with an officer and another soldier as his passengers. They were involved in an accident with another vehicle but fortunately Drive's speedy reactions saved his passengers from serious injury (or death), himself escaping with minor injuries. He was treated as something of a hero by his military buddies during the days following the accident. Here it seemed was the source of the driving fears. Yet he had responded quickly and calmly, his presence of mind having averted any serious harm. He was a hero for a day or two yet he carried fear back into civilian life. There were no other traumatic experiences in his tour and he never fired his weapon or experienced combat at any point.

The trauma signature in the natal chart shows a problem with beliefs – the way that meaning is ascribed to what has occurred (Uranus-Jupiter in Sagittarius in the 3rd house). Furthermore with the square to his Venus-Mars conjunction in Virgo in the 12th house we can see that he has internalized persecutory and critical messages on a deep unconscious level. He had experienced intense criticism in the past. His will (Mars) needed to create crisis (Virgo) in order to experience his deep feelings of inadequacy (Venus Virgo). In so doing he gained the potential to understand them.

With the evidence in the natal chart and the incongruity between his successfully negotiated trauma and his fierce hallucinations (Mars 12th house), I was alert to further layers unfolding regarding the experience he was having.

In *Waking the Tiger,* Peter A. Levine links trauma to an organism's incapacity to complete its survival response. Incompleteness leaves the body-mind in a state of excited suspension which becomes exhaustive to the entire system, initiating a vicious cycle whereby the self constantly recalls the stimulus (the traumatic event) without ever being able to bring the cycle, or gestalt to completion. Levine writes:

A maladaptive response to a life-threatening event never completes itself. An example of this is when the nervous system unceasingly and unsuccessfully searches for appropriate responses. As it fails to find this critical information, the emotions of rage, terror, and helplessness escalate. This escalation spurs further activation and compels the search for significant images. Since the images it finds are associated with traumatic emotions, the images themselves may evoke further activation without supplying the appropriate response to complete the process…the result is a continuing and ever-escalating spiral in which we search for images…all of the images are related to highly aroused, similar emotional states, but are not necessarily useful to our survival at that moment. They are the fuel of the 'trauma vortex.'[11]

I knew that Drive needed to delve deeper into his own "trauma vortex." His trauma signature refers to the importance of his beliefs (Uranus-Jupiter), and of messages that he had taken into himself (Mars-Venus Virgo) of disempowerment on a deep unconscious level (12th house). So I asked about them, using the invitational approach.

Drive remembered his struggles in school to conceptualize information in a linear form (Uranus-Jupiter in Sagittarius in the 3rd house). His dyslexia resulted in him being placed in the lowest class and held back academically. He remembered an experience as a young boy when play-fighting with his younger sister over a small toy which, by complete accident got thrown, chipping his sister's tooth. His father stormed into the room hearing the younger girl crying and began to beat his son as punishment. The father did not believe Drive's insistence of his good intentions (Uranus-Jupiter, trauma from not being believed, in the 3rd house – the sibling, the words spoken). Instead he beat Drive savagely using verbal persecutory messages saying that he "was a piece of shit and would amount to nothing."

Later when Drive was given extra tuition due to his dyslexia and began to thrive, his shamed father canceled it. It was revealed that the father had learning difficulties for which he was vilified and beaten. He passed this experience on to his son (Sun-Pluto-Saturn in Libra/Scorpio in the 2nd house). This was the source of the rage which erupted from father to son, since Drive was blameless. He had internalized a disconnection between what he was doing and the resulting intense punishment. He was doing nothing wrong, yet he was beaten and traumatized.

In the stressful situation in Afghanistan Drive also did nothing wrong. On the contrary, he did something good. But he internalized a residual shame and anxiety about some kind of comeback or punishment that would befall him. Even though he had succeeded in saving people, in reality he felt that he might fail now while driving and actually cost someone's life.

I did not explore this experientially through regression work, but we can see that with Uranus conjunct Jupiter, and with Jupiter the ruler of the South Node of the Moon, and also conjunct the South Node, that we're looking at the repeat of a series of prior-life experiences in which Drive was falsely blamed for something that he had done in good conscience.

We can also see issues in Drive's chart about speaking out. With the 3rd house square to the 12th house, we can see that over a number of lifetimes, he had been silenced from speaking and was carrying the impact of events as a powerful series of fearful visions. Drive had been punished, imprisoned and in all likelihood killed (Venus rules the 2nd house of survival, square to Uranus trauma signature) repeatedly for his struggle to articulate his experience, the misperception of others and their subsequent persecution of him for being stupid, worthless or different.

Peter Levine's concept of the trauma vortex consists of many layers, of which the incident in the jeep and the beating by his father were but the first couple in Drive's case. The investigation of these first layers gave Drive a context for understanding his hallucinatory experiences on the road and offered a glimmer of hope that the light of such awareness might end his nightmare.

Trauma and the Imagination

Drive experienced a compulsive grasping for images during extreme stress situations. The images conflated driving with violent beatings. This rush of imagery within the traumatic moment exemplifies the Uranus archetype as a sudden event in consciousness – the "need to have a whole picture immediately."[12] This reveals the limitations of the extant ego structure (Moon) and thinking processes of conscious memory (Mercury) such that attempts to create security for the individual based on their conscious prior experiences are doomed to failure. Ironically this failure itself fuels the trauma vortex.

Levine suggests that healing the trauma demands its recreation. This re-experiencing carries a symbolic charge that can be extraordinarily powerful. The psyche is thus able to complete the cycle of response in order to liberate itself from the trapped emotions, inducing a feeling of psychic descent into the plug-hole of entropy.

However, it is not necessary to literally undergo the trauma again. Levine writes, "When we don't become invested in finding a literal truth, we remain free to experience the full and compassionate healing afforded by the rhythmic exchange between the trauma and healing vortices that occur in renegotiation."[13]

In utilizing the imagination – the creative aspect of an individual's will – we are able to generate a "healing fiction" (to borrow a phrase from James Hillman) in which the polarity of the trauma vortex is reversed into an integrative flow. This is one of the critical potentials of Evolutionary Astrology – that through its symbolism we are able to regain our vitality, strength and resourcefulness in understanding the trauma anew and completing what we previously could not.

Levine places a Jungian emphasis on the process of active imagination in which the individual is able to process trauma through internal dialogue, imaginative journeying and/or path-working. This approach is sympathetic to our understanding of the *Evolutionary Axis* as a living symbolism operating within (yet transcendent of) space and time which assists us in visualizing an intended path of evolution for an individual.

The astrology reading can constitute a form of path-working whereby astrologer and client co-create an imaginal space in order to elucidate the potentialities latent within the natal chart.

The Road to Healing

When trauma signatures are found in the chart, we might consider using regression work and psychotherapy to make the most of the trauma-potential paradox of Uranus/Aquarius. Many techniques can be profoundly healing, including the Deep Memory Process (developed by Roger Woolger and practiced in conjunction with Evolutionary Astrology by Patricia Walsh), Alchemical Hypnotherapy, and Psychosynthesis Therapy. Hypnotherapeutic induction and/or the facilitation of encounters with the higher self can enhance connection with the material under consideration. The approach of reliving and re-contextualizing previously traumatic events presents an opportunity to liberate the client from being further impacted by them.

The astrology reading is, at its best, both an identification of the relevant dynamics and a first step toward healing. It affords the client access to a painful past in a way that is both compassionate and hopeful – the very same signatures that depict trauma also contain an implicit message of liberation.

Alongside on-going therapeutic work, counseling or the above-mentioned regression methods, the client may enter a relationship with their own process that is enlivened by the understanding catalyzed by Evolutionary Astrology. Future psychotherapies could gain much from this form of astrology, just as astrologers still have much to usefully integrate from the advances of depth psychology in the twentieth century.

Trauma and the Psyche's Defense System

> When Innocence has been deprived of its entitlement, it becomes a diabolical spirit.
> - Donald Kalsched

In *The Inner World of Trauma: Archetypal Defenses of the Personal Spirit*, Donald Kalsched argues that trauma tends to provoke a series of defense mechanisms in the psyche which subsequently become hyper-vigilant and can damage the nascent identity of the individual they are designed to protect.[14] The idea is that the trauma does not produce the defense mechanism, because it is already present.

This is the Saturn structure, a defense mechanism that is innate to the psyche. Through Kalsched's work, what Levine calls the trauma vortex is exposed in part as an aggressive and chaotic element of the psyche's self-protection, a component of the Saturn defense structure run amok.

Just as some immune system disorders and forms of cancer can force the body's own defense mechanisms into an over proliferation which then threatens the body's integrity, so a traumatizing event symbolized by Uranus can push the Saturn defense system into a form of overdrive which exacerbates and perpetuates the trauma. In cases like this, the Saturnian defense system becomes a disruptive and dissociative element of the psyche which sabotages attempts at healing. The paradox, as Kalsched explores, is that the internal defense mechanism becomes as destructive as the impact of the original event:

> Most contemporary analytic writers are inclined to see this attacking figure as an internalized version of the actual perpetrator of the trauma, who has 'possessed' the inner world of the trauma victim. But this popularized view is only half correct. The diabolical figure is often far more sadistic and brutal than any outer perpetrator, indicating that we are dealing with a *psychological* factor set loose in the inner world by trauma – an archetypal traumatogenic agency within the psyche itself.
>
> No matter how frightening his or her brutality, the function of this ambivalent caretaker always seems to be the protection of the traumatized remainder of the personal spirit and its *isolation from reality*. It functions, if we can imagine its inner rationale, as a kind of inner 'Jewish Defense League' (whose slogan after the Holocaust, reads 'Never Again!'). 'Never again,' says our tyrannical caretaker, 'will the traumatized personal spirit of this child suffer this badly! Never again will it be this helpless in the face of cruel reality...before this happens I will disperse it into fragments (disassociation), or encapsulate it and soothe it with fantasy (schizoid withdrawal), or numb it with intoxicating substances (addiction), or persecute it to keep it from hoping for life in this world (depression)...

In this way I will preserve what is left of this prematurely
amputated childhood – of an innocence that has suffered
too much too soon!'[15]

The archetype of Saturn the protector is transformed by the
Uranus event into a tyrant.

The Power of Astrology and the Path to Healing

Many of us are drawn to astrology to answer questions about our
lives, to engage with our potential and to explore the symbolism of
our life path. It is because of this visionary aspect of astrology and
its unusual and cultish status in our present culture that astrologers
tend to be optimistic. Those who do readings tend to be inspired by
a sense of possibility, the potential that could be actualized through
understanding the natal chart. I am one of these people.

Yet for the last ten years, I have worked with people who are
sincere about their desire for self-actualization but who at times
seem in desperate contention with inner forces that are resistant to
change. These can be explored using both astrological and therapeutic symbolism. And while I cannot claim to have thoroughly
integrated the powerful crossover potential between astrology
and psychotherapy, I have some initial observations and working
knowledge I want to share.

One level of resistance people face as they work on themselves
is symbolized by the Pluto placement – the intense unconscious attraction to a certain mode of self-understanding and expression.
I've found it powerful to relate all subsequent astrological insights
to this central compulsion – the orientation of the soul to a certain
way of experiencing reality over multiple lifetimes.

As seen in the case studies I've presented thus far, sometimes
the chart uncovers work for which longer-term healing work is indicated. We've seen that the Saturn archetype includes a defense
system that, when gone awry, can find people turning on themselves with more consistent brutality than their abusers did.

As a therapist working with traumatized individuals over
many thousands of hours I have repeatedly experienced the capacity of the individual psyche to torture, punish and demonize itself
for the very things that hurt it so much. In long-term therapy fo-

cused around recovery of traumatized aspects of identity, this destructive capacity cannot be allowed either to overwhelm the work or to be ignored.

Hypnotherapy and regression work can provide essential support in clearing prior-life traumatic memories but are not in themselves sufficient to resolve the infection of the psyche's internal ordering system (Saturn) by the trauma virus (Uranus). This kind of healing requires rapport with a person in the current life who can support the individual as they temporarily dismantle their own defenses in order to build them up again on more solid foundations. This requires an act of will in the form of conscious intention and alliance between therapist/astrological counselor and client.

The internal workings of the psyche are reflected in the mirror of the therapeutic alliance. The persecutory aspect of the distorted Saturn principle can play out safely in the counselor-client relationship where steps can be taken towards understanding and healing it. In therapeutic work this can involve a significant commitment over years. In our contemporary cultural context of quick fixes, this may seem like a long time, but it is a comparatively short one from the perspective of the soul and the countless prior lifetimes it has undergone.

How this more long-term dynamic might be identified and addressed in a one-off natal reading is a matter of personal taste and capacity.

Every astrologer should be in a position to refer clients to a good psychotherapist for further exploration of issues emergent from a natal reading which are too demanding, problematic and/or involved for a single session to address. Those with therapeutic qualifications or who are developing an astrological counseling practice may wish to offer time-limited follow-up sessions for this purpose. To offer more than that outside of licensed therapeutic practice, I suggest that one should have some understanding and experience of the major personality disorders and of core transference and counter-transference dynamics.

Childhood and Karma

We are most prone to the threat of non-being in our early childhood relationships (what psychology terms object relations) and any prolonged breakdown in these relationships will engender a lasting imprint of fear around this perceived lack of identity or inner void. It is my opinion that these early childhood conditions in which we do not seem to enjoy conscious choice are in fact a playing-out of prior karma. And in a sense the extremely powerful emotional and psychic states that a child undergoes at this time hold memories and traces of these prior karmas. In this way the child's fear of non-being (emergent when the primary caregivers are absent or unsympathetic) mirrors prior-life fears, compulsions and dependencies. As every parent will attest, children are not blank slates but complex, layered identities each with their own unique quality often apparent from birth (which itself illustrates the central premise of astrology that we are born at the precise moment when the movements of the heavens mirror our karma).

To fully appreciate the radical conflux of depth psychology and Evolutionary Astrology is to enter a territory wherein underlying prior-life traumas are a critical issue. This is not a stance that mainstream psychotherapy has been moved to adopt. Many of psychology's greatest thinkers have neglected to explore the idea of prior lives as an idea, or as a potential originator of experience. This is in contrast to my own psychotherapy practice in which I have experienced numerous clients entering spontaneous prior-life recall.

To really begin to get to grips with the complexity of what might be going on between prior-life karma and early childhood experience, we will have to integrate and utilize tools from a number of disciplines, including depth psychology, astrology, hypnotherapy, regression work, and the great spiritual teachings of the world. In the interface of these different traditions lies the thread of a psychology and astrology of the future.

Chapter 4

Putting It All Together: Evolutionary Astrology Step-By-Step

When studying charts it can be very useful to separate the core components to be analyzed so that they are not lost within the mass of symbols and information within the chart. In the following case study analysis we will take a closer look at the core elements of the chart as we have been exploring them throughout this book so that you might begin to organize the material in a cohesive manner.

When it comes to our analysis there is the question of which to prioritize: house, sign or planet? While I see an archetypal equivalence in terms of meaning between a planet and the house and sign it rules, for the start of my analysis I proceed in the order of planet, house and sign. I start with the planet Pluto as the defining signature of deep psychological orientation. I then move to the house. Since the planet Pluto is a generational signature, the house placement represents the unique expression of Pluto for the individual in question. I then move to the sign, which brings in further information about how we interact with and respond to the generational archetype.

It must be remembered throughout such example charts that all the symbolism within the natal chart needs to be related back to the consciousness of the individual whose chart it is, and their life experience. No amount of astrological ability or technical mastery will compensate for connection to the individual. These symbols remain a wonderful detailed set of potentials and possibilities arising out of the symbolism of the chart. These potentials are confirmed or become actualities through the actual experience of being open to the energetic reality of the person before you.

Case Study: Flo
Flo, April 8 1965, Bromley, UK 8:20 am (00E02, 51N24)

Figure 7. *Flo's Natal Chart.*

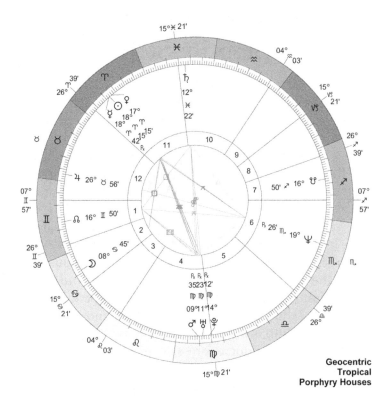

Step One: The Pluto Placement By House

Always start your analysis by examining Pluto by house and sign. In Flo's case, we see Pluto in the 4th house in Virgo (see fig. 7). With Pluto in the 4th house we combine the archetypes of Scorpio and Cancer, the deepest unconscious security (Pluto) of the individual is operating on the level of the emotional imprinting of early childhood (Moon) and the formation of the conditioned self. Here we see the potential for compulsive or unresolved emotional and psychological material from prior lives and from deep within the unconscious (Pluto) to play out within the family home (4th house).

Underlying this position is the need to transform (Pluto) the pre-existing conditioning and sense of personal security (4th house). Always with Pluto in the 4th house there will be a need to explore the nature of personal security and how much of that security is based on dependent relationships with others, particularly family members. This issue of dependency will have originated in prior life emotional entanglements (Pluto) in which the individual has projected all their personal safety needs onto others (4th house/ Moon) with very mixed results. There is a bottom line intention (Pluto) to explore the nature of these personal security attachments (4th house) in order to limit excessive dependency and heal negative past experiences.

What are the ways in which such prior dependency could have played out? As one possibility, we can consider the universal experience that people we depend upon let us down. Pluto relates to betrayal fears based on unconscious security needs. The conditioned self represented by the Moon is also sensitive to security issues. To clarify the difference between the two, the conditioned self (ego) is afraid of change, of having its personal routines and agendas influenced in a primarily conscious fashion. These are concerns that can be articulated about the nature of one's environment, whether that is safe and secure and will provide emotionally for the individual. Betrayal is then a seeming act of rebellion against those needs, a conscious experience of becoming unsafe.

When Pluto is involved, one betrayal represents all the times the person has ever been betrayed; one present loss becomes archetypal. It is this degree of intensity that can make its impact on people's lives both so profound and potentially so damaging.

Feelings of betrayal may originate in the intense feeling of disappointment and loss in an individual who feels let down by another (who may or may not have intended that). Betrayal can be intentional, non-intentional, or occupy the grey area in between. In many ways the source does not matter since the pain any kind of loss causes is real pain. But when it comes to recovery and to an increased acceptance of reality it is important to gain clarity about the actual wounding experience. Ultimately in the healing process there is only a choice between acceptance and non-acceptance of what has occurred. Understanding why things have happened is important to people at this level of integration. Astrological analysis can really help people at this stage.

To clarify the levels of this experience let's consider a hypothetical example of a woman with a Pluto 4th house/Cancer. Her mother has a problem: through some failure to individuate, some flaw in her own self-awareness, she did not realize the needs of her daughter or the impact of her actions. The mother's stress impacted her daughter through diminished care for her. The Pluto level then operates by resonance – this particular child has incarnated with repeat memories of being isolated or left abandoned and the deep unconscious structures of the identity formed within childhood contain this hidden strata of meaning. It is this level of prior experience that brings an extra (Plutonian) emphasis, an extra power to the maybe relatively ordinary experience of a mother misunderstanding or misrepresenting the daughter.

This does not require regression work to explore. I have shared a good deal of regression work in the previous parts of this book in order to illustrate the experiential truth of this kind of prior life analysis. However most of my work, both as a psychotherapist and an astrologer does not involve regression work. This is because the early childhood experience of the individual and the patterns in their relationships can be used like Ariadne's thread to follow to the heart of the labyrinth, the core of their past material. From people's personal experience in this life we can trace back the archetypal resonances that underpin that experience in prior lives. Profound healing work can be undertaken in this way.

In exploring this theme of the subtle but profound distinction between the level of security (primarily conscious) impacted upon by the Moon, Cancer and the 4th house and by the level (primarily unconscious) represented by Pluto, Scorpio and the 8th house I'm making both a general point about how to read charts and also pointing out the level of depth that can be revealed in just the house and sign of a particular Pluto placement. In this case, the 4th house suggests that difficulties with one or both of the parents may be just the tip of the iceberg – the parents acting as a trigger for feelings, memories and struggles of much deeper and longer lasting origin. Looked at in this way the difficulties with the family of origin become an opportunity for the individual to break free of long-standing past patterns, the stress involved becoming a catalyst to examine the nature of personal dependencies in order to reduce their negative impact.

Another potential with any strong emphasis of Cancer/4th house or Capricorn/10th house is that of gender identity issues. There could be a basic confusion about gender identity, a rejection of conventional gender values, a recent gender switch (from previous life to this one) or suffering due prior or current life judgments about what it means to be a particular gender.

Step 2: Pluto Placement By Sign

Next we consider the sign Pluto is in. How does Pluto being in Virgo add to our understanding? Virgo as an archetype corresponds to the need to analyze experience and to critique any excessive egocentricity, even to humble the self to better understand how to serve. Virgo represents the need to discriminate between all the information gathered in the more out-going Gemini expression of Mercury. Through this internalizing of the mental life the Virgo archetype is very sensitive to the kinds of messages that we receive from others – what psychotherapists call introjects. Introjects are internalized messages that imply value statements about the person.

With the tendency in the Virgo archetype to seek to overcome egotism through self-analysis and humility, a key problem is the tendency to be overly prone to negative introjects, internalizing negative messages from others. Some of these messages are overt. But they can also be covert. A child might internalize messages that her emotions are wrong or bad as the result of a primary caregiver routinely failing to meet her emotional needs. Unfortunately, a child doesn't possess the skills to objectively evaluate this experience, and instead can infer that she is the cause of her maltreatment. It is the lingering roots of these feelings that can see children painfully blame themselves when their parents have relationship problems or get divorced.

Psychoanalyst Melanie Klein's work has focused on this dilemma faced by the child: when things go wrong who is at fault?[1] To the Pluto in Virgo consciousness, so sensitive to internalized negative thoughts and feelings, this is a very important question. In order to save mother from a total association with the negative, Klein sees the child as psychologically splitting the experience of mother into one good breast that provides and one bad one that withholds. If the child can hold this split it can lead to the crucial insight that Klein named the "depressive position" which corresponds to the realization that mother is neither Angel nor Devil, merely human. She who withholds also provides.

This adaptation in thinking is critical in order for one to feel a healthy correspondence to reality. But if the primary caregiver is genuinely struggling or falling apart, and the child's experience of withholding considerably outweighs her experience of providing, an imbalance in the child's response is likely. The Pluto in Virgo child (or child with Virgo emphasis under stress in the natal chart) is particularly susceptible to this kind of internalization: I am bad, it is my fault. This often leads to a legacy of guilt, and the potential towards taking excessive responsibility for the difficulties in one's life.

Such guilt within the Pluto in Virgo consciousness can lead to a psychology of masochism, whereby the individual is attracting certain situations and internal states that are self-punishing in order to atone for, or ameliorate the internal guilt. This mind is often filled with repetitive negative messages running like a tape loop that are easily triggered by negative accusations and internal processes of judgment. When this foundation of guilt is allied with cold or invasive parenting and prior-life trauma, this internal dilemma can be of sufficient intensity to cause personality disorders (as was the case with Kay from the earlier chapter who had been diagnosed Borderline Personality Disorder). In other cases while there may not be clinical intervention, the anxiety and hallucinatory feeling of self-failure will be at the root of much personal suffering.

In all likelihood when this individual is under stress (and therefore reminded of any childhood deprivation or prior life dependency/betrayal/abandonment) they will tend towards emotionally dominating their environments since these unconscious forces emanate powerful waves into their surroundings. They may try to control situations or people around them or take the more passive approach of emotionally acting out in the hopes that others respond.

With Pluto in Virgo there is a need to explore the issue of right work. Deep down the individual seeks to serve the community or the larger social world. With Pluto in the 4th house, events in the early home-life of the individual may shape psychological habits and routines that play out in the workplace. Or the parents may have influenced (directed or thwarted) the career path in some critical fashion. It would be surprising if this individual did not carry some sense of burden or responsibility from the family life into the workplace.

Many students of this method want to rush on to the rest of the chart but I always encourage them to stay with the core symbolism of the Pluto placement for as long as possible in order to create as deep a set of potentialities as can be for the individual in question. By exploring the rest of the chart and through dialogue with the client we can then narrow our focus to the most relevant potentials. But it's important at the beginning to start with a wide net of possibility so that nothing is missed. A deep exploration of the Pluto material leads us to the questions we wish to ask of the chart and the client.

Step 3: Any Planets Conjunct Pluto?

The next step in our analysis is to consider any planets conjunct Pluto, which add further detail to our understanding of the core (Pluto) issues. While I am teaching a methodology, I personally try to carry it loosely, the method as scaffolding for my intuition and insight rather than dominating it. In the end, it is just important that you consider all of the necessary elements in your analysis. Don't get too hung up on the order or the method, especially if it feels limiting.

In Flo's chart with Uranus conjunct Pluto we see a trauma signature (as previously explained in the chapter on Uranus). This adds to our analysis the element of past mental (Uranus) and psychological (Pluto) trauma relative to the 4th house and Virgo. This makes it explicit that there are underlying prior life memories of abandonment and loss of personal security (4th house), betrayal and core fear (Pluto) and disassociation or loss of the capacity to mentally cope (Uranus) with the events that occurred. The nature of Flo's traumatic memories are implied by our in-depth analysis of the Pluto placement, which now becomes a matter of emphasis – the Uranus conjunction showing increased likelihood of mentally scarring events. So there will have been core lack of safety in prior-life families (and also likely in the current family) that led to a sense of breakdown or fracturing instead of safety or love.

Uranus under stress (here conjunct Pluto and Mars) in the 4th house or with the Moon/Cancer can indicate damage to the emotional body in prior lives of such significance that it is held in the subtle mind, or long-term memory. These traumatic memories will be of sufficient 'charge' to magnetize relationships and events around the individual in order to expose the latent damage. This damage may have involved experiences where the person was separated forcefully from the family, separated far too young from the parents (leading to profound separation anxiety) and/or systematically undermined within the family. With Pluto conjunct Uranus the likelihood is that these kinds of experiences have been repeated over lifetimes. As a result, they may have now reached a fever pitch of intensity.

That Uranus is in the 4th house with Pluto emphasizes the importance of any gender issues underlying the prior life and current life experience. The trauma signature makes clear that to the extent this person has experienced judgment or repression because of gender, or has experienced confusion themselves through their gender orientation, that these experiences have had traumatic outcomes.

That Mars is conjunct Uranus and Pluto adds that these traumatic memories within the families of origin, or tribe or society in which the individual lived involved an undermining of their instinctual body, their physical will. This in itself will have included violent or suppressive experiences that left the person physically restricted or confined in some fundamental way. There is potential rage buried within relative to how their instinctual desires have been thwarted by prior experiences.

Step 4: The Nodal Axis and Squares to the Nodes

As we reach this point in our analysis and look to the South Node of the Moon *we already have many questions to bring to our inquiry.* For instance, what if any information can we discover about Flo's experiences of being restricted or thwarted in self-expression? In what ways were Flo's current family (or prior-life families) experienced as unsafe or abandoning? In what way did her primary caregiver (usually the mother) express a profound dilemma to the child in this life? In what way was Flo overly dependent on others in the past that left them feeling profoundly misunderstood? In what way does she need to remove conditions of external dependency in order to feel more truly individuated? What, if any, traumatic gender issues or experiences took place in the past?

Flo's South Node of the Moon is in Sagittarius in the 7th house. Before considering the nodal meaning specifically, it is important to look for any planets in a square aspect to the nodes, as those planets are crucial in the analysis. In Flo's chart, we notice her Mars-Uranus-Pluto conjunction in the 4th house in Virgo is square to the nodes. This square adds to our analysis that the Mars-Uranus-Pluto placement represents a skipped step in evolutionary terms. These issues have somehow thwarted the movement from the South Node to the North Node in the past. So this adds even more emphasis to Flo's Pluto placement! The resolution of the issues symbolized by the Mars-Uranus-Pluto conjunction are of central importance, as they represent a missing link in Flo's past development. Something has tripped her up, profoundly delaying her growth or aspirations in the past.

With Pluto square the nodal axis of the Moon we can recognize a signature that speaks of the profundity of the fork in the road that the soul, or deep self, has come to in its development. The choices Flo makes in this life are ever more important as they represent a dilemma that has been building over multiple lifetimes that is now seeking resolution. Through understanding the symbolism of the South Node of the Moon through the lens of Pluto we can begin to understand the nature of these choices.

Flo's South Node of the Moon is in the 7th house, emphasizing the issues of dependency that we have already explored by adding relevance to their impact on her later adult relationships. Psychologically, the events of Flo's early childhood experience will potentially play out in challenging ways as her displaced childhood feelings overwhelm her adult relationships.

I will point out here that everyone experiences a degree of transference, of the projection of early material, onto adult partners or close friends. The difference here is one of emphasis. With this particular chart signature we can infer that a profound lack of safety, anger and confusion from childhood will impact with unusual severity on Flo's adult relationships. Going further, Flo's prior life relationships (7th house) have somehow trapped her will (Mars square), frustrated and fractured her emotional body (Uranus square) and led to profound insecurity and crisis coupled with a deep need to transform these feelings (Pluto in 4th house Virgo square the South Node of the Moon).

History has not been kind to the feminine aspect. Western civilization was built on a pyramid model of power in the hands of the few (primarily men) and with an underclass of slavery and very limited options for women. In Greek and Roman cultures (the forerunners of modern democracies), slavery and the lack of women's socio-political power were simply societal givens. Equality was understood to only apply, even in principle, to a select few. So being female, how might Flo's 4th house Pluto-Uranus-Mars in Virgo emphasis play out through the 7th house South Node of the Moon? This could represent arranged marriage, or of marriages that favored the social or material standing of the family but that were intensely personally restrictive to her. In the Venus/Libra/7th house archetypes we see a resonance with all cultures that have practiced this kind of approach to marriage.

Other potential traumatic memories that can be signified by Flo's Pluto-Uranus-Mars conjunction (in square to the nodal axis) include the disturbingly common cultural practice of extensive dowry requirements, of female infanticide, and the pressure to have children to provide the labor required to meet survival needs.[2] These experiences can directly relate to a lack of safety within the home, and can represent a fundamental rejection of the instinctive will for a woman caught in the crossfire of such expectations. We can further imagine that a woman in one of these situations might experience a complete humiliation of the egoic will or the value of her individual as a possible expression of the Virgo trauma signature.

By holding this level of underlying karmic material in mind, and by (potentially) relaying it to the client, we are able to help, if necessary, to contextualize the difficult childhood experiences and high levels of internal anxiety that this individual will have experienced. This represents one of the greatest gifts of this work, and can activate a profound healing process for the individual in question. Further, when space is meaningfully held, detailed information from the field can be intuited and communicated to the client, heightening the experience of the reading and increasing the potential for meaningful exchange. It is important to stay curious and inquisitive throughout the entire process to receive such information, which often becomes apparent through synchronicity and/or grace. It is a good practice to ask the client to pay attention to thoughts that arise during the reading, and to note their responses in the digestion period following the reading – recording their thoughts, feelings and dreams over the coming days for important details that come into awareness.

The link between the 4th and 7th houses in Flo's chart also suggests struggles between her family of origin and prospective partners. Perhaps the family rejected her partner or acted destructively towards the unwanted partner. We can also consider the possibility that because of the lack of safety in the family, Flo attracts partners who act more like de facto parents than intimate equals. These kinds of partners infantilize Flo, keeping her in a regressed state of emotional expression.

Remember that Libra as an archetype is learning balance, so it often expresses itself in extremes. The individual with a strong Libra signature may fluctuate wildly between excessive dependency and then long periods of isolation from others to protect the part that can become over dependent. This swinging back and forth can be as problematic as excessive proximity or prolonged isolation.

With the link between the 7th and 4th houses and the Virgo emphasis there may be a strong tendency towards playing the role of peacemaker in the family, or a situation where Flo sacrificed her own needs in order to protect a weak parent. This may have led to feeling responsible for the extra burden of holding the family together to ensure her own survival. With the South Node of the Moon in the 7th house and Pluto in the 4th house we can be sure that her desire to remove all unnecessary and restrictive external dependencies (Pluto 4th) includes long-term patterns of suspending her personal will (Mars-Pluto) to her partner – a pattern that she is now seeking to bring to an end (the square to the nodal axis).

The evolutionary need for Flo to choose her individual will over controlling or dependent relationships is clear from the way in which the three skipped steps (Pluto, Uranus and Mars) integrate via the 1st house North Node. When we have squares to the nodal axis of the Moon in the natal chart, the unresolved material integrates through the node that last transited the position of the skipped steps, in Flo's case, the North Node at 15 Gemini. Just to repeat from the earlier chapter for clarity: Due to the retrograde motion of the nodal axis of the Moon the last node that was transited by the planet(s) squaring can be hard to calculate. An easy and practical way to find the resolution node is to visualize standing on the place of the skipped steps, (in this case 9-14 degrees Virgo) and to look into the middle of the circle of the chart and then turn to the left. The node that you see there is the integrating node.

One paradox of planets square the nodes is that they suggest that the North Node of the Moon is like the South Node as well, because the North Node must have been developed somewhat in the past. But the individual didn't fully integrate the North Node due to being tripped up over the material contained within the symbolism of the planets squaring the nodal axis, the skipped steps. In our example it is clear that in the past that Flo took steps to express her individuality and instinctual freedom to become who she really felt she was at a gut level. But unresolved anger, hurt, traumatic memories and judgmental, repressive or problematic experiences from within her family and relationships held her back.

Moving now explicitly to the South Node, what extra information can we find from its position in Sagittarius? To start, we can see that the potential issues or conflicts Flo experienced both within intimate relationships, and within the family center around her beliefs, and in particular her personal vision of meaning, religious worldview or conception of personal freedom. This includes the possible influence of dominant religious and cultural beliefs about right behavior, dress and modes of expressing intimacy. We can guess that cultural and religious clashes (South Node Sagittarius) over the rights of women, over notions of personal freedom in relationship (South Node 7th house) are likely to have been involved in the struggle for independent validation. It is likely that restrictive religious/cultural conditioning within the family and with partnerships has restricted personal development to an extraordinary or dramatic degree (noted by the trauma signature across the nodal axis from Uranus with Mars-Pluto square the nodal axis).

Flo will have had many different prior life experiences of different cultures and different cultural and religious customs (South Node Sagittarius, and North Node in Gemini acting as a de facto South Node because of the skipped steps). This is in part because of a strong personal leaning towards understanding life in all its variety and richness, but also includes a strong potential search for freedom, meaning and faith (nodes Sagittarius/Gemini). It is possible that the natural insight, integrity and intuitive understanding possible for Flo (South Node Sagittarius) was very difficult to communicate within the family home (South Node Square 4th house Pluto-Uranus-Mars) and this left her feeling inferior (Virgo) or vulnerable (Pluto 4th house). Sometimes individuals with signatures of this kind of prior cultural difference, allied to radical insecurity and alienation, find themselves as small children imagining themselves to be adopted or to have come from another land.

Through the South Node in Sagittarius we see the potential for feeling alien within one's intimate relationships, family or culture because of memories of very different cultural contexts that are very close to the surface of consciousness. With the Uranus square to the nodes we can see that these memories of different cultural expressions may have produced very traumatic feelings of alienation or disassociation from the current cultural context. This signature can also include prior-life memories of being uprooted from home and forced into a radically different cultural sphere. The individual may be very sensitive therefore to disruptions within the home, or to foreign environments and the level of safety they afford.

With the South Node of the Moon in the 7th house we have an issue around expectations in relationship (the 1st house being the instinctual self, the 7th the relational self, or persona) and we can expect to see strong expectations placed on others. In this case we see those expectations colored by the projected idealism that relationships should be a shared journey marked by optimism and faith (Sagittarius).

In Flo's chart we have one more square to consider as Saturn in Pisces squares the nodes from the 10th house. Here you may note that we started by considering one square, then integrated the South Node, and now we are considering the second square. This is an example of how the order in which you consider these variables may differ from chart to chart. Use your intuition here. Just make sure to integrate every variable. You may find that mixing up the order in which you integrate items gives you additional information or insight.

With the Saturn square we can see that at times the reality of Flo's relationships has been more restrictive. Although entered into with the hope of shared adventure, Flo's relationships actually led to a prison of disappointment (Saturn square the South Node) as partners were more judgmental and controlling than she would have ever dreamed possible. Saturn represents condemning behavior from others, and the square to the South Node in Sagittarius suggests Flo's naivety about this. These dynamics are the source of profound emotional frustration (Pluto square nodes and opposite Saturn), inner disintegration (Uranus square) and resentment (Mars square). These broken expectations as others fail to live up to the potential imagined by Flo become their own kind of betrayal and the resulting disillusionment re-emphasizes the evolutionary need for Flo to develop primary security from within.

Step 5: The Ruler of the South Node

We look to the ruler of the South Node of the Moon to express more about the nature of the past experiences. In this case, Flo's South Node ruler is Jupiter in Taurus in the 12th house.

Here we see that one of Flo's traumatic memories of being uprooted from home and placed into a radically different cultural sphere may have occurred through slavery. Neptune, Pisces and the 12th house are key signature in slavery because of the archetypal resonance with mass cultural experiences of disempowerment, sacrifice and surrender. The opposition of Jupiter to Neptune in Scorpio in the 6th house emphasizes the signature as we'll see.

With Jupiter in Taurus there may be memories of having struggled materially, or because of disempowering environments (such as being a slave) and Flo may have experienced life as being of little value or faced a struggle to survive on a material level. In the 12th house such a signature may represent deep fears, or dream/nightmares of poverty or a fear of a return to these previous experiences (12th house Jupiter in opposition to Neptune).

When Neptune is in Scorpio and is in stressful aspect to Pluto or the nodes of the Moon or their rulers, or is in a trauma signature with Uranus it can often be an indication of a core experience of betrayal. The potential for betrayal is there in the Pluto-Uranus placement and is now echoed by Neptune in the 6th house (the 6th house repeating the Virgo signature). Flo has experienced core betrayals in the past (Pluto/Scorpio), has felt deeply humiliated and undermined by this (6th house/Virgo) and has experienced a resulting material (Taurus) and existential struggle (Jupiter) to survive.

When we look at charts using this technique we can get insight that transcends typical astrological practice. Isolating Flo's Jupiter in the 12th house, we can find plenty of astrology cookbooks that describe this placement as showing an innate faith, or a protective guardian angel experience. In fact this may well be the case, however it is not necessarily Flo's dominant inner experience. Through the South Node Sagittarius and its ruler Jupiter there is perhaps a natural faith in Flo. But the irony here is that she is just as likely to have periods of radical insecurity, fear the breakdown of the personality structure (Pluto-Uranus 4th house) and fear a return to a situation of poverty (Jupiter in Taurus) and core disempowerment (South Node ruler in the 12th house opposite Neptune in Scorpio).

Step 6: Deeper Integration

Now that we've looked at the major components of our analysis, we can revisit some of the components, fleshing out deeper meaning in the context of the whole.

The Saturn skipped step indicates that struggles with consensus values and conditioning have dominated prior relationships and the struggle to individuate. There may be a profound sensitivity to the nature of judgments, about self or others and a tendency to carry a subconscious guilt. We can see a potential for a strong karmic link to the father in the current life as someone who shared prior life experience.

Saturn as a skipped step integrates via the **South Node** in Flo's chart and as such represents a need to go back into the past in order to reclaim something that was lost. The Saturn placement describes the nature of what needs to be reclaimed by returning to the past and the approach to relationship (South Node 7th house).

In this complicated signature, we have 2 skipped steps, each integrating via opposite nodes. The Pluto-Uranus-Mars skipped steps need to integrate through the North Node while the Saturn skipped step integrates via the South Node. The 1st house/7th house axis is then implicated as primary to Flo's evolutionary journey and suggests a profound need to explore and heal the relationship of self to other.

With Saturn opposite Uranus we see a compounding of the Uranus trauma signature, this time indicating actual physical damage (Saturn) to the individual in the past. This could include physical imprisonment, physical restraints (chains, heavy dress code or uniform), intense physical wounding, torture or mutilation or actual physical death.

Because Saturn is opposite Pluto it is also sitting on the polarity point of Pluto. Saturn then adds to our understanding of the polarity point and is then representative of the thing that Flo needs in order to transform and grow beyond her pre-existing limitations.

With Saturn as a skipped step, a trauma signature and also opposite Pluto we can see that one of the critical intentions of this lifetime in Evolutionary terms is to go back into the past (integration of skipped step via the South Node) nature of relationships (South Node in 7th house) and to transform the experience of personal authority (Pluto applying to Saturn) so that prior judgments (Saturn 10th house) can be seen clearly and not just internalized as persecutory anxiety and negative internal messages about the self (Pluto-Uranus 4th house Virgo).

The key to this process is through the polarity point of Pluto, which here is Saturn in Pisces in the 10th house. Flo needs to take responsibility (Capricorn) for the events of the past (skipped steps to the nodal axis of Pluto and Saturn) and through that act of maturity on an existential level to open the door to forgiveness. Explicitly

Flo needs to forgive her parents in this life (Pluto-Uranus-Mars 4th house, Saturn in the 10th house skipped steps) by understanding that they hold the keys to a drama that was enacted in her prior lives. Flo will also need to extend that forgiveness to herself.

Forgiveness can happen spontaneously when we understand difficult relationships as pointing out our karmic issues and traps that we needed to contextualize in this life in order to move forward. We realize that those who have hurt us, or with whom we have struggled have shared stories with us. They share certain karmic resonances or themes with us and in re-enacting those in the current life they are opening the possibility for conscious insight and healing to occur. *Note – this is very different from saying that everyone who did something bad to us this time around was paying us back for something we did.* This common view of karma is simplistic and mired in dualism. Not to say that it isn't ever true. It's just that karma tends to play out through patterns, through energetic structures or internalized feelings that become outward behaviors or habits through our personality expression. Understand these patterns and you can help people liberate from them.

The question of forgiveness, especially forgiveness of self, brings up the question of guilt for which self-forgiveness is required to resolve. The 10th house, Saturn and Capricorn represent the need to take responsibility for the wrong actions and negative judgments that individuals have held and acted on. It can be seen simplistically as dealing with authentic guilt: that I did something wrong and I wish to take responsibility for it. It can refer to heavy conditioning influences from the environment which may complicate that process.

However in Virgo, Mercury and the 6th house, the problem becomes split from actions or from obvious outside influences, and the internalization of guilty messages can occur that may or may not have any overt origin. Flo will have to approach this material from both vantage points.

With signatures such as Pluto-Uranus-Mars in Virgo in the 4th house opposite the Saturn in Pisces in the 10th house the likelihood increases that the unconscious nature of the self takes in such ferocious self-criticism and lacerating self-judgment that all sense of proportion around guilt or self-responsibility is completely skewed. So in all likelihood Flo is so intensely self-persecutory that she is likely to suffer paroxysms of guilt if she deviates even slightly from her own standards. With this kind of karmic pattern the analysis of what may have gone wrong for her must be explored carefully, because more often than not the individual with this kind of amorphous guilt is already punishing themselves before anything has even gone wrong. Just the thought of something possibly going wrong (Mercury ruling Virgo) is enough to trigger an extreme reaction.

This kind of guilt complex can literally infect every area of an individual's life, spreading a heightened inner suffering into even the most successful of their endeavors. Some will even rise to positions of great prominence through the intense dedication not to make mistakes, which would result in internal despair. This very fear of falling into the inner dark hole of failure can paradoxically drive one to achieve great success, the problem coming when the success brings greater and greater responsibility and need for delegation, therefore exponentially increasing the risk of something going wrong, thereby elevating the stress, which then compels the person to do extra work to somehow prepare for the inevitable.

This type of vicious cycle can only be broken by coming back to the emotional core through the child within, the inner spirit – the possibility in the moment of experiencing self-acceptance or at least owning the inner perfectionism and the implicit self-rejection that such a perfect standard contains.

Step 7: The North Node

The next step in our analysis is to move to the North Node of the Moon. Flo's North Node is in Gemini in the 1st house, in which we can see the need to allow the instinctual curiosity of the self to have full reign and to escape the strictures of the past. Here openness to new experience that has been suppressed in prior lives needs to come to the fore now and Flo needs to be allowed unchecked personal expression and to tell her story.

Methodologically we see that the North Node of the Moon, and the polarity point of Pluto (its opposition point) work together to facilitate the evolution of the individual on the primarily conscious (Moon) and unconscious (Pluto) levels. Here the new structures of consciousness (Saturn, 10th house) that emerge from the unconscious through the examination and removal of external dependencies (Pluto-Uranus 4th house) combine with the conscious need to embrace new physical and mental experiences that refresh the identity and revivify the life of the individual (1st North Node in Gemini).

The ruler of Flo's North Node is Mercury in Aries retrograde in the 11th house, and conjunct to the Sun and Venus. The Aries symbolism echoes the 1st house placement of the North Node and emphasizes her powerful need to express her individual will. The seeming paradox is that Mercury is retrograde. When the North Node ruler is retrograde there is a need to repeat certain insights and understanding from the past and apply them afresh to the evolutionary potential of the future. Powerful forces in the past have suppressed Flo's natural insight and she has lacked the courage, physical strength or simple freedom of opportunity within prior life contexts in order to be able to act on any insights she gained. In some critical way Mercury retrograde speaks of the need to digest already existing information, to understand its impact rather than to take on new information.

We add to the complexity of this configuration when we recognize that the Mercury-Sun-Venus conjunction in Aries in the 11th house is the focal point of a Yod pattern that is formed with Neptune and Pluto-Uranus-Mars. A Yod occurs when two planets in sextile are each quincunx a third planet. The planet being quincunxed is the apex, or focal point of the energy generated by the two planets in sextile. That the apex of Flo's Yod is in the 11th house and that Uranus is in aspect to it confirm this as another trauma signature.

We can reason that with the ruler of the node in the 11th quincunx Pluto-Uranus this trauma signature provides confirmation of prior life post-traumatic stress disorder compounded by the family experience (Mars-Uranus-Pluto 4th house). The retrogradation of the North Node ruler indicates that insight (Mercury) as to this predicament has occurred before but that it has been suspended because of the core disempowerment of the individual (Aries trauma signature in the 11th house).

With Mercury ruling the 2nd house cusp and the apex of the trauma signature we can add that these powerful past experiences have involved loss of life. This echoes the Pluto-Uranus-Mars opposition to Saturn – violent prior conflict leading to loss of life. With

Mercury retrograde ruling the 2nd house with multiple trauma signatures involving all the outer planets we can sometimes see a situation where the weight of past pain contributes to a kind of passive suicide, where the individual simply gives up the ghost.

Validation from Flo's Life Experience

Now let's take a look at how some of these chart dynamics played out in Flo's current life.

When Flo was a child, her mother would have breakdowns (Uranus 4th) and that energy would dominate the home environment. On one occasion her mother left home after telling the children that she was going to end her life. Flo's older brother, distraught, left in pursuit, searching local roads and the railway bridge for his supposedly suicidal mother. When he later found her walking an alternative route back to the family home she beamed with delight that her child had wanted to find her so badly, feeding on her son's stress as an affirmation of love. Flo was at an age (under ten years old) where she could not fully grasp the situation, and her mother's narcissistic wounding had great impact.

Flo's mother was so out of control that she routinely became the focus of her father's confusion and increasing ire. The feelings of instability were such that the young Flo would attempt to cover for her mother, cleaning rooms in the house to compensate for her mother's collapse, so that her father would still think that she was on top of things in the household. In the stress signified by the 4th house/ 7th house dynamics in her chart, Flo attempted to save the appearances of contended family life in a way that could only ever be a temporary band aid over a gaping wound. This created the potential pattern of future care-taking in her adult relationships and workplace environments, even when the odds were stacked against this behavior ever leading to a truly positive outcome.

To resolve such a dilemma Flo initially needs to be supported to articulate (North Node Gemini) information she already possesses (ruler in retrograde) in order to express any anger or rage (Mars skipped step, 1st house North Node, Mercury in Aries) or unresolved grief (Saturn skipped step) that has blocked both her voice and her capacity to act on her own insights in past environments.

By stepping in to protect her mother (who made her feel unsafe and never met her needs) Flo also paradoxically managed to split her off from her father, elder brother and sister (who escaped the mother's crazy behavior by isolating their experience to intellectual pursuits within the home via reading and discourse). That the father was never able to resolve this split with his wife before he died (relatively young), that the brother emigrated to Australia, and that the elder sister, after a very brilliant early career as a psychologist, had a break down and was never able to work again, all indicate the impact of the larger tensions within the family home.

The elder sister's story is very interesting, for she followed the father through career and intellect pursuits, yet expressed rebellion through substance abuse and sexual acting out. Her breakdown came as she was unable to clear the hidden dynamics symbolized by her own mother, who she had tried to reject outright. Interestingly this plays into Flo's deepest secret fear that she will end up a bag lady – homeless and broken down (the expression of the South Node ruler Jupiter in the 12th house in Taurus as it applies through the 4th house trauma signatures). This projection of fear is likely a re-imagining of something that has already occurred in the karmic past and continues to resonate into the present through the energy of fear. Flo's mother, in fits of Christian charity, would frequently invite homeless people into the family home at Christmas. While well intentioned, because of her dissociative personality, her mother never managed the situation well, with the consequence that some of these individuals frightened the children. This story exemplifies one way prior life scenarios can be carried into the current life in an illustrative form that we can then actively process.

That Flo has a strong will is evidenced by her Sun-Venus-Mercury placement in Aries. That it is in the 11th house as the apex of a Yod from Pluto-Uranus and Neptune shows that her will was born in a crisis that contains the seed of core psychological issues from the past (Pluto), the core challenge of individuation (Uranus), and the ultimate aspirations or meaning of the self (Neptune). Finding a place of safety from which to re-engage the parts of the will that might be in suspended animation as a result of prior trauma and lack of support (Aries in the 11th house quincunx Pluto-Uranus in the 4th house) is central to the individual's capacity to renew the will and to renew the vitality of life that may have been muted by the early home life and prior restrictions (1st house North Node).

Saturn square to the nodal axis reveals the issue of heavy prior judgment, and of strict hierarchical conditioning as the predominant way Flo's experience has been conditioned in the past. In the current family Flo's older sister summarized the position of the feminine within the household as being like that of a black person in a benevolent white family – individually you are alright but your kind are not. The father ironically claimed to abase himself before her, itself a witty if condescending response that actually reinforced hierarchy within the family. The sister's insight here speaks volumes about the memories contained within the field of the family – memories of slavery and enforced hierarchy just under the surface.

In a wonderful expression of the South Node in Sagittarius, and one bright light in Flo's story, her father bought her a horse in response to seeing her struggle. Riding and taking care of the horse became part of her self-preservation response in that environment – an indication of part of the integration of the Saturn skipped step. Flo made a commitment to take up riding again as part of her recovery.

Flo is now an executive in a television production company and must manage many people and multiple programs simultaneously. Flo experiences herself re-living core anxieties through this process. In one sense she re-enacts the stress of her early life in her work role which involves constantly putting out fires and feverishly working to prevent disaster on the set. Initially Flo became known in the trade for saving projects in crisis. During her Uranus opposition, after the successful completion of one particularly stressful project, Flo had to leave work due to pneumonia and sustained permanent damage to her health.

Flo experiences a great deal of stress and feelings of being profoundly let down by others when directors and editors she's hired mess up a shoot. It is as if her job and the level of authority and responsibility that she has (Saturn in Pisces in the 10th house) causes her to experience the underlying guilt, shame and stress from her prior life (and current life) issues. The 10th house is the arena where they explicitly play out.

Flo's Healing Journey

While reading Flo's chart, what she described as my "rabbit in the hat" moment occurred, one that was essentially simple but in its timing and significance became of great import. I expressed to her the evolutionary desire encapsulated within her chart for her to avoid relationship dependency due to feeling trapped by expectation and the need to develop her independence, validate her instinctive will and have freedom of choice. This was timed after a prolonged discussion of her troubled early home-life, the intense narcissism and idealism of her mother, and the breakdown of the parental relationship.

For an individual with such patterns of internal guilt to hear a validation of what they have already done is a crucial step in self-acceptance. In several critical situations Flo had avoided the temptation to settle down with men who fundamentally did not understand how independent she was and wanted her to play a role as an appendage in their life. Yet as exemplified by the chart complex, Flo questioned her choices and had in many instances felt internalized guilt and fear that she might have somehow fundamentally failed in her life. Validating this experience for her, and the underlying motivations for her impulses opened up the door for healing to take place.

Through astrological and ongoing counseling, Flo began questioning the origins of her anxiety for the first time. Instead of internalizing feelings of being not good enough at her job, which she then works ever harder to compensate for, Flo instead began to see that the anxiety is itself a product of feelings of lack within and that its antidote is self-acceptance. Flo started to think of her anxiety as a virus which, when active, can infect whatever it touches. She had the realization that her thinking process itself is suspect. So she is now developing a new self-awareness that will both hold a container for the part of her that feels anxiety while also maintaining a self-accepting and even forgiving stance toward herself and others.

This new understanding reached a pinnacle when she called in a director, an old friend, to save a shoot that was in danger of going over budget. But he fell into a depression and became anxious himself and failed to make the right decisions or manage the situation well. Flo discovered this too late in the day to fix it and felt betrayed and in shock as all the responsibilities that he failed to manage landed on her with no time to resolve them. This incident occurred merely hours before a meeting of ours in which the resulting shock was still present like a post-traumatic stress response. As we held space for that response and witnessed how this man's anxiety matched and triggered her own, Flo realized a self-acceptance that flowed into her crown and deep into her being. She was able to move past the judgment of herself as wrong, lacking or a secret failure. This was a major breakthrough.

Another shift occurred for Flo regarding her mother. In one session we were able to hold a ritual space where Flo dialogued with her mother as if she were on her death bed. In speaking to her mother from that independent place within, Flo was able to recognize the suffering of the being within her mother and acknowledge to her that they had only ever had one authentic conversation in their life. To see Flo being real with her mother, if only within the heightened visualization in counseling, was incredibly touching. I witnessed Flo moving beyond her confining past paradigm as existing simply to compensate for her mother's inadequacy and to alleviate her mother's loneliness and suffering. By understanding her birth chart, Flo was able to see that her mother played out issues in this life that she herself still struggled with, and must have been overwhelmed by in the past. This allowed compassion to then flow towards her mother.

Then, in a moment that, while relatively common in my work never ceases to amaze me, Flo's mother spontaneously engaged in the second authentic conversation of their life – the week after Flo's visualized ritual with her in our session. To contextualize this conversation, it is important to know that Flo's mother is senile and living in a special assisted-living home. Sometimes when Flo visits she is not sure if her mother is aware who she is. Out of the blue, Flo's mother began to tell her that she is preparing for a change, that it is nothing to be scared of, she is just preparing for a journey which is natural and which she is excited about. She told Flo that her coming journey (death) is a natural deepening of what has already occurred in her life and she is looking forward to it. She said that she was aware of how Flo was there for her at critical times in her life and how she supported her. In a moment in which all of her confusion seemed to disappear, she offered Flo an acknowledgment of their real relationship. In the days that followed, Flo's mother returned to a confused state, but their relationship was forever changed.

Since this event Flo has been able to relate more directly to the child within herself also. She was able to recognize that childhood disruptions of moving house and changing schools were intensely traumatic for her and that they brought out residual anxieties and feelings of a profound lack of safety. She has been able to begin to do work on this level, holding space for the inner child and the core of her emotional body through acknowledgment of the past pain.

For Flo, reclaiming her voice and telling her story was truly evolutionary. It took knowing that she deserves to do so, that she is inherently valuable enough to sing the song of self. This single act overcomes her trauma of loss of self value, inner aloneness and her encounter with the central anxiety of lack within.

Harvesting the Gifts of the Method

Evolutionary Astrology holds the unique promise of enabling us to have access to areas of intimate personal experience that are central to a person's deepest feelings about themselves. It is extremely validating to the individual to have this level of their identity made acceptable within a therapeutic astrological context. To have someone name a core fear alone can be very transformative. It is important at this point to acknowledge the power and profundity of this work. It is to be used with the utmost care and respect. Please take care when approaching clients with this technique, which can easily stir up some of our deepest and most challenging complexes.

My best advice is to approach each reading with curiosity and compassion. If you can hold space for these, you hold space for healing to occur. The minute you feel that you know what the client needs to do, it's time to step back and reassess your approach. Even if you are correct on some level, it pays to always leave space in a reading for the client's sense of authority and self-authorship. If presented with a heavy hand, this material can potentially cause more harm than good. Openly share the material according to your analysis and then ask them what they think. Let them know that if something you say doesn't feel right, that it's of the highest importance to trust their own instincts. The healing process originates within the client, not within the astrologer. Remember that and you'll do good work.

Don't get caught in the trap of holding yourself to a high standard of "accuracy." Remember that each astrological archetype carries multiple possibilities of expression. If you name something and it doesn't ring true for your client, there is no great loss. Just stay inquisitive, ask questions, and work with the client proactively to reveal the message contained within the chart. We do our best to narrow down the core meaning of the chart, but ultimately the client will reveal more to you than you could know on your own. Ultimately the reading of a chart occurs in the fusion between the archetypes and the consciousness of the individual concerned.

We can't know where our clients are in terms of their self awareness and process without asking. We might name something in the chart only to have the person refuse, resist or deny it but then later validate our findings. The value of taking the risk to engage on a deep level is to offer a possible lifeline to the individual. Just don't be attached to your analysis. If the client takes you in a different direction, follow their lead.

To be able to contextualize the origins of complex feelings in the client is one of the true privileges of this work. The impact is so immediate. It is also something to be cautious of, as it is apparent that some people will need validation so badly that this could lead to the potential for being manipulated.

Problems can arise through the conscious and unconscious expectations of the individual pulling on the astrologer with the result of drawing from them insights or points of view with which the astrologer has no real authority. This can occur as part of a two-fold process: the astrologer's sincere desire to help, alongside an unconscious tension experienced because of the client's level of need or suffering. If you rush to offer information to the client in an attempt to alleviate their pain too quickly (perhaps stemming from your own discomfort), confusion can result. We cannot take away people's pain. We can however help people orientate to why they felt pain, and in exploring those origins encourage an understanding that may lead away from suffering. This is profound in itself.

In recognizing our limitations we are able to offer what we can: the contextualization of the individual life as meaningful, as having evolution and purpose. Through understanding the client's struggles we might help assist their sense of potential in this life, and help them accept and enjoy their humanity. Embrace their purpose. This is good enough.[3]

Endnotes

Introduction

[1] Keith Hackwood and Mark Jones "Dancing the Twelve Steps of Soul: Exploring How Astrology Can Impact Upon and Inform Therapeutic Work" in *Psychosynthesis: New Perspectives* (Glastonbury, UK: PS Avalon 2009) p.253.

[2] David R. Hawkins, M.D., Ph.D., *Transcending the Levels of Consciousness* (Sedona, AZ: Veritas Publishing, 2006) p. 81.

[3] Paramahansa Yogananda, *Autobiography of a Yogi* (Los Angeles: Self-Realization Fellowship, 1946) p. 188.

[4] Plotinus, *Ennead 2*, 3rd Tractate *Are the Stars Causes?*

[5] Nicholas Berdyaev, *The Meaning of the Creative Act* (San Rafael: Semantron Press, 2009) p.12.

[6] Jeffrey Green, *Pluto: The Evolutionary Journey of the Soul* (Woodbury: Llewellyn 1985) p. 3.

Chapter 1

[1] Peter D. Ouspensky, *Tertium Organum* (Whitefish: Kessinger Publishing, 2004).

[2] Green, *Pluto: The Evolutionary Journey of the Soul*, p. 7.

[3] I am using the word ego in a primarily psychoanalytical sense, originally from Das Ich (Freud) - The "I." Assagioli deepens this view in his work. Point 5 in the classic egg diagram provides a proper illustration: http://en.wikipedia.org/wiki/Psychosynthesis.

[4] Roberto Assagioli, *The Act of Will* (Amherst, MA: The Synthesis Center Inc., 2010).

[5] These are archetypal gender terms and not specific sexes – i.e. a man could be mother-home just as a woman could be father-society depending on their role within the family.

[6] Why Waldorf Works, http://www.whywaldorfworks.org/02_W_Education/history.asp (2011).

7   Rudolf Steiner, "Facing Karma" in Robert A McDermott, ed., *The Essential Steiner* (Herndon, VA: Lindisfarne Books, 2007).

8   Brother Lawrence, *The Practice of the Presence of God* (Peabody, MA: Hendrickson Publishers, 2004).

9   David R. Hawkins, M.D., Ph.D., *Transcending the Levels of Consciousness* (Sedona, AZ: Veritas Publishing, 2006) p.99.

10   Rudolf Steiner, "Facing Karma".

11   **Cnut the Great** (c. 985 or 995 – 12 November 1035), also known as **Canute**, was a king of Denmark, England, Norway and parts of Sweden. Henry of Huntingdon, the 12th-century chronicler, tells how Cnut set his throne by the sea shore and commanded the tide to halt and not wet his feet and robes. Yet "continuing to rise as usual [the tide] dashed over his feet and legs without respect to his royal person. Then the king leapt backwards, saying: "Let all men know how empty and worthless is the power of kings, for there is none worthy of the name, but He whom heaven, earth, and sea obey by eternal laws." He then hung his gold crown on a crucifix, and never wore it again "to the honour of God the almighty King". This incident is usually misrepresented by popular commentators and politicians as an example of Cnut's arrogance. Excerpt from Kathryn Westcott, "Is King Canute Misunderstood," http://www.bbc.co.uk/news/magazine-13524677 (BBC News Online, 2011) .

12   Thomas Moore, *Dark Nights of the Soul: A Guide to Finding Your Way Through Life's Ordeals* (New York: Gotham Books, 2004) p. 191.

13   Nathan Schwartz-Salant, *The Borderline Personality: Vision and Healing* (Brooklyn: Chiron Publications, 1989) p. 55.

14   Jakob Merchant, private conversation, January 2011.

15   Robert Johnson, *We: Understanding the Psychology of Romantic Love* (San Francisco : Harper & Row, 1983).

16   T.S. Eliot, Four Quartets (Orlando: Harcourt, 1943) p. 2.

17   William Glasser, *Choice Theory: A New Psychology of Personal Freedom* (New York: HarperCollins Publishers, 1998).

18   William Glasser, *Choice Theory: A New Psychology of Personal Freedom*.

19   Colin Wilson, *A Criminal History of Mankind* (London: Mercury Books Limited, 2005).

20   Anthony Storr, *Feet of Clay* (New York: Free Press Paperbacks, 1996).

21   David R. Hawkins, M.D., Ph.D., *Power Versus Force,* (Carlsbad, CA: Hay House, 2002).

22   T.S. Eliot, Four Quartets (Orlando: Harcourt, 1943) p. 58.

23   Martin Heidegger, *Being and Time* (New York: Harper, 1962).

[24] This question was posed to a group of students by a teacher of mine who was struggling with a cancer from which he soon passed away.

[25] Ouspensky, *Tertium Organum.*

[26] B.L. Benderly, 'Rape free or rape prone' (Science 82, vol. 3, no. 8, 1982).

[27] For example, in World War II the state sanctioned enforced prostitution of thousands of young Japanese women.

[28] Henryk Skolimowski, *A Sacred Place to Dwell: Living With Reverence Upon The Earth* (Element Books, 1993) p. 6.

[29] James Lovelock, *Gaia, A New Look at Life on Earth* (New York: Oxford University Press, 1979).

[30] Chogyam Trungpa, "Choiceless Magic," in *True Perception : The Path of Dharma Art* (Boston & London: Shambhala, 2008), p. 111.

[31] Jeffrey Green, *Uranus: Freedom from the Known* (Woodbury, MN: Llewellyn 1985).

[32] By the late 1960s, infighting within organizations such as NOW, Students for a Democratic Society (SDS) and the Mattachine Society led to warring factions, some of which separated and became more radical offshoots like the Weather Underground Organization and the Black Panther party. Such infighting broke down the strength of these organizations, ultimately leading to their demise or reduced effectiveness. See: http://hnn.us/articles/11316.html, http://www.encyclopedia.com/topic/Students_for_a_Democratic_Society.aspx, http://www.history.com/topics/civil-rights-movement.

[33] Gary Lachman, *The Dedalus Book of the 1960s: Turn Off Your Mind* (Sawtry, UK: Dedalus Ltd., 2008).

[34] Friedrich Nietzsche, *Beyond Good and Evil* (London: Penguin Classics, 1973) aphorism no. 156.

[35] Ernest Becker, The Denial of Death (New York: Free Press, 1973).

[36] David R. Hawkins, M.D., Ph.D., *I: Reality and Subjectivity* (Sedona,AZ: Veritas Publishing, 2006).

Chapter 2

[1] I refer to the perennial philosophy as the "universal recurrence of philosophical insight independent of epoch or culture, including universal truths on the nature of reality, humanity, or consciousness" (as quoted from Wikipedia http://en.wikipedia.org/wiki/Perennial_philosophy). Two brilliant texts on the subject are Karl Jaspers, *The Perennial Scope of Philosophy* and Aldous Huxley, *The Perennial Philosophy.*

2   For further insight, see the following text from Stanislav Grof, *When the Impossible Happens: Adventures in Non-Ordinary Reality* (Boulder: Sounds True, 2006) p. 165: "The existence of past-life experiences is an unquestionable fact that can be verified by any serious researcher who is sufficiently open-minded and interested to check the evidence. It is also clear that there is no plausible explanation for these phenomena within the conceptual framework of mainstream psychiatry and psychology. They (past-life experiences) represent a formidable conceptual challenge for traditional science, and they have a paradigm-breaking potential. Having observed hundreds of past-life experiences and experienced many of them myself, I agree with Chris Bache (1988) that 'the evidence in this area is so rich and extraordinary that scientists who do not think the problem of reincarnation deserves serious study are either uninformed or boneheaded.'"

3   Stanislav Grof, *The Holotropic Mind: The Three Levels of Human Consciousness and How They Shape Our Lives* (New York: HarperCollins, 1993).

4   James Hillman, *Suicide and the Soul* (New York: Harper & Row, 1964).

5   D.W. Winnicot *Playing and Reality*(New York: Basic Books, 1971).

6   We may also note here that this entire generation of people (roughly 1964-68) was born with a trauma signature relating to a profound crisis in identity.

7   Grof, *When the Impossible Happens: Adventures in Non-Ordinary Reality*.

8   Grof, *When the Impossible Happens: Adventures in Non-Ordinary Reality*.

Chapter 3

1   Judith Lewis Herman, *Trauma and Recovery*, (New York: Basic Books, 1992).

2   James Hillman, *The Myth of Analysis* (New York: HarperPerennial, 1992) p. 254.

3   Mark S. Micale, "The Decline of Hysteria" (Cambridge, MA: *Harvard Mental Health Letter* **17** (1): 4–6. PMID 10877868, July 2000).

4   Tracey Jenkins & Jennifer Dunne, *Domestic Abuse THE FACTS: A Secondary Research Report,* Equal Opportunities Commission, http://www.assemblywales.org/cc_3__da10_-_ehrc.pdf (August 2007).

5   Catriona Mirriees-Black, "Domestic Violence: Findings From A New British Crime Survey Self Completion Questionnaire," http:/rds.homeoffice.gov.uk/rds/pdfs/hors191.pdf (London: Home Office, 1999) p. 40.

6 D.E.H. Russell, *Sexual Exploitations: Rape, Child Sexual Abuse, and Sexual Harassment* (Los Angeles: Sage Publications, 1984), as quoted in Judith Lewis Herman, *Trauma and Recovery* (New York: Basic Books, 1992)

7 Richard Tarnas, "World Transits 2000–2020," Archai Journal 2 (Fall 2010) p. 2.

8 Richard Tarnas, *Prometheus the Awakener* (Oxford: Auriel Press, 1993).

9 Adyashanti, "The Everlasting Inheritance," http://www.adyashanti.org/index.php?file=writings_inner&writingid=29 (2006).

10 Stanislav Grof, *When The Impossible Happens: Adventures in Non-Ordinary Realities* (Boulder, CO: Sounds True, 2006) p.143.

11 Peter Levine, *Waking the Tiger: Healing Trauma* (Berkeley, CA: North Atlantic Books, 1997) p. 212-213.

12 Levine, *Waking the Tiger: Healing Trauma*, p. 31.

13 Levine, *Waking the Tiger: Healing Trauma*, p. 211.

14 Donald Kalsched, *The Inner World of Trauma: Archetypal Defenses of the Personal Spirit,* (London: Routledge, 1996).

15 Kalsched, *The Inner World of Trauma: Archetypal Defenses of the Personal Spirit.*

Chapter 4

1 Melanie Klein, *Love, Guilt and Reparation: and Other Works 1921-1945* (London: Hogarth Press, 1975).

2 To explore this further, see Steve Taylor, *The Fall* (New York: O Books, 2005).

3 If you'd like to further explore the dynamics of the therapeutic relationship, I recommend the book *Power in the Helping Professions* by Adolf Guggenbuhl-Craig. Though out of print now it is currently available in a free online version at http://www.creativespirit.net/learners/counseling/docu14.htm. This book explores some of the issues of unconscious expectation and the stress it can produce within the counseling process in a sober and insightful way.

Bibliography

Schucman, Dr. Helen. *A Course In Miracles: Text, Workbook for Students and Manual for Teachers*. Mill Valley, CA: Foundation for Inner Peace, 1989.

Assagioli, Roberto. *Psychosynthesis: A Manual of Principles and Techniques*. London: Thorsons, 1965

Assagioli, Roberto. *Transpersonal Development: The Dimension Beyond Psychosynthesis*. London: Thorsons, 1993.

Assagioli, Roberto. *The Act of Will: A Guide to Self-actualisation and Self-realisation*. Amherst, MA: Psychosynthesis & Education Trust, 1999.

Becker, Ernest. *The Denial of Death*. New York: Free Press Paperbacks, 1973.

Becker, Ernest. *Escape From Evil*. New York: Free Press Paperbacks, 1975.

Berdyaev, Nicolas. The Meaning of the Creative Act. San Rafael, CA: Semantron Press, 2009. (Victor Gollancz 1955)

Bradshaw, John. *Bradshaw On: The Family – A New Way of Creating Self-Esteem*. Deerfield Beach, FL: Health Communications Inc., 1988.

Clow, Barbara Hand. *Chiron: Rainbow Bridge Between the Inner and Outer Planets*. St. Paul, MN: Llewellyn Publications, 1993.

Fernandez, Maurice. *Neptune, the 12th House and Pisces*. Victoria, BC: Trafford, 2004.

Gainsburg, Adam. *Chiron: the Wisdom of a Deeply Open Heart*. Springfield, VA: Soulsign, 2006.

Glasser, William. *Choice Theory – A New Psychology of Personal Freedom*. New York: Harper Collins, 1998.

Green, Deva. *Evolutionary Astrology: Pluto and Your Karmic Mission*. St. Paul, MN: Llewellyn Publications, 2009.

Green, Jeffrey. *Pluto: The Evolutionary Journey of the Soul*. St. Paul, MN: Llewellyn Publications, 1985.

Green, Jeffrey. *Uranus: Freedom from the Known.* St. Paul, MN: Llewellyn Publications, 1988.

Green, Jeffrey and Forrest, Steven. *Measuring the Night: Evolutionary Astrology and the Keys to the Soul.* Chapel Hill, NC: Seven Paws Press/Boulder, CO: Daemon Press, 2000.

Green, Jeffrey and Forrest, Steven. *Measuring the Night Volume 2.* Chapel Hill, NC: Seven Paws Press/Boulder, CO:Daemon Press, 2001.

Grof, Stanislav. *When the Impossible Happens: Adventures in Non-ordinary Realities.* Boulder, CO: Sounds True, 2006.

Grof, Stanislav. *Psychology of the Future: Lessons From Modern Consciousness Research.* Albany, NY: State University of New York Press, 2000.

Guggenbuhl-Craig, Adolf. *Power in the Helping Professions.* Putnam, CT: Spring Publications, 1971.

Hawkins, David R. *Healing and Recovery.* West Sedona, AZ: Veritas Publishing, 2009.

Hawkins, David R. *Transcending the Levels of Consciousness.* West Sedona, AZ: Veritas Publishing, 2006.

Herman, Judith Lewis. *Trauma and Recovery: From Domestic Abuse to Political Terror.* New York: Basic Books, 1992.

Jamison, Kay Redfield. *Touched With Fire: Manic-Depressive Illness and The Artistic Temperament.* New York: Free Press Paperback, 1993.

Johnson, Robert A. *The Psychology of Romantic Love.* London: Arkana, 1983.

Kahn, Michael. *Between Therapist and Client: The New Relationship.* New York: Holt Paperbacks, 1991.

Lachman, Gary. *Turn Off Your Mind: The Mystic Sixties and the Dark Side of the Age of Aquarius.* New York: Sidgwick and Jackson Ltd, 2001.

Laszlo, Erwin. *Science and The Akashic Field: An Integral Theory of Everything.* Rochester, VT: Inner Traditions, 2004

Lawrence, Brother. *The Practice of the Presence of God.* New York: Revell, 1999.

Levine, Peter. *Waking The Tiger: Healing Trauma.* Berkeley, CA: North Atlantic Books, 1997.

Levoy, Gregg. *Callings: Finding and Following an Authentic Life.* New York: Three Rivers Press, 1997.

Magee, Bryan. *The Great Philosophers: An Introduction to Western Philosophy.* New York: Oxford University Press, 1987.

Marcus, Rose, ed. *Insights Into Evolutionary Astrology: A Diverse Collection of \Essays By Prominent Astrologers.* St. Paul, MN: Llewellyn Publications, 2010.

Miller, Alice. *The Drama of Being a Child: The Search for the True Self.* London: Virago Press, 1987.

Newton, Michael. *Journey of Souls: Case Studies of Life Between Lives.* St. Paul, MN: Llewellyn Publications, 1994.

Parfitt, Will. *Psychosynthesis: New Perspectives and Creative Research.* Glastonbury, Somerset (UK): PS Avalon, 2009.

Schwartz-Salant, Nathan. *The Borderline Personality: Vision and Healing.* Brooklyn, NY: Chiron Publications, 1989.

Skolimowski, Henryk. *A Sacred Place to Dwell: Living With Reverence Upon the Earth.* London: Element Books, 1993.

Steiner, Rudolph, Robert A. McDermott, ed. *The Essential Steiner.* Edinburgh: Floris Books, 1996.

Storr, Anthony. *Feet of Clay: A Study of Gurus.* New York: Harper Collins, 1996.

Storr, Anthony. *Jung: Selected Writings.* London: Fontana Press, 1983.

Tarnas, Richard. *Cosmos and Psyche: Intimations of a New World View.* New York: Viking Penguin, 2006.

Taylor, Steve. *The Fall: The Insanity of the Ego in Human History and the Dawnings of a New Era..* Hampshire: O-Books, 2005.

TenDam, Hans. *Exploring Reincarnation. London:* Arkana, 1990.

Tolle, Eckhart. *The Power of Now.* Novato, CA: New World Library, 1999.

Walsh, Patricia L. *Understanding Karmic Complexes: Evolutionary Astrology and Regression Therapy.* Bournemouth: Wessex Astrologer, 2009.

Wilson, Colin and Seaman, Donald. The Serial Killers: *A Study in the Psychology of Violence.* London: Virgin Books, 2007.

Wilson, Colin. *Super Consciousness: The Quest for the Peak Experience.* London: Watkins Publishing, 2009.

About the Author

Mark Jones is a licensed Psychosynthesis Therapist and astrologer from Bristol, UK. Educated at the Universities of Warwick and Manchester and with the Synthesis organization in Bristol, Mark is internationally known for his work in the field of Evolutionary Astrology. With over a decade of experience as a therapist and astrologer, Mark specializes in past-life analysis and on-going psychological counseling. Mark is a graduate of Noel Tyl's Masters astrology program and is a certified Evolutionary Astrologer.

Mark teaches and lectures in the U.S. annually. His teaching schedule is available online at www.plutoschool.com.

In early 2011 Mark unveiled his online Pluto School of Evolutionary Astrology. His school features at-your-convenience downloadable lessons, mp3 audio workshops, and video downloads.

Contact the author for information about workshops, private readings and counseling. He can be reached at markjones@plutoschool.com.

Please visit:
www.plutoschool.com

Study Astrology at The Pluto School

Learn evolutionary astrology with Mark Jones. Mark's complete Foundational Course in Evolutionary Astrology is now offered on-line at www.plutoschool.com. Enrolled students can study at their own pace, and gain access to special online conference calls with Mark in addition to online course materials.

The Foundational Course is based on the material presented in this book. The course consists of 12 modules which will teach students how to give an Evolutionary Astrology reading based on the concepts presented in *Healing the Soul*. Classes include written and audio material, as well as self-tests and recommendations for additional study. At the end of the course, students are eligible to pursue certification in Evolutionary Astrology with Mark Jones.

Learn more and enroll today:
www.plutoschool.com/about-pluto-school